## SHONA CRAWFORD POOLE

Shona Crawford Poole was born of
Scots parents at Seaford, Sussex, in
1943. She was educated at nine
schools, all in Britain, and is now a
Londoner by choice. She started her
career in journalism on weekly news-
papers, and then wrote features for the
*Daily Express* before joining *The Times*
eight years ago. She is now Deputy
Features Editor of *The Times*, as well
as cookery columnist. Ms Poole travels
extensively for work as well as for fun,
returning home with collections of
recipes, food and cooking utensils. She
is married to graphic designer Jasper
Partington.

# SHONA CRAWFORD POOLE
# COOKING FOR CHRISTMAS
## & OTHER FEASTS
### A UNIQUE COLLECTION
### OF RECIPES FROM ALL OVER THE WORLD

Hamlyn Paperbacks

COOKING FOR CHRISTMAS
& OTHER FEASTS
ISBN 0 600 20003 5

First published in Great Britain 1980
by Hamlyn Paperbacks
Copyright © 1980 by Shona Crawford Poole

Hamlyn Paperbacks are published by
The Hamlyn Publishing Group Ltd,
Astronaut House,
Feltham,
Middlesex, England
(Paperback Division: Hamlyn Paperbacks,
Banda House, Cambridge Grove,
Hammersmith, London W6 0LE)

Typeset, printed and bound in Great Britain by
Hazell Watson & Viney Ltd, Aylesbury, Bucks

*Cover photograph by Tessa Traeger*
*Line drawings by Marilyn Day; diagrams on*
*pages 136 and 138 by Jasper Partington*

To Jasper

# CONTENTS

# ACKNOWLEDGEMENTS

Christmas foods are made each year with so much love and warmth and nostalgia that in gathering this collection of recipes it has been hard to resist the temptation to include everything I found which fits the theme. So many people shared with me their traditions, their recipes and their memories that the choices about what to leave out were the hardest to make. So to everyone who helped, thank you.

My gratitude goes especially to Rita Slack, Krystyna Lyskowska, Eva Markus, Erkki Toivanen, Katie Stewart, Per Adolf Antell, Violeta Comati, Eulalia Sancho, Philip Vega, Flavio and Tiziana Andreis, Victoria Omotosho, Gabriel Ronay, Jacques Dandel, George Lanitis and Lois James.

I would also like to thank Elizabeth Cuthbert, Dr B. Stillfried, Myrna Lazarus, Carmen Gumucio, Sir Alvin Braynen, Raquel Braune, Yves Mabin, Ghizela Ringrose, Thordur Einarsson, Theresa Sherman-Pennoh, Margarita Sierra, Ray Mountain and Elizabeth Waldron.

For permission to quote passages from F. Marian McNeill's *The Scots Kitchen. Its Traditions and Lore with Old-Time Recipes*, I wish to thank Blackie & Son. Extracts from Elizabeth David's *French Country Cooking,* and from *The Best of Eliza Acton* edited by Elizabeth Ray, are reprinted by courtesy of Penguin Books. William Kimber & Co. have been generous in their permission to quote from *Chef to Queen Victoria. The Recipes of Charles Elmé Francatelli* edited by Ann H. Currah. My gratitude is also due to the Hutchinson Publishing Group, and to Crown, for the passages from Theodora FitzGibbon's *The Food of the Western World.*

For permission to write this book I am particularly grateful to my employer, *The Times,* and its editor William Rees-Mogg.

And for their good company, and for asking for so many second helpings, thank you friends, and thank you family.

# USEFUL FACTS AND FIGURES

## Notes on metrication

In this book quantities are given in metric and Imperial measures. Exact conversion from Imperial to metric measures does not usually give very convenient working quantities and so the metric measures have been rounded off into units of 25 grams. This table below shows the recommended equivalents.

| Ounces | Approx g to nearest whole figure | Recommended conversion to nearest unit of 25 |
|---|---|---|
| 1 | 28 | 25 |
| 2 | 57 | 50 |
| 3 | 85 | 75 |
| 4 | 113 | 100 |
| 5 | 142 | 150 |
| 6 | 170 | 175 |
| 7 | 198 | 200 |
| 8 | 227 | 225 |
| 9 | 255 | 250 |
| 10 | 283 | 275 |
| 11 | 312 | 300 |
| 12 | 340 | 350 |
| 13 | 368 | 375 |
| 14 | 396 | 400 |
| 15 | 425 | 425 |
| 16 (1 lb) | 454 | 450 |
| 17 | 482 | 475 |
| 18 | 510 | 500 |
| 19 | 539 | 550 |
| 20 (1¼ lb) | 567 | 575 |

*Note* When converting quantities over 20 oz first add the appropriate figures in the centre column, then adjust to the nearest unit of 25.

As a general guide, 1 kg (1000 g) equals 2·2 lb or about 2 lb 3 oz. This method of conversion gives good results in nearly all cases, although in certain pastry and cake recipes a more accurate conversion is necessary to produce a balanced recipe.

**Liquid measures** The millilitre has been used in this book and the following table gives a few examples.

| Imperial | Approx ml to nearest whole figure | Recommended ml |
|---|---|---|
| ¼ pint | 142 | 150 ml |
| ½ pint | 283 | 300 ml |
| ¾ pint | 425 | 450 ml |
| 1 pint | 567 | 600 ml |
| 1½ pints | 851 | 900 ml |
| 1¾ pints | 992 | 1000 ml (1 litre) |

**Spoon measures** All spoon measures given in this book are level unless otherwise stated.

**Can size** At present, cans are marked with the exact (usually to the nearest whole number) metric equivalent of the Imperial weight of the contents, so we have followed this practice when giving can sizes.

### Oven temperatures

The table below gives recommended equivalents.

| | °C | °F | Gas Mark |
|---|---|---|---|
| Very cool | 110 | 225 | ¼ |
| | 120 | 250 | ½ |
| Cool | 140 | 275 | 1 |
| | 150 | 300 | 2 |
| Moderate | 160 | 325 | 3 |
| | 180 | 350 | 4 |
| Moderately hot | 190 | 375 | 5 |
| | 200 | 400 | 6 |
| Hot | 220 | 425 | 7 |
| | 230 | 450 | 8 |
| Very hot | 240 | 475 | 9 |

## Notes for American and Australian users

In America the 8-oz measuring cup is used. In Australia metric measures are now used in conjunction with the standard 250-ml measuring cup. The Imperial pint, used in Britain and Australia, is 20 fl oz, while the American pint is 16 fl oz. It is important to remember that the Australian tablespoon differs from both the British and American tablespoons; the table below gives a comparison. The British standard tablespoon, which has been used through this book, holds 17·7 ml, the American 14·2 ml, and the Australian 20 ml. A teaspoon holds approximately 5 ml in all three countries.

| British | American | Australian |
|---|---|---|
| 1 teaspoon | 1 teaspoon | 1 teaspoon |
| 1 tablespoon | 1 tablespoon | 1 tablespoon |
| 2 tablespoons | 3 tablespoons | 2 tablespoons |
| 3½ tablespoons | 4 tablespoons | 3 tablespoons |
| 4 tablespoons | 5 tablespoons | 3½ tablespoons |

### An Imperial/American guide to solid and liquid measures

*Solid measures*

| IMPERIAL | AMERICAN |
|---|---|
| 1 lb butter or margarine | 2 cups |
| 1 lb flour | 4 cups |
| 1 lb granulated or castor sugar | 2 cups |
| 1 lb icing sugar | 3 cups |
| 8 oz rice | 1 cup |

*Liquid measures*

| IMPERIAL | AMERICAN |
|---|---|
| ¼ pint liquid | ⅔ cup liquid |
| ½ pint | 1¼ cups |
| ¾ pint | 2 cups |
| 1 pint | 2½ cups |
| 1½ pints | 3¾ cups |
| 2 pints | 5 cups (2½ pints) |

*Note* When making any of the recipes in this book, only follow one set of measures as they are not interchangeable.

# INTRODUCTION

All Christendom celebrates Christmas with feasting. It is a time of traditional dishes as richly varied, as odd and as pleasing as the peoples who have made them. Rituals and recipes have survived immense journeys through time and across great distances. Often they have evolved to meet the needs of modern living or transplantation to quite different climates. But in many places people cling to old and sometimes touchingly inappropriate eating customs.

The universal ingredients of Christmas celebrations everywhere are the preparation of special foods and the enjoyment of them in the company of as many members of the family as can gather for the occasion. Foods bought ready-prepared for every day are made lovingly at home. Family recipes are consulted, old methods honoured, and ingredients which would be an unthinkable extravagance at any other season are generously measured.

In the weeks before the festivities, evocative smells of Christmases long forgotten waft from kitchens busy with homely sounds of mixing and baking, steaming, roasting, simmering and sizzling. It is all a great to-do for the cooks.

In some countries the choice of Christmas foods is made not from a traditional selection as it is in Europe and America, but from a general list of party dishes which can be served on any sufficiently festive occasion, and it is fascinating to discover why particular foods appear only on days of religious or personal celebration. Often the reason is the simple one that the dishes involved hours of tedious preparation – and still do without the help of food mills and mixers.

In the splendid wealth of the world's Christmas eating styles almost every imaginable delicacy is served. There is a precedent somewhere for serving dishes as simple or elaborate as anyone's taste could run to or skill devise. Every recipe in this book is an essential part of Christmas for someone although not everything included is in the class of such unbreakable traditions as Christmas pudding in England, rice pudding or porridge in Scandinavia, Italy's fruit cake *pannettone*, or Spain's almond nougat *turrón*. These are sweet things without which Christmas wouldn't be Christmas in the countries where they are eaten.

Some of the recipes are for dishes peculiar to quite small regions, while others have been popular for so long or have travelled so far that it has been hard to choose which recipes to include from the apparently endless variations possible.

If selecting recipe variations was a problem, deciding what to leave out was a greater one. Written recipes are rare in large areas of the world, and it is usually in just such places that the foods chosen for Christmas celebrations are least governed by tradition. So rather than dip more or less at random into these cuisines I have taken only short detours along unmarked tracks. At the opposite extreme there are, on the well-travelled ground of Europe, so many customs and recipes woven across the borders that disentangling them would be a historian's life's work.

What I have tried to produce is a practical cookery book, gathering between two covers an entertaining and useful collection of Christmas recipes for family meals and all kinds of Christmas parties. Some call for considerable skill and expensive ingredients, others cost little in time, effort or cash.

Being a professional journalist and an incorrigible cook, writing this book has been a voyage of discovery for me, not because I had not previously attempted to reproduce in my own kitchen the tastes and smells of meals remembered in faraway places or eaten in foreign restaurants, though there were many discoveries of that kind too. I came across lots of new flavours, combinations, techniques and ideas which have greatly enriched my own repertoire. But the really rewarding discoveries were of a different kind. The biggest was learning to trust my own judgement. In everyday cooking I adjust recipes constantly, adding more or less of some ingredients to improve the flavour, and cooking a dish for a longer or shorter time than the recipe stipulates because experience and common sense tell me when it is, or isn't, ready. And, like everyone else, I improvise for unexpected guests, when the shops are shut and I have forgotten something, and often, simply for amusement.

So to every reader of this book, and especially to those whose cookery schools are their own kitchens, I want to say be brave, and have fun.

# PRACTICALITIES:
# A TABLESPOON IS LEVEL

To cook rice of the fresh harvest, says a recipe from south-east Asia, add a little less water. Now where I live, rice of many kinds can be bought loose or packaged, dry, pre-cooked, boil-in-the-bag, heat-in-the-can, and take-away, anything but 'of the fresh harvest'. And I mention it here only to illustrate the plain fact that the magic of good cooking can never quite be pinned down even in the most detailed recipes. There are just too many variables. Quite apart from matters of taste, which are another whole story, ingredients differ from one season to the next, one manufacturer to another, and between breeds and strains. They differ because of how they are grown, harvested, packaged, transported and stored. One clove of garlic can weigh anything from one-tenth of an ounce to half an ounce, and its size is not all. Only your own nose and taste buds will tell whether the garlic in your kitchen, of whatever size, is pungent or mild.

In a book which draws its recipes from so many places there are inevitable difficulties in defining, and sometimes obtaining, ingredients. Peppers and chillies are as good an example as any. The attributes and subtle variations of members of the capsicum family are the subject of much discussion by initiates, and rightly a matter of great importance to those who use them daily. For those who do not, too much precision, beyond a knowledge of whether the varieties called for are mild or hot, is seldom essential to enjoyable cooking and eating. (When handling chillies it is a good idea to wear rubber gloves as the volatile oils in their flesh and seeds can irritate the skin. If not wearing gloves, wash your hands thoroughly in soap and water after working with them. For most recipes, unless otherwise stated, the stalks and seeds of chillies should be removed and the flesh torn into small pieces.)

Techniques of cooking vary widely too because they have evolved to meet local needs and conditions. So while standardizing the recipes, I have tried to preserve the methods used in the countries of origin wherever this is practical. Electric mixers and blenders are a boon to busy cooks, but not everyone has one, and not every machine copes well with every kind of job. So, except where making a recipe by hand involves an unthinkable amount of work, this is the method I have described. Most of us know our own mixers and blenders well enough to work out timings, and a glance at the appliance handbook should resolve any uncertainties.

# SOUPS

Almond soup is a Christmas Eve favourite in Spain where almonds often appear again in the meal in both stuffings and in the traditional sweets. This delicate, milky-white soup is served cold, garnished with white grapes, powdered cinnamon, or, more festively, with a scarlet rose petal floating in each bowl.

### Almond Soup – Sopa de Almendras – Spain

*Serves 8*

200 g/7 oz blanched almonds
4 cloves garlic
4 tablespoons olive oil, mild
salt

4 teaspoons wine vinegar
white grapes (optional)
cinnamon (optional)

Crush the almonds with the garlic, olive oil and salt to a smooth paste using a pestle and mortar, or an electric blender. Gradually add 2·25 litres/4 pints water. Check the seasoning and chill.

Just before serving the soup, stir in the vinegar and serve in individual bowls garnished as described above.

Chestnut soup has been made for centuries throughout Europe. This version is adapted from an early nineteenth-century English recipe.

### Chestnut Soup – England

*Serves 10*

1 kg/2 lb chestnuts
2·25 litres/4 pints well-flavoured
   poultry or veal stock
salt

powdered mace
cayenne pepper
450 ml/¾ pint single cream

Using a sharp knife slit the shiny brown skin of each chestnut on the domed surface. Lay them, in a single layer, flat side down on a roasting tray. Pour 300 ml/$\frac{1}{2}$ pint water into the tray, and roast them in a moderately hot oven (200° C, 400° F, Gas Mark 6) for about 8 minutes. Peel the chestnuts while they are still hot.

Put the peeled chestnuts in a large, heavy-based pot, and cover them with the stock. Bring to the boil, skim, cover, and simmer for about 45 minutes or until the chestnuts are easily broken by pressing them with a wooden spoon. Strain the chestnuts and reserve the stock.

Rub the chestnuts through a fine sieve or reduce them to a purée in an electric blender with a small amount of the stock. Rinse the pot and return the chestnuts to it. Gradually stir in the stock and season the soup to taste with salt, ground mace and cayenne.

Bring the soup to the boil, reduce the heat, and just before serving, stir in the cream. Serve the soup very hot, but do not boil it again once the cream has been added.

The flavour and sweetness of fresh chestnuts can vary. If the chestnuts are very sweet the soup may be too sweet for some tastes. This can be modified by stewing the chestnuts in water and adding fresh stock to the purée.


Another festive looking soup is the Polish beetroot and mushroom consommé, *barszcz*, traditionally served on Christmas Eve with *uszka*, 'little ears' of mushroom-stuffed dough which are poached and served in the soup, or deep-fried and handed round separately. Both of the recipes which follow are equally authentic, but the first, which involves the advance preparation of a fermented beetroot stock, does have a finer flavour and is worth the little extra trouble that making it calls for.


### Fermented Beetroot and Mushroom Consommé – Barszcz – Poland

*Serves 4–6*

*Fermented stock*      1 litre/1$\frac{3}{4}$ pints water
450 g/1 lb fresh, raw beetroot      25 g/1 oz dark rye bread, cubed

About one week before making the soup, prepare the fermented beetroot stock. Peel and slice the beetroot. Put the slices in a large glass or pottery jar and cover them with the water which has been boiled and allowed to cool to lukewarm. Add the cubes of dark rye bread and cover the jar with a lid of perforated paper. Leave it in a warm place

18°–20° C/65°–68° F for a few days. Strain the stock and use it immediately, or bottle the strained stock for using later.

*Soup*
450 g/1 lb fresh, raw beetroot
225 g/8 oz mixed stock vegetables
50 g/2 oz dried mushrooms,
   boletus type

600 ml/1 pint fermented stock
salt
sugar
1 clove garlic, crushed
lemon juice

Soak the mushrooms in water for several hours, then cook them in the soaking water until soft. This usually takes about 2 hours, but the time can vary a great deal. Add the chopped stock vegetables and crushed garlic, and cook until they too are soft.

In a separate pot cook the beetroot in as little water as possible before peeling and grating them coarsely. Do wear gloves to handle the cooked beetroot as their brilliant juice stains fingers bright red.

Add about 1 litre/1¾ pints of water to the mushroom and vegetable mixture. Add the beetroot, and bring the pot quickly to the boil. Strain the mixture and add the fermented beetroot stock. Season to taste with salt, sugar and lemon juice. Serve in soup cups with 'little ears', *uszka* (see page 4).

### Beetroot and Mushroom Consommé – Barszcz – Poland

*Serves 4–6*

75 g/3 oz dried mushrooms,
   boletus type
1·25 kg/2½ lb fresh, raw beetroot
1½ tablespoons red wine vinegar

salt
sugar
lemon juice

Cover the dried mushrooms with about 900 ml/1½ pints boiling water and leave them to soak for several hours. Cook them uncovered until tender in the soaking liquid. This takes about 2 hours, by which time the liquid will have reduced to about 6 tablespoons. Strain the mushroom stock through a fine sieve.

Peel the raw beetroot and grate them coarsely. Wear gloves for this colourful operation. Add 1 litre/1¾ pints of cold water to the grated beetroot in a large pot, bring to the boil, reduce the heat, and simmer uncovered for about 10 minutes. Add vinegar, and simmer partly covered for another 30 minutes. Strain the beetroot stock through a fine sieve, extracting as much of the juice as possible.

Combine the beetroot and mushroom stocks in a clean pot, and bring the consommé quickly to the boil. Season to taste with salt, sugar and lemon juice. Serve in soup cups with 'little ears', *uszka* (see below).

### 'Little Ears' – Uszka – Poland

*Serves 4–6*

| | |
|---|---|
| *Filling* | salt |
| 50 g/2 oz dried mushrooms, | pepper |
| boletus type | *Dough* |
| 1 small onion | 150 g/5 oz plain flour |
| 1 tablespoon vegetable oil | 1 egg |
| 25 g/1 oz white bread | water to mix |
| 20 g/¾ oz white breadcrumbs | |

Cover the dried mushrooms with boiling water and leave them to soak for several hours before cooking them until tender in as little water as possible. Fry the onion, peeled and finely chopped, in the oil until golden. Soak the bread in water and squeeze out the excess moisture. Strain the cooked mushrooms. Put the bread, onions and mushrooms through the fine blade of a mincer. Add the breadcrumbs to this mixture and season to taste with salt and pepper. Fry the mixture, using a little more oil if needed, until it makes a smooth, pleasant-smelling paste.

To make the dough, sift the flour into a bowl. Beat the egg and blend with the flour and enough water to make a ball of firm dough. Roll out the dough as thinly as possible on a well-floured board, and cut into circles about 5 cm/2 inches in diameter with a plain edged pastry cutter or the rim of a wine glass. Spoon small blobs of filling on to the centre of each piece of dough, moisten the rim with water, and fold the circles in halves, sealing the edges firmly. Do not overfill the cases or they will burst when cooking. Now make the stuffed half circles of dough into 'little ears' by bringing the points together round your finger and pressing to join them securely.

The prepared uszka can be deep frozen at this stage for poaching later, in which case defrost them completely before cooking.

To poach the uszka, drop them in handfuls into a large pot of boiling, salted water. Reduce the heat, and simmer each batch for about 5 minutes, or until the dumplings are tender, and the dough cooked. Keep them warm in a covered bowl until all are cooked before arranging them in individual bowls and pouring the hot barszcz over them.

To fry the uszka, heat a large pan of deep fat or oil to about 180° C/ 350° F. At this temperature a 2·5-cm/1-inch cube of day-old bread will fry to a crisp, golden brown in about 90 seconds. Cook them in small batches until they are golden. Drain them on kitchen paper and serve immediately.

Fried uszka may be deep frozen and reheated from frozen on a baking tray in a moderately hot oven (200° C, 400° F, Gas Mark 6).

The Finns too are not content with soup alone and often serve it with *piirakkaa*, small, boat-shaped pies made with a rye crust and a variety of fillings. A clear soup or broth most frequently begins the elaborate Christmas meal. This vegetable broth is full of flavour.

### Vegetable Broth – Kasvisliemi – Finland

*Serves 8–10*

| | |
|---|---|
| 1 medium carrot | 12 radishes |
| 2 medium parsnips | 450 g/1 lb fresh peas, preferably |
| 450 g/1 lb Jerusalem artichokes | in the pod |
| 1 small beetroot | 50 g/2 oz parsley |
| 4 stalks celery | 6 whole allspice |
| 225 g/8 oz hard white cabbage | 6 black peppercorns |
| 1 large onion | 2 bay leaves |
| 2 medium leeks | salt |

Peel the carrot, parsnips, Jerusalem artichokes and beetroot and chop them roughly. Roughly chop the celery, cabbage, onion (do not peel), and leeks. Put all the vegetables, herbs and spices into a large stock pot. Cover them with 2¾ litres/4¾ pints of water, bring the liquid to boiling point, cover, and simmer for about 2½ hours. Strain the stock and reserve the vegetables for another use. Salt the vegetable broth to taste and serve it very hot in warmed soup cups or bowls with *juustipiirakkaa* (see page 82).

According to Sir Walter Scott fat brose was once the Christmas Day breakfast soup or gruel of his compatriots, and it would certainly have kept out the raw, chill, Scottish winters. 'In olden times, all, gentle and simple, had fat brose on Yule Day morning.'

In *The Scots Kitchen. Its Traditions and Lore with Old-Time Recipes*, F. Marian McNeill, writing in 1929, describes how this now almost extinct concoction was made. Half an ox head, a cow heel, or a good piece of hough (shank of beef) was covered with water and boiled until an almost pure oil floated to the top. A ladle full of this fat broth was poured over a handful of lightly toasted oatmeal and a pinch of salt in a bowl. The mixture was quickly stirred to form knots, returned to the pot for a minute or two to reheat, and served.

A comparable practice born of harder times survives in Sweden where *dopp i grytan*, dip in the pot, was traditionally eaten at mid-morning on Christmas Eve with rye bread, schnapps and pickled herrings. Today it more often appears as a token ritual item in the elaborate smörgåsbord served at lunchtime on Christmas Eve or as the first part of a longer evening meal. Dopp i grytan is the stock in which the Christmas ham and a variety of sausages for the smörgåsbord have been cooked. Pieces of rye bread are dipped in the pot or kettle of hot stock and eaten with the fingers.

It would be difficult to find a simpler soup than *aïgo bouïllido*, literally translated boiling water, which begins the traditional Christmas Eve meal in Provence. Two large cloves of garlic, 1 tablespoon of olive oil, 1 bay leaf and salt are boiled in about 900 ml/1½ pints of water for about 15 minutes. Two raw eggs are broken into a tureen, then the boiling liquid is poured over them and beaten with a wooden spoon.

Aïgo bouïllido is followed by *cardons aux anchois*, a vegetable of the artichoke family cooked and served with an anchovy sauce, and *cacalaus*, cooked snails with garlic mayonnaise or a fresh tomato sauce mixed with thyme, savory and fennel, and garnished with thorns of the acacia or judas tree. The final cooked dish, *anguilles en catigout* – eels, chopped bacon and mushrooms simmered in white wine is followed by a salad. Then come thirteen more traditional items; dates, oranges, apples, pears, mandarins, almonds, walnuts, raisins, figs, chestnuts, black nougat, white nougat and *fougasse*, a circular, latticed loaf of flour and olive oil flavoured with aniseed.

This feast puts to excellent use the superb garlic and herbs which, grown in the dry sunshine of southern France, taste so much better than those cultivated almost anywhere else.

In Peru, a substantial fish soup often begins an otherwise modest meal by American and European standards of Christmas eating. *Antichuchos*, skewers of marinated bull's heart, are accompanied by *papa rellena*, meat balls enclosed in mashed potato and fried till crisp and golden, and an escarole salad. A fruit compote usually completes the meal.

## Fish Soup – Chupe de Pescado – Peru

*Serves 6*

| | |
|---|---|
| 15 g/½ oz butter | 450 g/1 lb cooked crab meat or |
| 2 medium onions | shelled shrimps |
| 1 clove garlic | cayenne pepper |
| 1 tablespoon tomato pureé | 1 litre/1¾ pints milk |
| 225g/8 oz goat cheese, grated | 6 small potatoes |
| 50 g/2 oz rice | 6 slices eel or lobster |
| salt | 1 red pepper (mild) |
| oregano | 6 eggs |

Melt the butter in a large, heavy-based pot and add the onions, peeled and quartered, and the garlic, crushed with a little salt. At 2-minute intervals add in the following order, tomato purée, half the grated cheese, rice, and finally salt and oregano. Cook this mixture gently for about 5 minutes. Add the crab or shrimp, and the cayenne. Cover and cook over a low heat until the rice and onions are cooked to a mush. Add a little water if the mixture becomes too dry before the rice is completely cooked. Rub the mixture through a sieve. Rinse the pot and return the purée to it. Add the milk, stir well, check the seasoning and set the soup aside while the garnish is prepared.

Boil the potatoes in their skins until tender. Peel them and keep them warm on a large plate in a very low oven. Brush the slices of eel or lobster with oil and grill them lightly. Keep warm in the oven. Trim and de-seed the pepper and grill it lightly before scraping off the skin. Cut it into six pieces and keep warm. Finally, poach six eggs in boiling salted water, drain, and keep warm.

Bring the soup to the boil, and serve it in large heated soup plates. Arrange a potato, a slice of eel or lobster, a piece of pepper, a poached egg and a portion of the remaining goat cheese on each plate. Pour boiling soup over the pieces and serve.

Soup is an indispensable element of the Christmas meal in Hungary. This one is delicious.

### Fish Soup – Hal Leves – Hungary

*Serves 6*

head, tail, liver, hard and soft roe of a big fish, say pike or sturgeon
salt
1 bay leaf

25 g/1 oz plain flour
25 g/1 oz butter
6 tablespoons soured cream
lemon juice
50 g/2 oz rice

Put the fish pieces in a large, heavy-based pot, cover it with cold water, add a tablespoon of salt, and bring to the boil. Skim the liquid, add the bay leaf, cover the pot and simmer until the fish is tender. Strain the liquid and reserve it. As soon as the fish is cool enough to handle remove all the bones, break the flesh into pieces, and keep it warm.

Rinse the pot and melt the butter in it over a low heat. Stir in the flour and cook the roux for a minute or two without allowing it to colour. Gradually blend in about 1·5 litres/2½ pints of the fish stock and cook the soup over a low heat until the mixture has thickened slightly. Stir in the soured cream, and season to taste with salt and lemon juice.

Wash the rice and add it to the soup. Simmer the soup, covered, until the rice is tender, stirring occasionally to make sure the grains are not sticking to the bottom of the pot. To serve the soup, divide the pieces of reserved fish between large, very hot soup plates and pour over them the boiling soup.

Lighter fish soups are an excellent beginning to hearty meals. Both the following recipes, the Edwardian recipe for lobster soup and the older recipe for a traditional English oyster soup, call for a good fish stock. A well-flavoured fish stock is quickly prepared by boiling the bones and trimmings of any white fish, and a cod's head, if available, with one or two roughly chopped onions, carrots and celery sticks, a bay leaf, a bouquet of fresh herbs, salt and pepper. Cook the stock for about 20 minutes then strain it through a fine sieve. It can of course be reduced by fast boiling for a stronger flavour.

# Rich Lobster Soup – England

*Serves 6–8*

1 small whole lobster, cooked
50 g/2 oz butter
1 bay leaf
1 sprig parsley
salt

pepper
2 teaspoons lemon juice
40 g/1½ oz cornflour
900 ml/1½ pints good fish stock
300 ml/½ pint single cream

Remove the lobster flesh from the shell, and reserve the claw meat for garnishing the finished soup. Wash the shell, pound it with the butter and put the mixture into a heavy-based pot with the bay leaf, parsley, salt, pepper, lemon juice and cornflour. Cook these ingredients together very gently for about 10 minutes without allowing them to colour. Add the fish stock, roughly chopped lobster meat and coral, and simmer the soup gently for about 40 minutes.

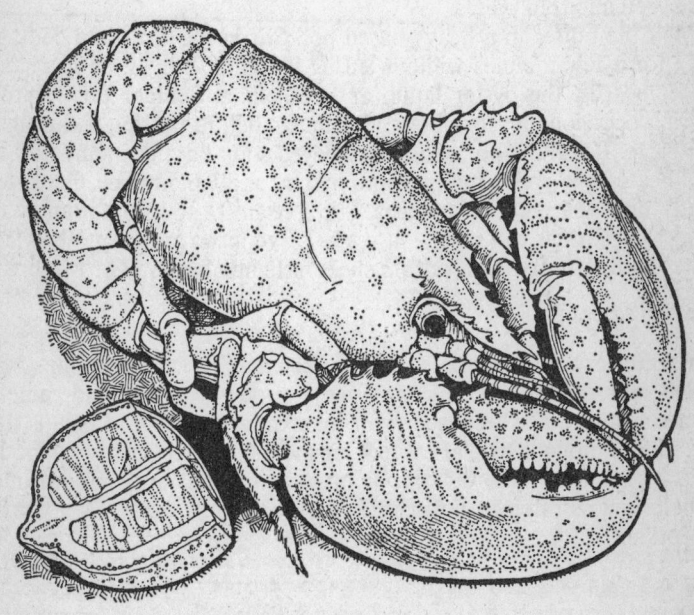

Strain the soup very carefully through a sieve lined with muslin, to make sure all the gritty shell fragments are extracted. Rinse the pot and return the strained liquid to it. Stir in the cream and reserved claw meat cut in dice. Reheat the soup gently but do not allow it to boil again after the cream has been added. Serve in warmed soup cups or bowls.

### Oyster Soup – England

*Serves 6*

| | |
|---|---|
| 12 fresh oysters | pepper |
| 50 g/2 oz butter | 2 egg yolks |
| 40 g/1½ oz plain flour | 125 ml/4 fl oz milk |
| 750 ml/1¼ pints good fish stock | 175 ml/6 fl oz single cream |
| salt | lemon juice |

Open the oysters, reserving the liquid in the shells. Separate the flesh from the shells, remove and reserve the beards, and cut the flesh from each shell into four pieces.

Melt the butter in a heavy-based pot. Stir in the flour and cook the roux for a few minutes without letting it colour. Stir in the fish stock, oyster beards, the oyster liquid and seasoning. Simmer this mixture, stirring occasionally, for about 15 minutes before passing it through a fine sieve. Rinse the pot, return the sieved soup-base to it, and add the well-beaten egg yolks, milk, cream, oysters and lemon juice. Cook very gently until the mixture thickens. Stir constantly and do not allow the soup to boil or it will curdle at once. Serve in warmed soup bowls or plates with thin dry toast or thin slices of lightly buttered brown bread.

For centuries thrifty housewives have been making splendid soups from giblets and carcasses of chickens, geese, turkeys, poultry and game of all descriptions, but because few of them appear on festive menus they are seldom thought special enough for mention when Christmas food is discussed. The Danish *kråsesuppe* of goose giblets, apples and prunes, embellished as often as not with butter dumplings, *boller*, is a worthy exception.

# Giblet Soup with Apples and Prunes – Kråsesuppe – Denmark

*Serves 6–8*

| | |
|---|---|
| 225 g/8 oz prunes | 6 peppercorns |
| 1 set goose giblets, neck, wings and feet | 1 blade mace |
| | 450 g/1 lb cooking apples |
| 2 large carrots | 25 g/1 oz sugar |
| 1 large onion | 25 g/1 oz butter |
| 1 stalk celery | 25 g/1 oz plain flour |
| salt | 4 teaspoons wine vinegar |

Cover the prunes with boiling water and leave them to soak, preferably overnight. Stone the prunes and reserve the soaking liquid. Set both aside.

Wash the goose giblets. Divide each wing into two pieces, and the neck into three. Put the giblets in a large pot, cover them with cold water, bring to the boil and skim. Chop the vegetables roughly and add them to the boiling stock with salt, the crushed peppercorns and the mace. Cover the pot and simmer gently for several hours until the giblets are tender.

Strain the stock, and if necessary reduce it by fast boiling to about 2 litres/3½ pints, and set it aside. Reserve the giblets and vegetables.

Slice and peel the apples. Cook them with the prunes and sugar in the soaking water until the fruit is tender. Strain and set aside fruit and juice.

Melt the butter in a large, heavy-based pot. Stir in the flour and cook the roux gently for a minute or two without allowing it to colour. Stir in the fruit liquid and the giblet stock.

Chop the vegetables and the meat from the goose giblets into small pieces. Add the meat, vegetables and fruit to the soup. Add the vinegar and check the seasoning, adding more sugar, salt, vinegar and pepper to taste. Serve in warmed soup bowls or plates with butter dumplings, *boller* (see below).

# Butter Dumplings – Boller – Denmark

*Serves 6–8*

| | |
|---|---|
| 175 g/6 oz butter | 4 eggs |
| 225 g/8 oz plain flour | 1 egg yolk |
| 475 ml/16 fl oz boiling water | salt |

Melt the butter in a heavy-based saucepan. Stir in the flour and cook the roux gently for a minute or two without allowing it to colour. Gradually stir in the boiling water, and continue to cook slowly until a lump-free ball of dough is formed. Remove the pot from the heat and beat in the eggs and egg yolk one at a time. Add salt to taste. Shape the dough into little balls using two teaspoons.

The boller can be cooked in the soup, or separately in stock, or in boiling salted water. Drop them into the boiling liquid, a few at a time so that it does not go off the boil which would make the dumplings soggy. They are ready when they rise to the surface. Serve with kråsesuppe in warmed soup bowls or plates.

In Italy quite small areas and even single towns have long held traditions of eating particular dishes on Christmas Eve, traditions of which their nearest neighbours have often only vaguely heard.

*Cappelletti*, little hats of pasta, are made with various stuffings. Tuscany, Umbria, Emilia, Romagna and Rome all have their own characteristic fillings. The following recipe is from Perugia where *cappelletti in brodo* are made for the Christmas Eve dinner.

Many Italian cooks who buy ready-made pasta for everyday meals make their own for special occasions, and to pasta lovers the delicious flavours of home-made stuffings fully justify the work of making the filled varieties. Making pasta does require patience and a fair amount of space. It is not something to do in a hurry or in a tiny kitchen.

### Cappelletti in Broth – Cappelletti in Brodo – Italy

*Serves 8–12*

*Filling*
175 g / 6 oz lean pork
175 g / 6 oz lean veal
50 g / 2 oz ham
50 g / 2 oz calf's brains
1 small carrot
1 small stalk celery
25 g / 1 oz butter
4 tablespoons dry Marsala

50 g / 2 oz grated Parmesan
salt
pepper
nutmeg
*Dough*
250 g / 9 oz flour, hard gluten or
    strong bread flour if possible
salt
3 large eggs

*These quantities make about 84 cappelletti. Allow at least 300 ml / ½ pint of well-flavoured chicken or veal broth for each serving.* Chop the pork, veal, ham, cleaned brains, carrot and celery finely. Melt the butter in a heavy-based pot. Add the chopped meats and vegetables and cook gently for 5 minutes. Add the Marsala and cook for about 20 minutes more. Put the mixture through the fine blade of a mincer. Mix in the grated cheese and season with salt, pepper and nutmeg. Set the mixture aside to cool.

To make the pasta, sift the flour and salt and heap in a mound on a large pastry board. Make a well in the centre of the flour and break the eggs into it. Fold the flour over the eggs and knead until a soft, elastic dough is formed.

To roll the pasta, divide it into two or four pieces – smaller amounts are easier to manage unless you have a very large board and an extra long rolling pin. Place the first piece of dough on the floured board and roll it lightly. Lift it, drape it over the rolling pin to stretch it gently, sprinkle it with flour and roll again. Continue to lift, stretch, flour and roll until the pasta is extremely thin. Lay the pasta, which should now be almost like a piece of fabric, on a clean cloth on a table or over the back of a chair. Roll out the remaining dough using the same technique of rolling and stretching the pasta.

To assemble the cappelletti spoon teaspoonfuls of the filling on to one sheet of the rolled pasta at about 3·75-cm/1½-inch intervals. Cover with a second sheet of pasta. Using a crimped or plain-edged pastry cutter about 3·75 cm/1½ inches in diameter, or the rim of a wine glass of suitable size, cut through both layers of pasta, centring the cutter over each blob of filling, to form little circular parcels.

Cappelletti may be made the day before they are to be eaten. Lay them in a single layer on a large floured board or dish and cover them with a floured cloth. Keep them in a cool place, but not in a refrigerator.

To cook the cappelletti, prepare a large pot of boiling chicken or veal broth. Drop the cappelletti carefully into the bubbling liquid, a few at a time so that it does not come off the boil. They are ready when they rise to the surface of the broth which takes only about 4 minutes.

Serve cappelletti in their broth in large soup plates. Hand round separately a bowl of freshly grated Parmesan.

# FIRST COURSES

Travellers, especially people who travel on business, often eat few dishes which do not appear on hotel menus anywhere. The distinctly local character of freshly baked breakfast rolls can easily be the only sign that one is in one capital, or continent, and not another, unless there is time and opportunity to explore further than the city's central block.

A selection of authentic recipes for dishes which have travelled far, and are often poorly made, seems a useful offering. Their association with Christmas is real enough although the strength of that association varies. Christmas dinner without *tortellini* would raise eyebrows in Bologna, and *cannelloni*, the other pasta dish in this section, comes not from Italy but from Spain where the Catalonians have evolved their own seasonal variation.

For those who can afford them, *foie gras*, oysters, lobster, and caviar are internationally popular openings to Christmas dinner, especially in the cities where older local traditions have loosened their hold. These delicacies are much too good and too expensive to spoil by careless presentation.

Many more dishes which can be served as a first course, or between soup and the main dish, are included in later chapters. On the infinitely varied cold tables of northern and eastern Europe are dozens of dishes which could have been drawn into this section. But as *smörgåsbord* and cold table dishes are so often, with the addition of various hot items, a meal in themselves, these recipes will be found under other headings.

The *tamales* of Mexico and Ecuador posed much the same problem. In those countries they are eaten at the beginning of the Christmas meal, while versions made elsewhere are served at different times. So, as descriptions of how to make them are repetitive, and because we are perhaps more likely to make them for a Christmas party than for the main family meal, tamales and their relations can be found, fitting a little uneasily, in the chapter on pies.

# Cannelloni – Canalones – Spain

*Oven temperature Moderate 180° C, 350° F, Gas Mark 4*

*Serves 8*

450g/1lb lean beef
225 g/8 oz chicken livers
2 medium onions
4 tablespoons olive oil
450 g/1 lb tomatoes
4 tablespoons tomato purée
4 cloves garlic
1 tablespoon wine vinegar
oregano
sugar

salt
pepper
cannelloni (2–4 pieces per person
depending on the size of the
tubes)
750 ml/1¼ pints béchamel sauce
(see page 181)
50 g/2 oz Spanish Manchego
cheese or Parmesan, grated
paprika (optional)

To prepare the filling, first mince the beef and chicken livers using the finest blade of the mincer. Peel and chop the onions finely. Heat the oil in a heavy-based pot and fry the onions for a few minutes. Add the minced beef and chicken livers and fry them with the onions until both are lightly browned.

Peel the tomatoes (dip them for a moment in boiling water and the skins should rub off easily), discard the seeds and roughly chop the flesh. Add chopped tomatoes and tomato purée to the meat mixture. Fry it over a low heat for a few minutes more before adding the garlic, crushed with a little salt, the wine vinegar, and oregano, sugar, salt and pepper to taste. Cover the pot and simmer gently for about 1 hour. You may need to add a little water during the cooking, but the finished consistency of the filling should be solid enough not to run out of the pasta tubes.

While the filling is cooking, boil the pasta according to the directions on the packet.

To assemble the dish, first spread a thin layer of the filling over the base of a well-buttered shallow, ovenproof dish. Ideally, the dish should hold all the cannelloni in one layer without too much space around the edges. Fill the pasta tubes with the meat mixture and lay them side by side in the dish. Pour the béchamel sauce over the cannelloni, sprinkle the dish with grated cheese, and bake in a preheated moderate oven for about 40 minutes. A very light sprinkling of *pimentón* or paprika over the cheese before the dish goes into the oven will give the finished dish those toffee-coloured blisters which make cheese toppings look so appetizing. A bowl of freshly grated Manchego or Parmesan can be handed round separately.

Although béchamel sauce does not freeze successfully by itself, it seems to come to no harm when incorporated into pasta dishes like cannelloni. If you can spare a baking dish good enough to go to the table, this recipe is a candidate for advance preparation and freezing. Freeze it ready to go into the oven, but do thaw it completely before baking. The pasta would not come to grief, but a favourite dish might.

Christmas dinner in Bologna, Italy, begins with *tortellini*. According to a romantic local legend, these little rings of deliciously stuffed dough were the invention of a love-lorn cook who, catching sight of his master's wife sleeping naked, cooked and served pasta fashioned in the shape of her navel as a token of his hopeless passion.

Tortellini are fun to make. For grand occasions they are served in a well-flavoured broth, or as here, *ascuitta*, dry with butter and grated cheese. For everyday eating they may come with ragù Bolognese, a giant of a sauce compared with its pale and widely travelled imitator, and cheese.

### Tortellini Bolognese – Italy

*Serves 4–6*

*Filling*
75 g/3 oz lean pork
50 g/2 oz lean veal
50 g/2 oz breast of chicken or turkey
50 g/2 oz ham
25 g/1 oz mortadella sausage
50 g/2 oz calf's brains
25 g/1 oz butter
salt

pepper
nutmeg
2 large eggs
75 g/3 oz Parmesan, grated
*Dough*
500 g/18 oz flour, hard gluten or strong bread flour if possible
salt
3 large eggs

Chop the pork, veal, breast of chicken or turkey, ham, mortadella and cleaned calf's brains. Melt the butter in a heavy-based pot, add the pork, veal and chicken or turkey meat, and sauté gently until lightly browned. Add the ham, mortadella and brains, and season to taste with salt, pepper, and plenty of grated nutmeg.

Cover the pot and simmer for about 15 minutes. Put the mixture through a mincer, using the finest blade, and add the eggs and grated cheese. Mix all the ingredients together to make a smooth paste.

To make the dough, sift the flour and salt and heap in a mound on a large pastry board. Make a well in the centre of the flour and break the eggs into it. Fold the flour over the eggs and knead until a soft, elastic dough is formed.

To roll the dough, divide it into two or four pieces – smaller amounts are easier to manage unless you have a very large board and an extra long rolling pin. Place the first piece of dough on the floured board and roll it lightly. Lift it, draped over the rolling pin, to stretch it gently, sprinkle with flour, and roll again. Continue to lift, stretch, flour and roll until the dough is extremely thin. Lay the pasta, which should now be almost like a piece of fabric, on a clean cloth on a table or over the back of a chair. Roll out the remaining dough using the same technique. Cut circles of the rolled dough using a plain edged pastry cutter about

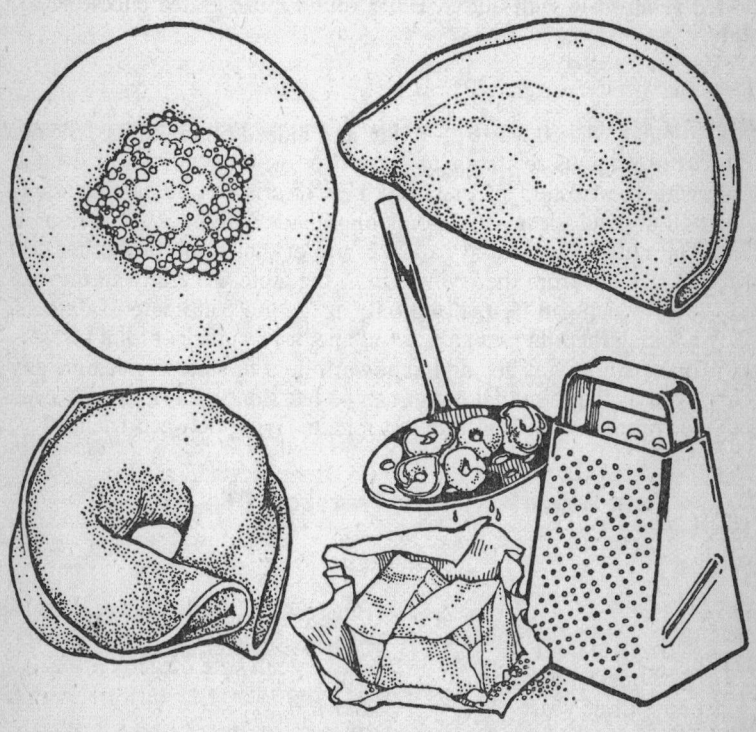

3.75 cm/1½ inches in diameter, or the rim of a wine glass of suitable size.

To assemble the tortellini, place about half a teaspoonful of filling on each circle of pasta. Then fold each circle in two so that the top edge lies just short of the under edge. Curling the pasta round a finger, bring the two points of each folded circle together to make a ring. Arrange the tortellini in a single layer on a floured board or dish and cover them with a floured cloth until wanted. They may be made the day before they are to be eaten. (See the diagram on the previous page.)

To cook the tortellini prepare a large pot of boiling chicken or veal stock, or boiling salted water. Drop the tortellini carefully into the bubbling liquid, a few at a time so that it does not come off the boil. They are ready when they rise to the surface. Scoop them out with a perforated spoon as they bob up to the top of the pot, and keep them warm until all the tortellini are cooked. Serve in a large warmed bowl dotted generously with butter. Hand round more grated cheese separately.


It is, to me, a wicked waste of caviar, and indeed of any of its delicious but less prestigious relations, to serve it on wilting canapés or even at table with the freshest of toast in a nest of crisp white damask. Only *blini* will do, and for my taste, only blini made with buckwheat flour at that. The nutty yeast-raised pancakes are at their mouthwatering best whisked straight from the frying pan to the table, generally an impractical ideal which can be realized only at the most intimate of dinners.

By cooking them in two pans simultaneously, sufficient blini for, say, six people, can be finished and kept warm in a fit state to outshine any toast. And as the prepared batter can be left standing for hours – even a day or more – what is a little last minute frying between friends?

### Yeast-Raised Buckwheat Pancakes – Blini – Russia

*Serves 6*

*Batter*
225 g/8 oz plain flour
225 g/8 oz buckwheat flour
2 teaspoons dried yeast
600 ml/1 pint milk
sugar

2 large eggs, separated
25 g/1 oz butter, melted
salt
*For frying*
75 g/3 oz butter, melted

Sift the plain flour into one large bowl and the buckwheat flour into a smaller one. Dissolve the yeast according to the instructions on the tin or packet using a little of the milk heated to lukewarm (about 43° C/ 110° F) and sweetened with a generous pinch of sugar.

Make a well in the plain flour, pour in the dissolved yeast and draw in the flour gradually. Beat the mixture with a wooden spoon, adding enough of the warm milk to make a thick, smooth batter. Cover the bowl with a cloth and leave the batter to rise in a warm place until it is light and bubbly and has doubled in bulk.

Beat in the buckwheat flour with enough of the remaining milk to produce a smooth batter with the consistency of double cream. Now beat in the egg yolks, melted butter, and salt to taste. Whisk the egg whites until they are stiff, but not dry, and fold them into the batter. Cover the bowl with a cloth and leave the batter to rise again in a warm place until it has doubled in bulk.

At this stage the batter can be left for several hours at kitchen temperature. If it is to be kept overnight, keep it in a refrigerator and remember to allow it plenty of time to come back to room temperature before cooking.

To cook the blini, heat one or more small, heavy frying pans and brush them lightly with melted butter. Pour batter to a depth of about 6 mm/$\frac{1}{4}$ inch into the pan, swirl it to the edges, and cook over a steady, moderate heat until the underside of the pancake is golden and small bubbles are bursting through on top. Flip it over and cook until the second side is golden too. Grease the pans before each addition of batter, and continue in the same way until all the batter is used.

To keep blini hot, stack them on a plate over a pot of simmering water and cover them loosely with a clean napkin.

Preparing the traditional accompaniments for caviar and blini – the separate bowls of soured cream, finely chopped hard-boiled egg, and finely chopped onion – can help to while away the time the batter takes to rise. Only a small jug of melted butter needs last minute action.


*Foie gras*, the liver of fattened goose, is especially popular in France where the famous and notorious geese of Strasbourg are subjected to force-feeding and killed for their over-developed and mouthwatering livers. Foie gras is on the Christmas table of every Frenchman who esteems it and can pay the always high asking price. There are few places outside France where uncooked foie gras can be obtained. But the familiar round, cream earthenware pots, and tins shaped like a long, inverted loaf of bread, are in good food shops the world over. Preserved foie gras is sold in three basic grades: *au naturel* is natural cooked liver with a little seasoning; *bloc* means cooked foie gras pressed with extra fat or a little stuffing; *purée, mousse* and *crème de* foie gras should be at least 75% cooked goose liver stretched with chicken or pork. Truffles are sometimes included with any of the three preparations.

Hot fresh toast may be served with all types of foie gras which is served straight from the pot, or, if it is tinned, whole or sliced on a plate. Foie gras au naturel can be baked in a raised pie crust with a protective coating of additional filling, and all types can be baked inside a loaf of melting *brioche* dough.

Cured and smoked hams, eaten raw, are a much sought after delicacy wherever they are still made by traditional methods. They become more difficult to find, even locally, and few ever reach the shops at all. In some villages in Cyprus an unusual ham, *hiromeri*, akin to Parma ham but with an even stronger flavour, is served at Christmas. A leg of pork is soaked in a wine brine for four to six weeks and then pressed to about a quarter of its original volume before being smoked in the chimney of the house all winter. Hiromeri is made in the autumn, and for Christmas it is the hiromeri from the previous winter's smoking that is enjoyed. Yellow melons, tied up and hung from the rafters since summer, are cut down to complement the pungent ham for the Christmas feast.

To make the best of cured meats of all kinds, never serve them straight from the refrigerator, but always at room temperature. If you want to make up portions more than a few minutes before serving, cover each plate with clear plastic wrap or kitchen foil to prevent the slices from drying out.

Smoked salmon should also be served at room temperature, with lemon wedges and thin slices of buttered brown bread.

Oysters too could not be simpler. Open them with an oyster knife, or any strong, short-bladed knife, starting on the hinged side and working round the shell. Serve them very cold, on their half shells, with lemon wedges and buttered brown bread.

Potted lobster can be prepared well in advance. It keeps perfectly in the refrigerator for several weeks with a covering of clear plastic wrap or kitchen foil. It is also suitable for deep freezing. Serve it with fresh toast and a bowl of lightly salted butter.

Christmas dinner in Chile begins with bite-sized chunks of freshly cooked lobster or king crab served cold on a crisp bed of chopped lettuce and topped with a classic olive oil mayonnaise. *Locos con salsa verde*, abalone with a green sauce of oil, vinegar, onions, lemon juice

20

and herbs, is a traditional alternative to lobster or crab. Also traditional is the table setting. The centrepiece is a bowl of red carnations and sweet basil set on a snow-white cloth.

Finally, two recipes for preserving meats to serve cold, either as a first course or as a lunch or supper dish, are included here.

A modern Swedish recipe for a brawn is made with pork and veal and set with gelatine.

### Jellied Pork and Veal – Fläsk-och Kalvsylta – Sweden

*Serves 10–12*

| | |
|---|---|
| 1 kg/2 lb lean pork | 5 cloves |
| 1 kg/2 lb knuckle of veal | 1 medium onion |
| 2 tablespoons salt | 1 medium carrot |
| 15 white peppercorns | 2 tablespoons white wine vinegar |
| 10 whole allspice | $\frac{1}{2}$ tablespoon gelatine |
| 3 bay leaves | |

Put the pork and veal in a large pot, cover them with cold water, and bring to the boil. Drain the meat and repeat the process. When the fresh water comes to the boil, skim the surface and add the salt, pepper and allspice, crushed, bay, cloves, and the onion and carrot, peeled and roughly chopped. Reduce the heat, cover, and simmer for $1\frac{1}{2}$ to 2 hours, or until the meat is tender. Remove the meat, and when it is cool enough to handle, cut it in small cubes and set aside.

Return the veal bones to the stock and cook them for another $\frac{1}{2}$ hour. Strain the stock and return about 950 ml/32 fl oz to the pot with the meat and cook for about 10 minutes. Add more white pepper to taste, and the vinegar. Soak the gelatine in 125 ml/4 fl oz of stock taken from the pot, and when it is soft, add it to the meat. Stir until the gelatine has dissolved completely.

Pour the meat and stock into one or more moulds, rinsed with cold water, and leave it to set in a cool place. Unmould on to a serving dish and cut in slices. Pickled beetroots are served with jellied pork and veal.

Spiced beef, a medieval recipe for preserving the meat, is still made on the east coast of the United States, in Ireland and northern England. Usually it is served cold, but in Ireland, where it is a traditional Christmas meat, it is sometimes eaten hot. The Irish cookery writer Theodora FitzGibbon gives this recipe in *Food of the Western World*.

Lean cuts such as brisket, rump, round, or tail-end should be used. For a 6 lb joint, 3 bay leaves, 1 teaspoon cloves, 2 chopped shallots, 1 teaspoon each mace and allspice, $\frac{1}{2}$ teaspoon crushed peppercorns, 3 tablespoons brown sugar, and chopped thyme and rosemary are all well mixed in a mortar. Then 1 lb coarse salt and 1 teaspoon salt-petre are added and mixed well in. This mixture is rubbed all over the meat, which is then laid on a bed of the same mixture. The meat is left for 2 days, more of the spiced mixture already in the bowl being rubbed in each day. Then 2 tablespoons treacle (molasses) is poured over and rubbed with the spiced salt mixture, into the joint. The meat is left for a week, being turned and rubbed each day. At the end of this time, it is tied up, covered with water, and simmered very gently with root vegetables for 5–6 hours. Then it is pressed between 2 dishes and weighted.

# FISH DISHES

Fish has a much more important place in traditional festive cooking than in everyday eating today.

Despite the year-round availability of many varieties brought about by faster transportation and freezing, less popular types can be difficult to find even in major cities. If you cannot buy live carp or fresh pike do not be deterred from trying some of these splendid recipes with more familiar fish like sole or turbot. In some cases you may think the result an improvement.

Many of the recipes for cold dishes make excellent first courses or attractive buffet choices, and nearly all of them will be popular with people who have an eye on their waistlines. In this chapter the number of servings given at the start of each recipe should be taken only as a rough guide. How much of each dish people will eat will depend not just on their appetites, but on whether the dish is served alone, or with others, and on what is to follow. The Swedish and Polish fish salads, for example, usually appear on the cold table which begins the Christmas meal, and several will be offered together.

Fish is the focal point of the Christmas meal in many places where dinner or supper on Christmas Eve is the principal family celebration. The custom usually stems from the fast day regulations of the Catholic Church which, for many centuries, forbade the eating of meat on Christmas Eve. Now the dishes are often eaten as much for their Christmas associations as in strict observance of religious dietary regulations.

Only strong sentiment could account for the survival of some festive fish recipes. The Scandinavian speciality of lye fish which is soaked for many days in a strongly alkaline solution of potash, is, even its admirers concede, an acquired taste. And mixed feelings about carp are evident in the instructions for its preparation. 'Muddy' is the most usual description of its flavour, a drawback acknowledged in the widespread practice of buying the fish live and giving it the run of the family bath for several days to wash away the taste of pond and river.

### Herring Salad – Sillsallad – Sweden

*Serves 6–8*

| | |
|---|---|
| 1 large salt herring | 2 tablespoons water |
| 350 g/12 oz boiled potatoes | 25 g/1 oz sugar |
| 350 g/12 oz pickled beetroot | white pepper |
| 50 g/2 oz pickled gherkins | 125 ml/4 fl oz double cream |
| 1 small onion | 2 hard-boiled eggs |
| 1 medium eating apple | parsley |
| 4 tablespoons wine vinegar | |

Soak the herring in cold water for at least 12 hours.

Clean, fillet, and dry the fish with kitchen paper. Dice the herring, potatoes, beetroot and gherkins. Peel and dice the onion. Peel, core and dice the apple. Mix all these carefully together.

Mix together the vinegar, water, sugar, and white pepper, and stir this dressing gently into the herrings and vegetables. Whip the cream and fold it into the salad.

Sillsallad can be heaped in a bowl to serve, or moulded and chilled. Either way garnish it with sliced or chopped hard-boiled eggs and finely chopped parsley. Pass round separately a bowl of stiffly beaten soured cream.

### Herrings with Apple and Cream – Śledzie w Śmietanie – Poland

*Serves 4–6*

| | |
|---|---|
| 450 g/1 lb salt herrings | salt |
| 1 small onion | sugar |
| 1 medium hard eating apple | lemon juice |
| 4 tablespoons double cream | parsley |
| 4 tablespoons single cream | |

Soak the herrings in cold water for at least 12 hours.

Clean and fillet the fish and dry them with kitchen paper. Cut the fillets into diagonal strips and arrange them on a dish. Peel and finely chop the onion. Peel, core and coarsely grate the apple. Whip together the double and single cream. Mix the onion and apple with the cream and season the dressing to taste with salt, sugar and lemon juice. Pour the dressing over the herrings and sprinkle the dish with chopped parsley. It is ready to serve at once.

In Fiji, where open air Christmas feasting centres on an enormous pit barbecue called a *lovo*, and the celebrations last well into the night, *kokoda* is one of the cold side dishes usually served.

### Marinated Raw Fish – Kokoda – Fiji

*Serves 6–8*

6 lemons
1 tablespoon salt
1 kg/2 lb white fish – haddock or
   grey mullet
2 large carrots

1 bunch spring onions
1 large green pepper
2 large tomatoes
2 fresh coconuts
cayenne pepper

Squeeze the juice from all six lemons and strain it into a deep bowl. Add the salt.

Skin and bone the fish and cut it into slices about 6 mm/¼ inch thick. Soak the fish in the salted lemon juice for at least 4 hours or overnight.

Grate the carrots and finely chop the spring onions, the de-seeded pepper and tomatoes. Drain the fish and add the vegetables to it.

Make coconut cream by putting the chopped coconut flesh into a blender with the coconut milk made up to 475 ml/16 fl oz with warm water. Strain the resulting liquid through a fine sieve. Press through all the cream and discard the residue.

Add the coconut cream to the fish and vegetables and chill the mixture. Sprinkle with cayenne pepper before serving.

### Jellied Carp – Kocsonyás Ponty – Hungary

*Serves 12–16*

3-4 kg/6-8 lb carp – preferably a
   whole fish
3 large onions
1 tablespoon paprika

3 large green peppers
3 large tomatoes
salt
3 hard-boiled eggs

Clean and fillet the carp. Put the head, bones, and roe in a saucepan with just sufficient water to cover them and bring to the boil. Skim the liquid. Add the onions, peeled and roughly chopped, paprika, and two peppers and two tomatoes, de-seeded and roughly chopped. Add salt to taste and simmer this stock for about 15 minutes.

Cut the fish fillets into pieces weighing about 150 g/5 oz each, and poach them very gently in the simmering stock until they are cooked through.

Carefully lift out the fish and arrange the pieces on a shallow serving dish big enough to present the fish in one layer without too much space around it.

Strain the stock through a fine sieve lined with two layers of muslin to remove the fat, and reserve the roe.

When the stock is on the point of setting, set aside enough to glaze the decorations, and pour the rest over the fish. Leave the dish in a cool place until the jelly has set firm before decorating it with slices of hard-boiled egg, green pepper, tomato and pieces of the roe. Melt the remaining jelly and glaze the decorations with it.

*Note*: If reducing the quantities of this recipe it may be necessary to add a little unflavoured gelatine to the strained stock to obtain a good set.

### Fried Carp – Karp Smaźony – Poland

*Serves 4*

| | |
|---|---|
| 675 g/1½ lb carp – preferably a whole fish | pepper |
| | flour |
| salt | vegetable oil |

Scale and fillet the carp and cut the fillets into diagonal portions. Sprinkle the fish with salt, pepper, and flour, and fry it on both sides until the flesh is cooked through.

Arrange the pieces on a warmed plate in the shape of a whole fish, and serve it with boiled potatoes.

Traditionally this is the main hot dish of the meal and is served after the cold fish dishes and soup. To avoid a mid-meal dash to the kitchen, the fish is sometimes fried lightly on both sides until golden and finished in a slow oven while the earlier courses are eaten.

In Austria carp fillets are dipped in egg and breadcrumbs before frying. The head, skin and bones of the fish are used to make stock for a carp soup which, with added vegetables and the fish roe, is another traditional Christmas Eve dish.

Eels are almost compulsory Christmas eating in parts of France and Italy, and there are many recipes for their preparation. Neapolitans eat them stuffed and fried accompanied by cauliflower salad, *insalata di rinforz* (see page 101). Steaks of skinned and filleted eel are flattened and stuffed with a mixture of hard-boiled egg yolks, butter, parsley and onion, all bound with raw egg yolk. The steaks are then tied to hold the stuffing in, and fried in butter and lemon juice. When they have cooled the threads are untied, and the pieces of eel are dipped in batter and fried in oil until golden.

In Rome they are often stewed with peas, as in the following recipe.

## Roman Stewed Eels – Anguille in Umido alla Romana – Italy

*Serves 4*

| | |
|---|---|
| 450 g/1 lb small eels | 300 ml/$\frac{1}{2}$ pint dry white wine |
| 1 clove garlic | 1 tablespoon tomato purée |
| 50 g/2 oz shallots or onion | 225 g/8 oz peas, fresh or frozen |
| 3 tablespoons olive oil | 2 tablespoons stock, fish or |
| salt | chicken |
| pepper | |

Cut the eels into 8-cm/3-inch slices and discard the heads. Peel and chop finely the garlic and shallots. Heat the oil in a heavy-based pot and fry the shallots and garlic until lightly browned. Add the pieces of eel, season with salt and pepper, and simmer, uncovered, until the liquid from the eels has evaporated. Add the wine, tomato purée, peas and stock and simmer the stew for about another 15 minutes, or until both the eels and peas are tender. Add more stock if needed during the final cooking. Serve the stewed eels in warmed soup plates with plenty of fresh, crusty white bread.

The English language edition of *Larousse Gastronomique* gives more than fifty recipes for eels, including *anguille à la provençale*, a magnificent eel stew with tomatoes, garlic and black olives. But for an older recipe for this traditional Christmas dish let us leave the great chefs and turn to Elizabeth David's *French Country Cooking* and her source, Madame Léon Daudet in *La France à Table*, 1935.

In a sauté pan put a little olive oil with a few strips of bacon, and let them turn very lightly brown. Next add about 1 lb each of sliced onions and 1 lb of the white part of leeks cut in rounds. Let these brown slightly and then add 1 lb of tomatoes cut in pieces and three or four cloves of garlic crushed, a bay leaf, salt, pepper, and a good pinch of saffron. On top of this put a layer of sliced raw potatoes and the eels cut in thick slices. Add water or white veal stock to cover.

Boil rapidly for 20 minutes, and season with a good measure of freshly ground pepper from the mill before serving. Pour the stock from the *catigau* over pieces of French bread in a deep dish and serve the eels and vegetables on another dish.

The unlikely combination of beer and gingerbread in this classic German recipe makes a rich, dark sauce which is slightly sweet. Traditionally each member of the family sharing the Christmas Eve carp saves one of the fish's large scales to bring luck in the coming year. (German gingerbread is dark, dense, and fairly sweet.)

### Carp in Beer – Karpfen in Bier – Germany

*Serves 6*

| | |
|---|---|
| 1 (1½-2-kg/3-4-lb) carp | 2 cloves |
| 3 tablespoons white wine vinegar | salt |
| 2 medium carrots | pepper |
| 1 large leek | 175 g/6 oz gingerbread |
| 1 large onion | 900 ml/1½ pints brown ale |
| 1 bay leaf | 1 large lemon |

Clean the carp but do not scale it. Soak the fish in cold water with the vinegar for about 1 hour.

In a pot or casserole big enough to hold the fish put the vegetables, cleaned and chopped, the bay leaf, cloves, salt and pepper. Add about 600 ml/1 pint of water, and bring the pot to the boil. Cover, and simmer the stock for about 1 hour.

Break the gingerbread into cubes and soak it in a third of the ale.

Drain the carp and put it into the simmering stock. Add the juice of the lemon (save the rind) and the rest of the ale. Cover and cook gently for about 20 minutes or until the carp is tender. Lift the fish out carefully and keep it warm on a serving dish.

Strain the stock and return it to the pot. Add the soaked gingerbread and boil this mixture briskly until it has reduced to about half the original quantity.

Strain the sauce over the carp and garnish it with curls of lemon rind.

The richest of the traditional carp dishes come from Czechoslovakia, and from Hungary, where it is baked with soured cream and potatoes.

## Carp in Black Sauce – Kapr na Ćerno – Czechoslovakia

*Oven temperature Moderately hot 190° C, 375° F, Gas Mark 5*

*Serves 4–6*

| | |
|---|---|
| 1 stalk celery | 1 teaspoon chopped lemon peel |
| 1 large carrot | 2 tablespoons redcurrant jelly |
| 1 medium parsnip | 6 tablespoons light beer |
| 1 large onion | 4 ginger biscuits |
| 25 g/1 oz unsalted butter | 1 tablespoon light brown sugar |
| 25 g/1 oz castor sugar | salt |
| 1 tablespoon water | 6 carp steaks, about 2·5 cm/1 inch |
| 150 ml/¼ pint red wine vinegar | thick |
| 600 ml/1 pint water | 10 prunes, stoned and chopped |
| 2 bay leaves | 25 g/1 oz sultanas, chopped |
| pinch thyme | 1 tablespoon almonds, slivered |
| 5 black peppercorns | 2 lemons |
| 5 whole allspice, crushed | |

Peel and chop the vegetables. Melt the butter in a heavy-based pot. Add the vegetables, lower the heat, cover the pot and cook them gently for about 10 minutes.

In another heavy-based pot dissolve the sugar in the 1 tablespoon water over a low heat, then bring to the boil and continue boiling until the sugar forms a dark caramel. Add the vinegar and keep the mixture boiling until it has reduced to about 4 tablespoons. Add 600 ml/1 pint water, bay leaves, thyme, peppercorns and allspice, lemon peel, red-currant jelly and the sweated vegetables. Bring to the boil, lower the heat and simmer the mixture, partially covered, for about 30 minutes before adding the beer, crushed ginger biscuits and brown sugar. Increase the heat and cook the mixture, uncovered, for about 5 minutes, or until it thickens a little. Strain the sauce through a sieve, discarding any vegetables that cannot be pressed through easily. Add salt to taste.

Butter an oven-to-table dish large enough to take the fish steaks in one layer. Arrange the carp in the dish and pour over the sauce. Sprinkle on the prunes, sultanas and almonds. Bake the fish in a preheated moderately hot oven for about 20 minutes or until it is just firm, basting once or twice during cooking.

Serve the fish from the dish in which it was baked.

Hungarian hospitality can have the overwhelming warmth of a hug from a friendly bear. You need to be hungry to enjoy it. Servings are usually substantial as the following recipe demonstrates. It is for a dish of Rascian carp as made by the renowned Hungarian chef Karoly Gundel.

### Rascian Carp – Ráczponty – Hungary

*Oven temperature Moderately hot 190° C, 375° F, Gas Mark 5*

*Serves 6*

| | |
|---|---|
| 3 kg/6 lb carp, preferably a whole fish | 2 large onions |
| | 2 large tomatoes |
| 350 g/12 oz smoked bacon | 3 large green peppers |
| 1 tablespoon salt | 75 g/3 oz butter, melted |
| 1 tablespoon paprika | 350 ml/12 fl oz soured cream |
| 1 kg/2 lb potatoes, parboiled | 2 tablespoons plain flour |

Scale and wash the carp and split it in two. Divide the fish into 6 pieces and score them deeply. Press thin rashers of bacon into the gashes and sprinkle the fish with salt and paprika.

Butter an oven-to-table dish large enough to hold the fish in one layer. Cover the base with the parboiled potatoes cut in slices. Lay the fish on top of the potatoes and cover it with thinly sliced onion rings, and the sliced tomatoes and peppers. Pour over the melted butter and bake in a preheated moderately hot oven for 30 minutes, or until the vegetables are half cooked.

Mix the soured cream with the flour and pour this mixture over the fish. Sprinkle the top with a little paprika and bake it for about another 30 minutes. Serve the fish, which needs no accompaniments, straight from the baking dish.

Fish, this time boiled or steamed salt cod, is the focal point of Portugal's Christmas meal, eaten on Christmas Eve. Its accompaniments are equally plain – boiled potatoes and cabbage. For pudding there is *filhós*, a kind of yeast-raised fritter, vermicelli, or *rabanadas*, French toast made with bread soaked in cinnamon-flavoured milk.

## Boiled Salt Cod – Bacahlau Cozido – Portugal

*Serves 4*

500 g/1 lb salt cod                    black pepper to taste
olive oil to taste

Cut the salt cod into four serving pieces and soak them in cold water
for at least 12 hours. Rinse the fish and put it in a pan with enough fresh
cold water to cover. Bring to the boil, skim and simmer, covered, until
tender. The exact time depends on how dry the salt cod was before
soaking.

Drain the fish and serve it with freshly boiled potatoes and cabbage,
all in separate dishes. Olive oil and black pepper are passed round so
that each person seasons his portion to taste.

Sea bream is traditional Christmas Eve fare all over Spain and each
region has its own special way of cooking the fish. In the Basque
country it is grilled over a wood fire with lemon, olive oil and garlic. In
Asturias it will usually be casseroled with white wine, garlic, pine kernels, olive oil, lemon, onions and parsley. Olive oil and garlic are
essential ingredients in much Spanish cooking, and for the baked sea
bream of New Castille, no substitutes will capture the flavour of Spain.

## Baked Sea Bream – Besugo Asado a la Madrileña – Spain

*Oven temperature Moderate 180° C, 350° F, Gas Mark 4*

*Serves 3–4*

1·5 kg/3 lb sea bream, preferably       2 cloves garlic
   a whole fish                         parsley
2 lemons, preferably thin-skinned       1 bay leaf
4 tablespoons olive oil                 salt
125 ml/4 fl oz dry white wine or        pepper
   dry sherry

Clean the bream and leave it whole. Make diagonal cuts at about
2·5-cm/1-inch intervals on one side of the fish and put a slice of lemon
in each cut. Put about 1 tablespoon of the olive oil in the bottom of a
shallow oven-to-table dish and lay the fish, cut side up, in the dish. Pour

over the rest of the olive oil and the wine or sherry. Sprinkle the fish with crushed or very finely chopped garlic, chopped parsley, the crumbled bay leaf and a generous seasoning of salt and freshly milled black pepper.

Bake the fish for about an hour in a preheated moderate oven. Serve the fish from the baking dish with fresh crusty bread and a crisp green salad dressed with olive oil and lemon juice.

So many people are impatient with fish cooked on the bone that we are sometimes wary of putting any fish in front of guests except the ubiquitous prawn cocktail. Two splendid recipes from eastern Europe solve this problem beautifully. The first, a soufflé of pike, comes from Poland. It is ideal for small lunch or supper parties and may, of course, be made with almost any fish you fancy. The second is the much better known Russian *kulebiaka*, a crusty fish pie that has the uncommon distinction of being elegant on a heroic scale — which is just as well since the work involved is considerable.

### Pike Soufflé – Suflet ze Szczupaka – Poland

*Oven temperature Moderately hot 200° C, 400° F, Gas Mark 6*

*Serves 4–6*

| | |
|---|---|
| 450 g / 1 lb pike | 75 g / 3 oz butter |
| ½ tablespoon salt | nutmeg |
| black peppercorns | pepper and salt |
| 1 bay leaf | 3 large eggs, separated |
| 1 blade mace | dry breadcrumbs |
| 150 ml / ¼ pint milk | |

Put the piece of pike in a pot, cover it with water, and add the salt, a few black peppercorns, crushed, the bay leaf and blade of mace. Bring to the boil slowly, reduce the heat, and simmer the fish gently until it is cooked through.

When the fish is cool enough to handle remove as many of the bones as possible. Put the flesh in a blender with about 150 ml / ¼ pint of the strained fish stock, and blend it thoroughly so that any small bones remaining in the flesh are rendered harmless.

Add another 150 ml / ¼ pint of strained fish stock to the milk. Melt the butter in a small, heavy-based saucepan and stir in the flour. Cook the roux over a low heat, stirring constantly for about 2 minutes before adding the fish and milk mixture gradually. Cook the sauce for another 2 minutes over a low heat.

Take the saucepan off the heat and beat in the puréed fish and the three egg yolks, well beaten. Season the mixture well with nutmeg, pepper and salt.

Whisk the egg whites until stiff and fold them gently but thoroughly into the fish mixture. Turn the soufflé into a 1¾-litre/3-pint soufflé dish which has been well buttered and dusted with dry breadcrumbs (this gives the mixture something to bite on as it rises).

Bake in the centre of a preheated moderately hot oven for about 45 minutes, or until the soufflé is well risen and golden. Serve it immediately with a crisp green salad and crusty bread or rolls.

Kulebiaka is a creation for which literally hundreds of recipes exist. Like so many long-established favourites they differ not only from region to region but from family to family. The following recipe is for a salmon kulebiaka made with shortcrust pastry and explains the method in detail. There are puff pastry versions too, and any number of possible fillings from an inexpensive and delicious everyday cabbage with hard-boiled egg and soured cream mixture to the festive fish kulebiaka below.

### Salmon Kulebiaka – Russia

*Oven temperature Moderately hot 200° C, 400° F, Gas Mark 6*

*Serves 8–10*

*Pastry*
450 g/1 lb plain flour
1 teaspoon salt
225 g/8 oz unsalted butter
75 g/ 3 oz vegetable fat
125-150 ml/4-5 fl oz iced water
*Filling*
3 litres/5 pints water
450 ml/¾ pint dry white wine
4 medium onions
1 stalk celery
1 large carrot
black peppercorns
4 teaspoons salt

1·25 kg/2½ lb fresh salmon,
    preferably in one piece
100 g/4 oz unsalted butter
225 g/8 oz mushrooms
2½ tablespoons lemon juice
90 g/3½ oz long-grain rice
250 ml/8 fl oz stock, fish or
    chicken
4 tablespoons dill leaves, chopped
3 hard-boiled eggs
*Glaze*
1 egg yolk
1 tablespoon single cream

To make the pastry sift the flour and salt into a large cold bowl. Cut the fats, which should preferably be chilled, into dice, and work the fats and flour together using your fingertips or a pastry blender until the mixture looks like fine breadcrumbs. Sprinkle the mixture with 8 tablespoons of the iced water and gather it into a ball. If the dough seems too crumbly add as much as required of the remaining iced water a drop or two at a time. Divide the pastry into two equal balls, dust both pieces with flour, wrap them separately in greaseproof paper and refrigerate them until firm – about 3 hours.

To make the salmon filling, first make a court bouillon by boiling together in a large pot the water and wine with one of the onions, coarsely chopped, the celery and carrot, also coarsely chopped, about 10 black peppercorns, crushed, and about $2\frac{1}{2}$ teaspoons of the salt. Lower the salmon into the boiling stock, reduce the heat to a simmer, and poach the fish until it is firm. This will take 8 to 10 minutes according to the thickness of the cut. Lift the fish out, and when it is cool enough to handle, separate it into small flakes, discarding skin and bones.

Now take a heavy frying pan and melt in it 25 g/1 oz of the butter. Slice the mushrooms thinly and fry them in the melted butter, stirring occasionally, until they are soft. Transfer the mushrooms to a bowl and mix them with the lemon juice, a pinch of salt and a little freshly ground black pepper.

Melt another 50 g/2 oz of butter in the pan and add all but 1 tablespoon of the remaining onions, finely chopped. Fry the onions until they are soft, but not brown. Season them with the remaining salt, and a little black pepper, and add them to the mushrooms.

Finally, melt the rest of the butter in the pan and fry the remaining finely chopped onion until it is soft, but not brown. Add the rice and stir it together with the onions until each grain is coated with butter. Now add the stock, bring the mixture to the boil, cover the pan tightly, reduce the heat to a simmer, and cook the rice for about 12 minutes or until the liquid is absorbed and the rice is tender. Remove the pan from the heat. Stir in the dill. (If you are using dried dill add only one generous teaspoonful.)

Now combine the mushroom and onion mixture with the cooked salmon. Add the rice and chopped hard-boiled eggs. Mix them together gently with a fork and adjust the seasoning, remembering to season more generously if the pie is to be served cold.

To assemble the kulebiaka, roll one piece of pastry dough to about 3 mm/$\frac{1}{8}$ inch thick on a floured surface, and trim it to a rectangle about 40 cm/16 inches long by about 18 cm/7 inches wide.

34

Butter a large heavy baking tin generously, and lifting the pastry by draping it over the rolling pin, place it on the tin stretching it as little as possible. Heap the salmon filling on to the pastry to within 2·5 cm/1 inch of the edge and brush the bare edge with the egg yolk mixed with the cream.

Roll out the second ball of pastry dough to a rectangle about 45 cm/18 inches long by about 23 cm/9 inches wide and place it on top of the filling. Seal the edges firmly with your fingers, a fork or a pastry cutter. Make three diagonal cuts in the top of the pie and decorate it with pastry trimmings. Brush the pie with the rest of the egg yolk and cream mixture, and rest it in the refrigerator for about 20 minutes before baking.

Pour a teaspoonful of melted butter into each of the holes on top of the pie and bake it in the centre of a preheated moderately hot oven for about 1 hour or until the pastry is crisp and golden. (If it browns too quickly cover the pie loosely with foil for part of the baking time, but remove the covering for the last 10 minutes of cooking to crisp the pastry.)

Serve the kulebiaka immediately with a jug of hot melted butter or soured cream, or serve it cold with soured cream.

# ROASTS

Back in fifteenth-century England swans and peacocks graced the festive tables of the rich and powerful. Dame Alice de Byrene was not, the records show, in the peacock eating class, but two swans, two pigs, twelve geese, two joints of mutton, twenty-four capons and seventeen coneys were roasted for the feast she gave for 100 people on New Year's Day 1413. Maybe she did not like peacocks, for by all accounts they are not good eating.

Two hundred and fifty years later for a Twelfth Night feast held at Ingatestone Hall, the Essex home of the Secretary of State Sir William Petrie, over seven pounds of meat per head were served. The household books show that 100 diners were offered nine pieces of boiled beef (about 20 lb to a piece); six pieces of roast beef (30 lb to a 'livery' piece); a haunch and leg of pork; two legs of veal; a whole young pig; a loin and breast of veal; two rabbits; ten beef, two mutton and four venison pasties – all these were 'very great'; three geese; two capons; two partridges; a woodcock; two teal and twelve larks; plus sauces, dressings, forcemeats, pastry and bread. Caterers these days think in terms of 100–175 g/4–6 oz portions.

Wild and tame fowl were popular Christmas gifts and payments in the Middle Ages, and were often presented alive to be kept in special pens, fed on such delicacies as raisins, white breadcrumbs and milk till they were needed in the kitchen. This custom and the difficulties of housing and feeding more than breeding stock of larger beasts through the winter months set a pattern of Christmas eating which is followed to this day.

Roasting is an art few of us practise for everyday meals when time is short and large joints and big birds would break the family budget. So ensure success by working out cooking times carefully, using the charts given with each group of recipes. The following check-list may also be useful.

- Roasting times are calculated for meat or poultry starting at room temperature – not straight from the refrigerator.
- Preheat the oven.

- Calculate cooking time on the oven-ready weight – this *includes stuffing*.
- Roasting is a dry cooking method. Never cover a roast closely with foil or a lid which will prevent steam escaping. Even the largest turkey will not burn or dry out if it is covered with a double thickness of muslin wrung out in water then dipped in melted butter and draped over the whole bird. Baste frequently, moistening the cloth with pan juices every 15 to 20 minutes throughout cooking time.
- To test a roast use a thin metal skewer and stick it into the thickest part of the meat. Pull it out and the colour of the juices which flow from the hole will tell you whether it is done. Appropriate juice colours are given in the introduction to each meat. Do not prod the meat too often or it will be less succulent.
- Rest roasts before carving. Leave them for at least 15 minutes in the oven with the heat turned off and the door open.
- Never over-stuff poultry or it may burst in the oven.

No stuffing should be so aggressively flavoured that it overwhelms the taste of the meat. In some cases the stuffing is intended only to flavour the flesh during cooking and not to be eaten at all. But usually the stuffing is food in its own right.

Recipes for stuffings have changed little over the centuries. Although white breadcrumbs are specified in many recipes, crumbs from a wholemeal loaf give a nuttier flavour and looser texture which you may prefer. An extra egg or two, beaten and added to a stuffing mixture will bind it more thoroughly if a denser texture is wanted.

A trussed bird need not look as if it has been caught in a game of cats' cradle. Sew or skewer the vent firmly to prevent juices escaping, then tie the legs together with string and tie the string round the tail. Pull the neck skin gently down under the back and fasten it with metal skewers or wooden toothpicks. Cut off the wingtips for the stockpot, and secure the wings to the sides of the bird with string tied under the back.

### Goose

Of all the domesticated birds, goose has the finest flavour. Its creamy white flesh cooks to a dark beige and has a rich, slightly gamey taste. One of the reasons the meat tastes so good is that goose is a fatty bird. Nowadays its fattiness is more often mentioned as a criticism, but it is an advantage too. Goose is the original self-basting bird.

Turkeys have been around a long time in Europe, but geese are

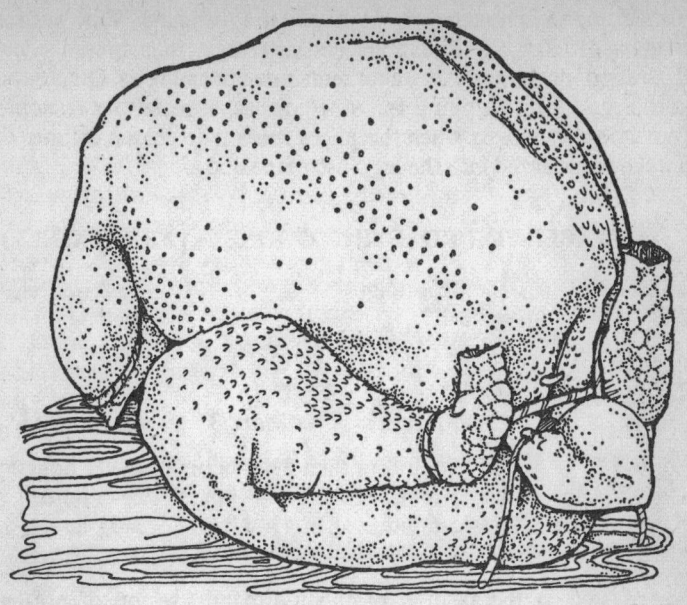

**Trussing a turkey – the legs are tied together with string, which is also tied round the tail. The wings are folded under the body and held in place with string**

indigenous and their appearance on the Christmas table goes back further. The Germans are especially attached to their festive goose, stuffing it with apples, nuts, raisins and prunes. Irish and Polish cooks often use mashed potato flavoured with onion and herbs. Sage and onion stuffing is the best known English recipe, and all these traditions have merged in American kitchens.

Although geese live to a great age, they are little use for eating when more than two years old. Choose a young bird with soft feet and legs which still have a little down on them. Grey goose is favoured in France, the larger white goose in England. Both are raised in North America where wild geese are still much more widely available than in Europe.

A goose usually weighs between 3 and 6 kg/6 and 13 lb. When shopping, allow about 450 g/16 oz per person. Frozen birds should be thawed slowly in the refrigerator for at least 24 hours.

I much prefer the slow roasting method for goose. The meat is evenly cooked and more of the fat melts out. Prick the bird on the legs, sides and lower breast with a sharp skewer or fork before roasting. Put it breast side up in a roasting tin for the first 15 minutes. Turn it breast side down for half the remaining cooking time, then breast side up again, raised on a rack, for the remainder. Basting is unnecessary. (Save the goose fat dripping for other dishes, especially a *cassoulet.*)

Your goose is cooked when the juices run a pale golden colour. Test with a skewer inserted into the leg close to the body.

### TIMETABLE FOR ROASTING GOOSE (AVERAGE ONLY)

| Weight of bird | Slow roasting method | | Fast roasting method |
|---|---|---|---|
| (including stuffing) | 200°C 400°F Gas Mark 6 | 160°C 325°F Gas Mark 3 | 200°C 400°F Gas Mark 6 |
| 3–4 kg/6–8 lb | 1st 15 minutes then 3½–4 hours | | 2½–2¾ hours |
| 4–5 kg/ 8–11 lb | 1st 15 minutes then 4–4½ hours | | 2¾–3 hours |
| 5–6 kg/11–13 lb | 1st 15 minutes then 4½–5 hours | | 3–3¼ hours |

Goose roasted in the fashion of the Normandy region of northern France is the finest goose recipe I have found. Blood puddings are a continuing part of French Christmas tradition, and this stuffing of black pudding, apples and port makes a magnificent dish.

### Goose with Black Pudding and Apples – Oie à la Normande – France

*Serves 6–8*

| | |
|---|---|
| 1 (4-5-kg/8-11-lb) goose | 5 tablespoons port wine |
| *Stuffing* | salt |
| 675 g/1½ lb blood (black) puddings | black pepper |
| | 100 g/4 oz medium oatmeal (optional) |
| 1 goose liver | |
| 1-2 cloves garlic | *Garnish* |
| 2 large eating apples | 2 kg/4 lb eating apples |

Skin the blood puddings and break them into a large bowl, picking out any visible pieces of white fat. Add the goose liver and crushed garlic and pound the mixture smooth. Peel and core the apples and grate them coarsely into the bowl. Add the port, season with salt and freshly ground black pepper, and mix all the ingredients thoroughly together.

Blood puddings vary enormously in the amount of liquid they will absorb. If the stuffing mixture appears too mushy add up to 100 g/4 oz medium oatmeal (ground oatmeal not oat flakes). This will swell during cooking so it is particularly important not to over-fill the bird if oatmeal is used. Stuff the goose loosely with this mixture, truss, and roast as directed on page 40. Serve the goose on a bed of hot, unsweetened apple purée.

### Goose with Apple and Prune Stuffing – Gaasesteg med Aebler og Svedsker – Denmark

*Serves 6–8*

| | |
|---|---|
| 1 (4-5-kg/8-11-lb) goose | *Gravy* |
| ½ lemon | 300 ml/½ pint giblet stock |
| *Stuffing* | 1 tablespoon cornflour |
| 675 g/1½ lb stoned prunes | 2 tablespoons redcurrant jelly |
| 1 kg/2 lb cooking apples | salt |
| salt | pepper |
| pepper | |

Remove any excess fat from the vent of the goose and rub the cavity with a cut lemon. Chop the prunes. Peel, core and roughly chop the apples. Mix them together with a seasoning of salt and freshly ground black pepper, and pack this simple stuffing into the goose. Truss the bird and roast as directed on page 40.

Make the gravy while the goose is resting after roasting. Pour most of the fat from the roasting tin into a bowl. Pour the stock into the roasting tin, and stir over a low heat to dissolve any hardened pan juices. Stir in the cornflour blended with a little cold water. Cook for 2 or 3 minutes before stirring in the redcurrant jelly. Season the gravy to taste with salt and freshly ground black pepper. Strain it into a serving jug. Red cabbage and sugar-browned potatoes are the traditional accompaniments to the Danish goose.

A typical German recipe for a Christmas goose also includes apple.

## Goose with Apple, Raisin and Nut Stuffing –
### Gänsebraten mit Äpfeln, Rosinen und Nüssen – Germany

*Serves 6–8*

| | |
|---|---|
| 1 (4-5-kg/8-11-lb) goose | 3 medium cooking apples |
| *Stuffing* | 50 g/2 oz blanched almonds or |
| 150 g/5 oz seedless raisins | hazelnuts |
| 1 goose liver | 3 tablespoons chopped parsley |
| 3 tablespoons butter | 1 teaspoon dried marjoram |
| 1 large onion | salt |
| 100 g/4 oz soft white breadcrumbs | black pepper |

Put the raisins in a bowl and cover them with boiling water. Set them aside to plump up.

Roughly chop the goose liver. Melt the butter in a small saucepan and fry the liver until it is just firm. Take the liver from the pan and set it aside to cool. Peel and finely chop the onion and fry it in the remaining butter until it is soft and transparent. Do not let the onion brown.

Chop the liver very finely and put it in a large mixing bowl with the fried onion and butter. Add the breadcrumbs, the apples, peeled, cored and roughly chopped, the nuts, roughly chopped, drained raisins, herbs, and a generous seasoning of salt and freshly ground black pepper. Mix these ingredients well and check the seasoning.

Stuff the goose loosely with this mixture. Truss, and roast as directed on page 40.

Red cabbage, sauerkraut, or noodles are usually served with goose in Germany. In Czechoslovakia sauerkraut is used for the stuffing. Its sharp flavour goes well with the rich goose flesh.

## Goose with Sauerkraut Stuffing –
### Pecena Husa se Zelim – Czechoslovakia

*Serves 4–6*

| | |
|---|---|
| 1 (3-4-kg/6-8-lb) goose | ½ teaspoon caraway seeds |
| *Stuffing* | 6 juniper berries |
| 2 medium onions | 1 large potato |
| 25 g/1 oz butter | ½ teaspoon salt |
| 450 g/1 lb sauerkraut, well drained | black pepper |

Peel and finely chop the onions. Melt the butter in a small saucepan and fry the onions gently until they are soft and transparent but not brown.

Put the sauerkraut in a mixing bowl with the onions, butter, caraway seeds and juniper berries. Peel the potato and grate it coarsely into the bowl. Season the mixture with salt and freshly ground black pepper and combine all the ingredients thoroughly.

Stuff the goose with this mixture. Truss, and roast as directed on page 40. Dumplings are served with goose in Czechoslovakia.

## Roast Goose with Sage and Onion Stuffing – England

*Serves 4–6*

| | |
|---|---|
| 1 (3-4-kg/6-8-lb) goose | 175 g/6 oz fresh white or brown |
| *Stuffing* | breadcrumbs |
| 1 large onion | 4 leaves fresh sage |
| 50 g/2 oz butter | 1 teaspoon salt |
| 1 goose liver (optional) | black pepper |

Peel and chop the onion finely. Melt the butter in a small saucepan and fry the onion gently until it is soft but not brown. If the goose liver is being included, chop it roughly and fry until it is just firm. Mix the onions, the liver, finely chopped, and butter with the breadcrumbs and the sage leaves, very finely chopped. Season the mixture with salt and freshly ground black pepper.

Stuff the goose with this mixture. Truss, and roast as directed on page 40. For a denser stuffing, bind the mixture with a beaten egg.

A potato stuffing for a 4–5-kg/8–10-lb goose consists of 1 kg/2 lb well mashed boiled potato mixed with a large onion, chopped and softened in 25 g/1 oz of butter, the liver, lightly cooked and finely chopped, and a finely chopped celery heart. Season with chopped parsley or thyme, nutmeg, salt, and pepper.

## Turkey

Wild turkeys were still plentiful in New England when the Pilgrim Fathers caught some for their first Thanksgiving dinner in 1621. Domesticated turkeys had been found by explorers in Mexico and central America a century earlier and were first imported to Spain in 1498. The earliest written record of their success in England comes in 1541 when Archbishop Cranmer, attempting to limit the gluttony of the higher clergy, laid down a list of 'greater fowls', among them turkey cocks, of which only one was permitted in a dish.

Turkeys are easily raised by traditional methods of husbandry as well as in factory farms. They should be properly hung to develop their full flavour – a process often skimped with frozen birds. This is one of the reasons fresh turkeys often taste better than frozen ones. If it must be a frozen bird, thaw it slowly in the refrigerator, for 48 hours for a large bird, 24 hours for a small one.

Turkeys can weigh anything from 2 kg/4 lb to 18 kg/40 lb, but few domestic ovens can cope with a bird of more than 9 kg/20 lb. When shopping allow about 350 g/12 oz per serving.

A perfectly cooked turkey is a rare bird if for no other reason than that the darker meat of the legs takes more cooking than the delicate white breast meat. The muslin basting method described on page 38 goes a long way to solving the problem of dry breast meat. The slow roasting method is generally better if time permits. For very large birds it is not always practicable.

Set the turkey on a rack in a shallow roasting tin and baste it every 15 to 20 minutes throughout the cooking time. It is ready when the juices run clear. Test with a skewer inserted into the thickest part of the leg close to the body.

## TIMETABLE FOR ROASTING TURKEY (AVERAGE ONLY)

| Weight of bird | Slow roasting method | Fast roasting method |
|---|---|---|
| (including stuffing) | 160°C 325°F Gas Mark 3 | 230°C 450°F Gas Mark 8 |
| 3–4 kg/6–8 lb | 3–3½ hours | 2¼–2½ hours |
| 4–5 kg/8–11 lb | 3½–3¾ hours | 2½–2¾ hours |
| 5–7 kg/11–15 lb | 3¾–4¼ hours | 2¾–3 hours |
| 7–9 kg/15–20 lb | 4¼–4¾ hours | 3–3½ hours |
| 9–10 kg/20–22 lb | 4¾–5¼ hours | 3½–3¾ hours |
| 10–12 kg/22–26 lb | 5¼–6 hours | 3¾–4¼ hours |

Turkeys are now so widely available that in many parts of the world, especially in cities and larger towns, older Christmas eating customs are being forgotten. Chileans stuff turkeys with apples and walnuts. In Ecuador they are filled with rice, almonds, eggs, raisins, prunes and peas, in Greece with pork and chestnuts, in France with chestnuts and

44

truffles. There are chestnut stuffings for turkey from every continent and there is surprisingly little to choose between most of them. The best I have found is a Milanese stuffing. The ingredients may look an odd mixture, but the flavour they produce is magnificent. (Tinned, whole chestnuts, even well drained, are a bit too wet for most stuffings. Fresh chestnuts, boiled or baked, and peeled, of course, or reconstituted dried chestnuts, have better flavour and texture.)

## Milanese Stuffed Turkey – Il Tacchino Ripieno – Italy

*Serves 10–12*

1 (4-5-kg/8-11-lb) turkey
1 black Perigord truffle
*Stuffing*
225 g/8 oz Italian pork sausages, fresh
225 g/8 oz minced veal
1 turkey liver
100 g/4 oz Parma ham
100 g/4 oz shallots or onions
225 g/8 oz stoned prunes
1 kg/2 lb chestnuts, cooked*
truffle parings

4 tablespoons olive oil
40 g/1½ oz Parmesan cheese, grated
1 tablespoon honey
4 tablespoons sherry
½ nutmeg
1 teaspoon salt
pepper
*To baste*
6 tablespoons melted butter
125 ml/4 fl oz dry white wine

*To prepare chestnuts, see pages 1–2.

Peel the truffle and slice it very thinly. Reserve the trimmings. Using your fingers, gently loosen the turkey skin away from the breast and upper legs, being careful not to break the skin. Tuck slices of truffle between the meat and the skin.

To make the stuffing, skin the uncooked sausages and break them into a large mixing bowl. Add the minced veal. Finely chop the turkey liver and Parma ham, and peel and chop the shallots. Add them to the bowl along with the prunes and prepared chestnuts, roughly chopped, and the truffle parings. Mix well. Put the oil in a large, heavy-based pot over a medium heat and sauté these ingredients gently together for about 10 minutes. Return the mixture to the bowl and add the grated cheese, honey and sherry. Grate half a nutmeg into the stuffing and add the salt and a generous grinding of fresh black pepper.

Stuff the turkey with this mixture, dividing it between the breast flap and the main cavity. Truss, and roast as directed on page 44, basting with the melted butter and wine.

A very similar Spanish stuffing is made adding 175 g/6 oz each of dried peaches and pine kernels, and omitting the honey and shallots. Thyme, marjoram, basil and bay are also added to this Catalan recipe. Serve very plain vegetables with these luxurious birds.

Another rich stuffing, American this time, uses pork, veal and cream to keep the meat moist, as well as chestnuts and truffles for a superb flavour.

## Two-Stuffing Turkey – United States

*Serves 12–18*

| | |
|---|---|
| 1 (5-7-kg/11-15-lb) turkey | 250 ml/8 fl oz double cream |
| 2 black Perigord truffles | 1 tablespoon paprika |
| *First stuffing* | 2 tablespoons chopped parsley |
| 1 turkey liver | 1 tablespoon chopped chives or |
| 1 tablespoon butter | spring onions |
| 1 tablespoon brandy | 1 teaspoon salt |
| 450 g/1 lb minced pork | black pepper |
| 450 g/1 lb minced veal | *Second stuffing* |
| 225 g/8 oz chestnuts, cooked* | 225 g/8 oz chestnuts, cooked* |
| 50 g/2 oz hazelnuts | salt and pepper |
| 8 tablespoons fresh white | *To baste* |
| breadcrumbs | 225 g/8 oz butter, melted |
| truffle parings | |

*To prepare chestnuts, see pages 1–2.

Peel the truffles and slice them very thinly. Reserve the trimmings. Using your fingers gently loosen the turkey skin from the breast and upper legs, being careful not to break the skin. Tuck slices of truffle between the meat and the skin.

To make the first stuffing, chop the turkey liver roughly. Melt the butter in a small saucepan over a medium heat and sauté the liver for about 3 minutes or until just firm. Flame it with the brandy and put the liver and juices in a large mixing bowl with the pork and veal. Break up the chestnuts and add them to the meats. Add the hazelnuts, finely chopped, the breadcrumbs, truffle trimmings, cream, paprika, parsley, chives, salt, and a generous grinding of fresh black pepper. Mix the ingredients thoroughly together, and when they are well blended put this stuffing into the main cavity of the turkey. Sew or skewer the vent.

To prepare the second stuffing, simply break up the chestnuts, season with salt and pepper, and pack them into the neck end of the bird.

Truss, and roast the turkey as directed on page 44, basting with melted butter. Bacon rolls, small pork sausages, cranberry sauce, bread sauce, brussels sprouts and roast potatoes are traditional accompaniments to turkey in the United States and Britain.


A very plain chestnut stuffing is easily made by rubbing cooked chestnuts through a coarse sieve and mixing them with salt and pepper. A beaten egg will bind the stuffing to give a firmer texture, and the addition of truffles, sliced or chopped, improves the flavour. Allow 100–175 g/4–6 oz of chestnuts per 450 g/1 lb of turkey.

The simplest turkey recipe I know is roasted without stuffing. Constant basting with honey and butter makes it crisp and black on the outside, while underneath the flesh is very moist and white. The method was taken to England by the Romans who cooked flamingoes, herons and other large birds in this way, and it is still used in the North. Butter and dark honey are melted together and painted over the bird several times until it is well coated. This turkey should be roasted in a moderately hot oven (200° C, 400° F, Gas Mark 6) for the first 30 minutes, then in a moderate oven (160° C, 325° F, Gas Mark 3) for the remainder of its cooking time. For a 7–9-kg/15–20-lb turkey use 450 g/1 lb honey and 225 g/8 oz butter.


Eggs, raw and hard-boiled, are used in this substantial Maltese stuffing recipe.

### Roast Turkey – Dundjan Mimli – Malta

*Serves 16–18*

| | |
|---|---|
| 1 (6-7-kg/13-15-lb) turkey | 25 g/1 oz pistachio nuts, shelled |
| *Stuffing* | 1 small onion |
| 1 kg/2 lb minced pork | 2 tablespoons chopped parsley |
| 225 g/8 oz fresh white | 1 teaspoon salt |
|    breadcrumbs | black pepper |
| 100 g/4 oz ham | 4-5 eggs |
| 50 g/2 oz Parmesan cheese, | 3 hard-boiled eggs |
|    grated | |

Put the pork in a large bowl with the breadcrumbs, the ham, finely chopped, the cheese and the pistachios. Peel the onion and grate it into the bowl. Add the parsley and salt, and freshly ground black pepper to taste. Beat the eggs and stir them into the dry ingredients, mixing until they are well blended. Chop the hard-boiled eggs and fold them into the stuffing.

Separate the skin from the flesh at the neck end of the turkey, using your fingers, and stuff this cavity, loosely to allow the mixture to swell during cooking. Use the remaining stuffing to fill the main cavity. Truss, and roast the turkey as directed on page 44.

*Peru a Brasileira* has a delicious dry neck dressing of toasted manioc meal, as well as a more conventional stuffing inside the bird, and it is considered one of Brazil's outstanding contributions to the culinary arts. Its preparation presents two small problems. Manioc meal can be difficult to find. Other names for it are cassava meal and *farine de manioc*, sometimes shortened to *farine*. The second problem is persuading a butcher not to chop the neck off the turkey. You want a really big flap of neck skin to encase the dry stuffing.

### Roast Turkey Brazilian Style – Peru a Brasileira

*Serves 16–20*

1 (6-8-kg/13-17-lb) turkey
1 set turkey giblets
1 stalk celery
1 sprig parsley
½ teaspoon salt
*Marinade*
1 medium onion
1 stalk celery
1 medium carrot
3 cloves garlic
4 tablespoons chopped parsley
¼ teaspoon powdered cloves
½ teaspoon salt
black pepper
500 ml/16 fl oz dry white wine
250 ml/8 fl oz wine vinegar

*Neck stuffing*
575 g/1¼ lb manioc meal
65 g/2½ oz butter
1 medium onion
2 medium tomatoes (optional)
4 tablespoons chopped parsley
1 portion reserved cooked giblets
5 drops Tabasco sauce
20 green olives, stoned
3 hard-boiled eggs
salt
black pepper
*Second stuffing*
250 g/9 oz fresh white
  breadcrumbs
175 ml/6 fl oz milk

2 rashers bacon, lean and fat
1 large onion
2 medium tomatoes
4 tablespoons chopped parsley
250 ml/8 fl oz giblet stock

1 portion reserved cooked giblets
salt
black pepper
*To baste*
250 ml/8 fl oz strained marinade
100 g/4 oz butter, melted

The day before you plan to roast the turkey cook the giblets and leave the bird in its marinade overnight.

Wash the giblets, neck, heart and liver, and put them in a pot with 900 ml/1½ pints cold water and bring to the boil. Skim off the froth, add the celery, roughly chopped, parsley and salt. Cover the pot and simmer for about 1 hour. Cool the giblets in the stock.

Strain the stock and reserve. Chop the giblets very finely, divide into two equal portions and reserve them for the stuffings.

Prepare the marinade in a bowl or dish large enough to hold the turkey. Peel and chop the onion, chop the celery and grate the carrot. Mix with all the remaining marinade ingredients. Pour some of this mixture into the turkey, and holding the bird over the bowl, turn to dampen the whole interior. Place the turkey in the bowl and turn it from time to time in the marinade. Leave overnight in a cool place.

To make the neck stuffing, spread the manioc meal on a shallow baking tray and toast it in a preheated moderate oven (180° C, 350° F, Gas Mark 4) for about 15 minutes or until it is a golden biscuit colour. Melt 25 g/1 oz of the butter in a large frying pan. Peel and chop the onion and tomatoes and sauté them gently in the butter. Add the parsley, one portion of reserved giblets, and the Tabasco sauce. Fry together for another minute or two. Now add the remaining butter and when it has melted remove the pan from the heat and mix in the toasted manioc meal. When it is well blended return the pan to the stove and stir the mixture over a low heat until it is crumbly.

Add the olives and chopped hard-boiled eggs and season the mixture to taste with salt and freshly ground black pepper.

To make the second stuffing, soak the breadcrumbs in the milk and set aside. Chop the bacon finely and fry it gently in a frying pan until the fat runs. Add the onion and tomatoes, peeled and finely chopped, and the parsley. Fry these together until the onion is golden brown. Add the 250 ml/8 fl oz of the reserved giblet stock and bring to the boil. Remove from the heat and press this mixture through a sieve into a large bowl. Add the remaining reserved giblets and the soaked breadcrumbs. Season the mixture to taste with salt and freshly ground black pepper.

Remove the turkey from the marinade and pat it dry. Stuff the neck loosely with the manioc stuffing and sew it up neatly. Any left-over stuffing can be served separately. Stuff the main cavity with the bread stuffing. Truss, and slow roast the turkey as described on page 44. Baste with a mixture of strained marinade and melted butter.

Hand-rearing capons for the table is still a wifely art in country districts in many parts of the world. Present-day Romans roast them for Christmas with a stuffing of sausages, cooked giblets, pecorino cheese and breadcrumbs. Any of the turkey stuffings already described can be made in smaller quantity for a capon or chicken. A lemon and thyme stuffing – made like the sage and onion stuffing on page 43 but adding grated lemon rind and fresh or dried thyme or lemon thyme in place of the sage – is particularly fresh and delicious.

## Game

Game, furred and feathered, is at its best in northern Europe and North America during the Christmas season. Wild boar is still sometimes available in France, Germany, and further east, and saddle of venison is a popular choice in Germany for the main Christmas meal. Small game birds, from pheasant which will serve two, to quail, two or three per person, are often served in the days before or after Christmas. These are seldom stuffed, although fruit, berries and herbs are sometimes inserted to add flavour during roasting. Spit-roasting is a particularly good method of cooking well-hung birds. Your cooker handbook will advise on timings. Remember to baste well. The following table gives oven roasting times for the most popular game birds and lists their traditional accompaniments.

### TIMETABLE FOR ROASTING GAME BIRDS
### (AVERAGE ONLY)

| Type of game | Oven temperature | Cooking time | Accompaniments |
| --- | --- | --- | --- |
| Grouse | 190°C 375°F Gas Mark 5 | 35 minutes | Game chips, fried breadcrumbs, bread sauce, clear gravy, watercress. |
| Partridge | 220°C 425°F Gas Mark 7 | 30 minutes | As grouse. |

| Pheasant | 200°C 400°F Gas Mark 6 | 50–70 minutes | As grouse plus red-currant jelly, cranberry sauce, roast or sauté potatoes. |
|---|---|---|---|
| Snipe | 230°C 450°F Gas Mark 8 | 15 minutes | Roast on toast to catch the juices. As grouse. |
| Teal | 220°C 425°F Gas Mark 7 | 15–20 minutes | Game chips, strong clear gravy, orange salad, watercress. |
| Widgeon | 230°C 450°F Gas Mark 8 | 20–25 minutes | As teal, with orange or sherry flavoured gravy. |
| Mallard | 230°C 450°F Gas Mark 8 | 25–35 minutes | As teal. |
| Quail | 230°C 450°F Gas Mark 8 | 15 minutes | Serve on toast. As grouse plus redcurrant jelly and bacon rolls. |
| Wood pigeon | 220°C 425°F Gas Mark 7 | 20–25 minutes | Thin gravy and watercress. |
| Woodcock | 220°C 425°F Gas Mark 7 | 15–20 minutes | Roast on toast. Fried breadcrumbs, game chips, lemon wedges and watercress. |

Venison is likely to become more widely available as new farming experiments, tied to conservation projects of the forests and hills the deer inhabit, increase.

### Roast Saddle of Venison with Red Wine Sauce – Rehrucken mit Rotweinsosse – Germany

*Oven temperature Moderate 180° C, 350° F, Gas Mark 4*

*Serves 6–8*

2·25-kg/5-lb saddle of venison
100 g/4 oz raw pork fat
50 g/2 oz lard

*Marinade*
750 ml/1¼ pints dry red wine
750 ml/1¼ pints water

5 juniper berries
2 cloves
8 black peppercorns
1 bay leaf
2½ teaspoons salt
*Sauce*
2 medium carrots
1 small onion
2 spring onions

3 stalks celery
2½ tablespoons plain flour
6 tablespoons double cream
1 teaspoon fresh lemon juice
*Garnish*
8 pear halves, poached or canned
4 tablespoons lingonberry or
    cranberry sauce (see page 184)

The venison must marinate for at least 8 hours at room temperature, longer if the meat is not from a young animal. Marinating it in the refrigerator for three days or more will improve the flavour and tenderize the meat.

To make the marinade, put the wine and water in a large pot and add the juniper berries, cloves and peppercorns, bruised, a crumbled bay leaf and the salt. Bring to the boil and set the liquid aside to cool. Put the venison in a dish just large enough to hold it and pour over the marinade. Turn the meat to wet it all over and marinate it, turning occasionally.

Remove the meat from the marinade and pat it dry. Strain the marinade and set the liquor aside for the sauce. Cut the pork fat into long, thin strips, and using a larding needle, insert two rows of lardons along each side of the meat at approximately 2·5-cm/1-inch intervals.

Melt the lard over a high heat in a roasting pan on top of the stove. Brown the venison evenly on all sides. Transfer the venison to a dish. Add the vegetables, peeled and roughly chopped, and cook them over a medium heat until they are soft and slightly browned. Reduce the heat, sprinkle the flour over the fried vegetables, and cook the mixture gently to brown the flour a little. Pour in reserved marinade to a depth of about 2·5 cm/1 inch. Set the venison on the vegetables and roast in a preheated moderate oven for about 1½ hours, basting occasionally with the pan juices.

Venison is usually served slightly pink, so roast it longer for well-done meat. Transfer the venison to a heated serving dish. Turn the oven off and return the joint to it to rest, leaving the door open.

To finish the sauce, strain the roasting juices into a measuring jug and skim off the excess fat. Make up to 350 ml/12 fl oz with reserved marinade. Heat this stock in a saucepan. Bring to the boil and add the cream, whisking briskly. Reduce the heat and simmer the sauce, stirring frequently, for about 5 minutes. Add the lemon juice and correct the seasoning to taste.

Pour the sauce over the venison and garnish the dish with pear halves filled with lingonberry or cranberry sauce. The pears may be warm or cold.

## Pork and ham

Suckling pig is the Christmas roast of the Caribbean, Pacific and Mediterranean islands and of much of southern and eastern Europe. In many places it was traditionally spit-roasted, and still is in those parts of the world where Christmas is celebrated in warm weather. Stuffings are as varied as the places it is eaten, from a simple flavouring of tamarind rind and banana leaves in the Philippines, to elaborate dressings of meat, fruit and spices in the Caribbean. Cubans stuff suckling pigs with rice and beans and nuggets of guava paste, and oddly the Rumanians use rum and olive oil basting liquor, a technique which would seem more appropriate to the West Indies.

Suckling pigs weigh from about 2 kg/4 lb to about 6 kg/13 lb cleaned weight, and can be bought fresh or chilled. It is usually necessary to order them in advance, and when shopping allow 350–450 g/ 12–16 oz per serving.

To truss a suckling pig, sew the stomach opening neatly after stuffing, or secure with skewers. Draw the back legs away from the body and tie with string, and the front legs forward and tie. If oven space does not permit the pig to be roasted in this extended pose, fold the legs underneath it and secure with skewers or string. Wedge the mouth open with a piece of crumpled foil which will be replaced after cooking with an apple, orange or baked potato. Protect the snout and ears with foil for part of the cooking time. Rub the pig with salt and place it on a rack in a shallow roasting tin. Baste it frequently during cooking. If it is necessary to protect its skin with foil, make the covering very loose and remove for the last half hour of roasting so that the skin will be crisp. The meat is cooked when the juices run clear. Test with a skewer inserted into the thigh.

# TIMETABLE FOR ROASTING SUCKLING PIG
## (AVERAGE ONLY)

| Weight of pig | Oven temperature |
|---|---|
| (including stuffing) | 200°C |
| | 400°F |
| | Gas Mark 6 |
| | |
| 2 kg/4 lb | 1½–1¾ hours |
| 3 kg/6 lb | 2¼–2½ hours |
| 4 kg/8 lb | 2¾–3 hours |
| 5 kg/11 lb | 3¼–3½ hours |
| 6 kg/13 lb | 3¾–4 hours |
| 7 kg/15 lb | 4¼–4½ hours |

Roast suckling pig is one of Spain's gastronomic triumphs and this recipe from the Basque country makes an impressive party dish.

### Roast Suckling Pig – Lechona Asada Vasca – Spain

*Serves 8–10*

1 (4 kg/8 lb) suckling pig
salt
olive oil
*Stuffing*
75 g/3 oz fresh white breadcrumbs
2 tablespoons milk
4 medium onions
225 g/8 oz minced pork
225 g/8 oz minced veal
1 liver of suckling pig
2 tablespoons chopped parsley

1 teaspoon dried thyme
1 teaspoon dried rosemary
125 ml/4 fl oz dry sherry
4 tablespoons brandy
2 eggs
1 teaspoon salt
black pepper
6 hard-boiled eggs
*Garnish*
1 red eating apple

Wash the pig, pat it dry, and rub it inside and out with salt.

To prepare the stuffing, put the breadcrumbs in a large bowl and moisten them with the milk. Peel and finely chop the onions and add them to the bowl with the minced pork, veal, and finely chopped liver. Add the herbs, sherry, brandy and beaten eggs. Season with salt and freshly ground black pepper and mix the ingredients thoroughly together.

Shell and slice the hard-boiled eggs. Line the inside of the pig with slices of egg, then pack it with the stuffing. Truss, brush with olive oil and roast as directed on page 54. Baste with the pan juices and additional olive oil if needed.

Serve the pig on a large dish with a shiny red apple in its mouth, and a thin gravy made from the skimmed pan juices. Whole, roasted red and green peppers and dark green watercress are often used as further embellishment.


Caribbean islanders enjoy highly flavoured food as the following recipe for suckling pig shows. 'Seasoning up' is a term used in the English-speaking islands for the marinade used to flavour the animal before it is stuffed.

### Roast Suckling Pig – Trinidad

*Serves 10–14*

1 (5-6-kg/11-13-lb) suckling pig
125 ml/4 fl oz peanut oil
*Marinade*
2 medium onions
2 cloves garlic
4 spring onions
1 bunch celery leaves
4 tablespoons cane or malt
  vinegar
4 tablespoons rum
2 teaspoons salt
2 tablespoons soy sauce
2 teaspoons cayenne pepper

*Stuffing*
2 medium onions
2 cloves garlic
50 g/2 oz butter
350 g/12 oz fresh white
  breadcrumbs
125 ml/4 fl oz milk
20 green olives, stoned
75 g/3 oz seedless raisins
2 medium tomatoes
1 small hot red pepper*
2 tablespoons capers
1 teaspoon thyme
1½ teaspoons salt
black pepper

* See note, page xv, on preparing chillies.


To prepare the marinade, peel and chop the onions finely, crush the garlic, and finely chop the spring onions and celery leaves. Mix well together in a small bowl with the vinegar, rum, salt, soy sauce and cayenne.

Wash the suckling pig and pat it dry. Paint it inside and out with the marinade and leave it to stand at room temperature for about 2 hours.

To make the stuffing, peel and chop the onions and garlic very finely. Melt the butter in a small pot and sauté the onions and garlic gently until tender but not brown. Transfer them to a large mixing bowl. Moisten the breadcrumbs with milk and add to the onions. Add the olives, roughly chopped, raisins, tomatoes, peeled and roughly chopped, hot red pepper, finely chopped, capers, thyme, salt and a generous seasoning of freshly ground black pepper. Mix the ingredients well together.

Scrape the marinade off the pig and reserve it. Stuff the pig loosely with the filling and sew or skewer the opening. Truss and roast as directed on page 54. Use the reserved marinade and the peanut oil to baste the pig.

### Roast Suckling Pig – Jamaica

*Serves 10–14*

| | |
|---|---|
| 1 (5-6-kg/11-13-lb) suckling pig | 175 g/6 oz seedless raisins |
| *Stuffing* | 1 hot red pepper* |
| 1 large onion | 1 tablespoon powdered ginger |
| 1 clove garlic | 1 lime |
| 50 g/2 oz butter | 3 tablespoons Pickapeppa or |
| 350 g/12 oz fresh white | Tabasco sauce |
| breadcrumbs | 1 teaspoon salt |

* See note, page xv, on preparing chillies.

Peel and chop the onion and garlic finely. Melt the butter in a small saucepan and sauté the onion and garlic until soft but not brown. Transfer them to a large mixing bowl and add the breadcrumbs, raisins, roughly chopped, hot red pepper, finely chopped, and ginger. Grate the lime rind finely into the bowl and mix the ingredients thoroughly. Sprinkle the mixture with the Pickapeppa or Tabasco sauce and salt, and mix again.

Stuff the pig loosely with this filling. Truss and roast as directed on page 54. Baste with pan juices and olive oil.

Pawpaw apple sauce (see page 186) or creole sauce (see page 182), or both, may be served with the last two recipes.

Roast loin of pork is a popular Christmas roast in Scandinavia. The following Danish recipe is especially simple and delicious. For this roast do not let the butcher remove the skin. Ask him to chine the joint for easy carving and to score the skin deeply at about 1·2-cm/ ½-inch intervals.

### Roast Loin of Pork – Stegt Svinekam – Denmark

*Oven temperature Hot 230° C, 450° F, Gas Mark 8; then*
*Moderate 180° C, 350° F, Gas Mark 4*

*Serves 8*

1 (3-kg/6-lb) loin of pork       6 cloves
75 g/3 oz dripping or butter     12 small bay leaves
salt

Place the joint skin side down in a roasting tin. Pour in boiling water to a depth of about 2·5 cm/1 inch and place the tin in a preheated hot oven for 15 minutes.

Take the pork from the oven, reduce the heat to moderate and pour off the stock, reserving it for basting. Dry the roasting tin and smear it with dripping or butter. Rub the pork well with salt. Push the cloves and bay leaves into the cuts in the skin and roast the pork, skin side up on a rack. Baste every 30 minutes with about 2 tablespoons of stock.

Roasted apple halves filled with redcurrant jelly, sugar browned potatoes (see page 87) and red cabbage (see page 95) are the usual accompaniments for this roast.

Roasted spare-ribs are a speciality of the Swedish smörgåsbord table which is at its most magnificent over the Christmas season.

### Roasted Spare-Ribs – Ugnsteket Revbensspjäll – Sweden

*Oven temperature Moderately hot 200° C, 400° F, Gas Mark 6; then*
*Moderate 180° C, 350° F, Gas Mark 4*

*Serves 4–6*

2·5 kg/5 lb spare-ribs, bones     ¼ teaspoon powdered ginger or
    cracked                      mustard
1½ tablespoons salt          225 g/8 oz tinned prune juice
½ teaspoon ground white pepper

Trim and wipe the meat. Mix together the salt, pepper and ginger or mustard. Lay the spare-ribs on a rack in a shallow roasting tin and place in a preheated moderately hot oven for 15 minutes. Reduce the heat to moderate and baste the spare-ribs with the prune juice. Return them to the oven and roast for a further 1 hour, basting occasionally, or until the meat is tender.

Cut the spare-ribs in pieces and arrange them on a warmed serving dish. Skim the pan juices and serve them separately. Apple sauce and cooked prunes are the usual accompaniments.

Baked hams appear on festive occasions wherever pigs are reared. Their variety, once rich beyond belief, is now diminishing as commercial products take the place of old and cherished curing arts practised in farm and cottage kitchens. Finland's sauna smoked hams, England's York and Bradenham hams, Ireland's Limerick hams, America's Virginia, Smithfield and Kentucky hams, France's Jambon de Paris, Germany's Mainz and Westphalian hams, Czechoslovakia's Prague hams, Spain's Asturias hams, all are distinctively flavoured and justly famous.

The best hams are made from the hind leg of a pig and may be dry cured or pickled, smoked or simply dried. Unsmoked hams are usually described as 'green'. Hams are sometimes baked in a crust which is later discarded to prevent them drying out. More usually though they are boiled, or parboiled, then baked with a decorative glaze or pastry case to be eaten hot or cold.

Buy a whole ham ready-cooked or boil an uncooked ham at home. Soak in cold water for 24 hours before simmering an uncooked ham in a mixture of white wine or cider and water and herbs. Allow 25 minutes cooking time per 450 g/1 lb. Never try to hurry the cooking by fast boiling which will dry the ham. Simmer it gently, covered, and cool it in its own stock.

### Ham in Pastry – Prosciutto in Crosta – Italy

*Oven temperature Hot 220° C, 425° F, Gas Mark 7*

*Serves 8–10*

| | |
|---|---|
| 1 (3-kg/6-lb) cooked ham | 450 g/1 lb prepared puff pastry (see page 163) |

Remove the skin and fat from the cooked ham. Roll the puff pastry to about 6 mm/¼ inch thick. Place the ham, top side down, in the centre of the pastry, and wrap the pastry over it, sealing the edges firmly. Set the covered ham seam-side down on a damp baking tin and decorate the top with pastry leaves or flowers fashioned from the trimmings. Bake in a preheated hot oven for about 35 minutes.

Serve the ham warm or cold. A white sauce is served separately with warm ham, and very sweet candied fruits in a heavy syrup flavoured faintly with mustard, *mostardi di frutta*, invariably garnish this dish.

To bake a ham, simmer it for half the cooking time, 25 minutes per 450 g/1 lb, then wrap it in foil and bake it in the centre of a preheated moderate oven (180° C, 350° F, Gas Mark 4) for the remaining cooking time. Half an hour before cooking is completed, turn up the oven to hot (220° C, 425° F, Gas Mark 7) and take the ham from the oven. Remove the foil and peel off the skin.

To finish the ham, score the fat with a diamond pattern of intersecting diagonal cuts, sprinkle the fat generously with brown sugar and pat it well in. Decorate with whole cloves pushed into the fat at the corners of the diamonds. Return the ham to the oven and roast for a further 30 minutes to set the glaze

Decorations can be varied to include halved glacé cherries or apricots, pineapple rings, and slices of any glacé fruit. These should also be patted with sugar or painted with honey before the final baking. Alternative glazes may be made with honey, marmalade, corn or maple syrup.

Serve glazed ham hot or cold. Spiced peaches or pears cooked in red wine go well with hot or cold ham, and cooked prunes are usually served in Scandinavia.

**Lamb**

Smoked leg of lamb called *hangikjöt*, boiled or braised and served with a white sauce flavoured with nutmeg, peas and mashed potatoes, is a national speciality much enjoyed at Christmas in Iceland. Roast baby lambs are eaten in Spain and in Sardinia, but the one country that really goes to town on lamb at Christmas is, of course, New Zealand. The festive looking crown roast and a boned, stuffed leg, known as *colonial goose*, are two favourite Christmas recipes.

The cut of lamb used for crown roasts is called best end of neck in England, rack in the United States, fair end in Ireland, *côtes or côtelettes premières* in France. It is made by joining together two or three of these joints, each consisting of 5, 6 or 7 cutlets. Allow at least two cutlets per serving when ordering a prepared crown roast from the butcher or making one at home by sewing the joints together after removing the chine bones and trimming the cutlet bones. A crown may be roasted with or without stuffing. In either case the exposed cutlet bones should be protected from charring with individual foil hats. These are replaced for serving with cutlet frills or small glazed onions.

### Crown Roast of Lamb with Raisin and Nut Stuffing – New Zealand

*Oven temperature Moderately hot 190° C, 375° F, Gas Mark 5; then Moderate 180° C, 350° F, Gas Mark 4*

*Serves 6*

| | |
|---|---|
| 1 12-cutlet crown roast | 150 g/5 oz seedless raisins |
| 50 g/ 2 oz butter or beef dripping | 50 g/2 oz shelled walnuts, broken |
| cornflour | $\frac{1}{4}$ teaspoon dried thyme |
| 1 tablespoon redcurrant jelly | $\frac{1}{4}$ teaspoon dried rosemary |
| *Stuffing* | $\frac{1}{4}$ teaspoon dried tarragon |
| 1 medium onion | 1 lemon |
| 1 clove garlic | $\frac{1}{2}$ teaspoon salt |
| 50 g/2 oz butter | pepper |
| 225 g/8 oz mushrooms | 1-2 eggs, beaten |
| 175 g/6 oz fresh brown or white breadcrumbs | |

To make the stuffing, peel and finely chop the onion and garlic. Melt the butter in a small saucepan and sauté the onion and garlic until soft and slightly browned. Add the mushrooms, finely chopped, and cook gently, covered, until the mushrooms have released their liquor.

Transfer the mixture to a large mixing bowl. Add the breadcrumbs, raisins, walnuts, thyme, rosemary and tarragon. Grate the lemon rind over the bowl and season the mixture with salt and freshly ground black pepper. Toss the ingredients thoroughly together before adding as much beaten egg as you need to moisten the mixture. This stuffing should be fairly loose.

Pile the stuffing into the crown. Weigh the roast and calculate the cooking time at 30 minutes per 450 g/1 lb.

Melt the butter or dripping in a shallow roasting tin and set the crown in it. Roast for the first 10 minutes in a preheated moderately hot oven then reduce the temperature to moderate for the remainder of the cooking time.

When the joint is ready put it on a warmed serving dish and return it to the oven, switched off and with the door open. Let the joint rest while making the gravy. Skim the pan juices and add chicken stock, or a mixture of stock and white wine. Thicken the gravy with a little cornflour mixed with cold water, and sweeten it with about 1 tablespoon of redcurrant jelly. Check the seasoning and adjust to taste.

Serve the crown roast with a jug of gravy, more redcurrant jelly, fresh peas and new boiled potatoes.

### Colonial Goose – (Stuffed Leg of Lamb) – New Zealand

*Oven temperature Moderate 180° C, 350° F, Gas Mark 4*

*Serves 6*

| | |
|---|---|
| 1 (2-kg/4-lb) leg of lamb, boned | black pepper |
| 25 g/1 oz butter | 1 egg, beaten |
| *Stuffing* | *Marinade* |
| 100 g/4 oz dried apricots | 2 large carrots |
| 125 g/4½ oz fresh white or brown breadcrumbs | 1 large onion |
| | 1 bay leaf |
| 50 g/2 oz butter | 2 tablespoons chopped parsley |
| 1 tablespoon clear honey | ¼ teaspoon salt |
| 1 small onion | black pepper |
| ¼ teaspoon dried thyme | 250 ml/8 fl oz dry red wine |
| ½ teaspoon salt | |

Ask the butcher to bone the leg or prepare it at home. Lay the meat, fat side down, on a wooden board. With a sharp, pointed knife, work the meat away from the bone at the top of the leg, down to the first joint. Now cut along the line of the bone from the opposite end of the leg. Work the flesh away from the bone, being careful not to puncture the skin in any other place. Sever the bone from all the flesh and ligaments and draw it out. Lay the meat out flat, making occasional shallow cuts until the piece is approximately the same thickness over its whole surface.

To make the stuffing, roughly chop the dried apricots and put them in a mixing bowl with the breadcrumbs. Melt the butter and honey together in a small saucepan. Add the onion, peeled and finely chopped, and cook over a low heat until the onion is soft but not brown. Add the cooked onion, butter and honey to the bowl with the thyme, salt, and a generous seasoning of freshly ground black pepper. Toss the mixture to blend the ingredients before binding it with the beaten egg.

Spread the stuffing in the middle of the boned lamb, and fold the meat into a neat parcel which will cook evenly. Sew the joint firmly with a needle and strong thread. Set aside.

For the marinade, peel and finely chop the carrots and onion. Put them in a bowl big enough to hold the stuffed lamb and add the bay leaf, crumbled, parsley, salt, freshly ground black pepper and wine. Stir the marinade and add the meat. Leave the joint to marinate in a cool place for 6 to 12 hours, or longer in the refrigerator, turning it from time to time.

To roast the lamb, pat it dry and set it in a shallow, generously buttered roasting pan. Spread the rest of the butter on the joint and roast it in a preheated moderate oven for about 35 minutes per 450 g/ 1 lb, basting occasionally with the pan juices.

Rest the colonial goose on a warmed serving dish in the oven, switched off and with the door open. Skim the fat from the pan juices and make a thin gravy by adding chicken stock or white wine. Serve the gravy separately and remove the trussing threads from the meat before carving.

Fresh peas and new potatoes, boiled and buttered, are the traditional accompaniments to colonial goose. Any of the garnishes served with goose or turkey go very well with this roast.

## Beef

A majestic roast of beef, hot for the main Christmas meal, or cold for a buffet table, is increasingly popular in Britain. The high price of beef now, and the smaller size of households, have made large roasts of beef a treat for special occasions.

Only prime cuts of well-hung beef will make a perfect roast, crusty brown on the outside and pale pink at the centre. Look for a joint with dark red meat, succulent and flecked with a light marbling of fat, and creamy white fat on the outside.

The timings suggested here are for good quality beef. If you are quite certain that the joint comes from a prizewinning animal reduce the cooking time a little.

## TIMETABLE FOR ROASTING BEEF (AVERAGE ONLY)

| Cut | Oven temperature 220°C 425°F Gas Mark 7 | | 160°C 325°F Gas Mark 3 | Degree of doneness |
|---|---|---|---|---|
| Fillet (whole) | 8–10 mins per 450 g/1 lb 14 mins per 450 g/1 lb 21–22 mins per 450 g/1 lb | | | Very rare, blue medium rare well done |
| Rib roast (2 ribs, about 2.5 kg/5 lb) | 1st 15 mins 1st 15 mins 1st 15 mins | then then then | 16 mins per 450 g/1 lb 25 mins per 450 g/1 lb 32 mins per 450 g/1 lb | rare medium well done |
| Rib roast (4 ribs, about 5 kg/11 lb) | 1st 15 mins 1st 15 mins 1st 15 mins | then then then | 15 mins per 450 g/1 lb 20 mins per 450 g/1 lb 36 mins per 450 g/1 lb | rare medium well done |
| Sirloin (boned and rolled) | 1st 15 mins 1st 15 mins 1st 15 mins | then then then | 15 mins per 450 g/1 lb 27 mins per 450 g/1 lb 37 mins per 450 g/1 lb | rare medium well done |

Fillet steak roasted in one piece makes surprisingly economical use of this expensive cut because shrinkage is minimal. Allow 100-175 g/4-6 oz, uncooked weight, per serving. Bard the meat with fine strips of pork fat or seal in the juices by browning it very quickly in hot beef dripping on top of the stove before roasting. A classic bearnaise sauce makes a wonderful accompaniment to the succulent meat which may be served in steak-sized chunks or thick slices.

For rib roasts allow 350-450 g/12-16 oz per serving, and for boned, rolled sirloin, 175-225 g/6-8 oz per person, uncooked weights.

### Roast Beef and Yorkshire Pudding – England

*Oven temperature Hot 220° C, 425° F, Gas Mark 7; then Moderate 160° C, 325° F, Gas Mark 3*

*Serves 6–8*

1 (2·5-3-kg/5-6-lb) rib roast
4 tablespoons beef dripping or
  butter
salt
black pepper

*Yorkshire Pudding*
100 g/4 oz plain flour
$\frac{1}{4}$ teaspoon salt
2 large eggs
150 ml/$\frac{1}{4}$ pint milk

Coat the meat with dripping or butter and season generously. Put the beef on a rack over a roasting tin and brown it in a preheated hot oven for 15 minutes. Lower the heat to moderate and roast the meat, basting occasionally, using the timing chart on page 63.

To make the Yorkshire pudding, sift the flour and salt into a mixing bowl and make a hollow in the centre. Mix the eggs with a little of the milk, add to the flour and stir to make a smooth paste. Gradually whisk in the rest of the milk and leave the batter to stand for at least an hour before baking it.

About 40 minutes before the beef is cooked, pour the batter into the roasting tin under the beef. The pudding will be ready when the beef is done and richly flavoured with its juices.

If lighter Yorkshire pudding is preferred make individual puddings. Divide 4 tablespoons beef dripping between 6 or 8 small baking pans and heat the prepared tins in the oven towards the end of roasting time. As soon as the meat is out of the oven, pour the batter into the tins and bake for 15 minutes on a high shelf. Leave the meat in a warm place to settle before carving.

Hot horseradish sauce, as it comes, or toned down with double cream, or English mustard are served with roast beef. Roast potatoes and any green vegetables are good accompaniments. Buttered baby beetroots are excellent too.


A Christmas barbecue? Well yes, in a word, or rather words – *pachamancha, hangi* and *lova*. These are the pit barbecues of the southern hemisphere and they are surprisingly alike at opposite sides of the globe. Pachamancha is the main celebration meal in the country districts on the coast and in the mountains of Peru. Pork, whole baby lambs, chickens, sweet and ordinary potatoes are wrapped in banana leaves and cooked in pits on heated stones. The stones are first warmed by fires, and when the flames have died the pits are lined with leaves, the food piled in and covered with more leaves, and earth from the pit digging heaped on top. Two or three hours later the food is dug out and morsels of tender meat and poultry distributed among the participants.

Baby lambs are also cooked in the New Zealand hangi, a Maori pit barbecue adopted by everyone and made now in urban back yards, on beaches and in the country. Foil has taken the place of leaves for wrapping the food but the principle is much the same. Baby lambs stuffed with *kumuru* (sweet potato), and pumpkin, are a hangi speciality.

Huge family parties gather to make the Fijian lova. Plaited coconut fronds protect the pork, chickens, fish, potatoes and other vegetables from heated river stones. Heart-shaped *taro* leaves enclose parcels of corned beef mixed with onion, chilli and coconut cream called *palusami*. Heaps of breadfruit and banana leaves topped with earth hold in the heat and smoke. *Kava*, the ceremonial drink of Fiji is drunk in great quantities. Offering beer is regarded as sophisticated.

Another kind of barbecue is also made for Christmas by the mixed blood Spanish-Indian Creoles of Peru. *Antichuchos*, skewers of bull's heart marinated in vinegar, onion, herbs and chilli, and *papa rellena* (see page 75), stuffed potatoes, are eaten to the accompaniment of lots of music.

# CASSEROLES

The casseroles, pot roasts, ragouts and sundry stews made for Christmas are hearty, warming recipes – forgiving dishes to be kept warm for latecomers, heated up for unexpected guests, and left unattended for hours at a time while everyone has a party.

*Christmas colombo* from Martinique is usually made with pork. The curry mixture, *poudre de colombo*, brought to the Caribbean in the middle of the last century by migrant Hindu workers, is a mild one. Most of the tropical fruits and vegetables for this bright, golden dish, can be found fresh, or tinned, in markets and speciality foodstores.

## Christmas Colombo – Martinique

*Serves 6–8*

*Curry paste*
¼ teaspoon turmeric
1 teaspoon ground coriander seeds
1 teaspoon ground mustard seeds
3 cloves garlic
2 hot red peppers, fresh*
*Casserole*
1·5 kg/3 lb pork
4 tablespoons peanut or coconut oil
2 medium onions
2 cloves garlic
1 tablespoon tamarind pulp
1 green mango

350 g/12 oz West Indian pumpkin
1 large green papaya (optional)
1 large aubergine
1 christophene (chayote)
450 g/1 lb dasheen (taro) or white tropical yam
125 ml/4 fl oz dry white wine or coconut milk
125 ml/4 fl oz chicken stock
1-2 hot peppers, fresh*
salt
1 teaspoon lime juice
2 tablespoons dry Madeira or *rhum vieux*

*See note, page xv on preparing fresh chillies.

To make the poudre de colombo or curry paste, put the turmeric, coriander and mustard in a small bowl or mortar. Add the garlic, peeled and roughly chopped, and the peppers, seeded and roughly chopped. Pound these ingredients to a paste.

Cut the pork into large cubes. Heat the oil in a heavy frying pan over a high heat and brown the pork lightly in several batches. Transfer the meat to a large, heavy casserole.

Peel and chop the onions and sauté them in the remaining oil over a low heat. Peel and finely chop the garlic and add to the onion with the curry paste. Fry together for a few minutes, stirring occasionally, then transfer the onion mixture to the casserole.

Add to the casserole the tamarind pulp, the mango, peeled and roughly chopped, the pumpkin, papaya, aubergine, christophene and dasheen, all peeled and sliced. Pour in the wine or coconut milk and chicken stock, and add one or more hot peppers, seeded and finely chopped. Bring slowly to the boil on top of the stove, reduce the heat, cover, and simmer very gently until both the meat and vegetables are tender, about 3 hours. Stir occasionally during cooking and add more stock if the stew becomes too dry.

Just before serving, add salt to taste and stir in the lime juice and Madeira or rhum vieux. Plain boiled rice is the usual accompaniment to this substantial stew which freezes well too.

A pot roast of boned loin of pork stuffed with prunes and apples and cooked in a wine and cream sauce is another pork dish served in Denmark and Sweden. In Cyprus *afelia*, pork cooked in red wine and handfuls of crushed coriander seeds, is invariably served on the day after Christmas, a day for visiting friends and erratic, leisurely meals. Afelia can be made in advance, left waiting, and reheated. It usually is.

### Pork and Coriander Casserole – Afelia – Cyprus

*Oven temperature Cool 150° C, 300° F, Gas Mark 2*

*Serves 12–16*

| | |
|---|---|
| 3 kg/6 lb lean pork | *Casserole* |
| *Marinade* | 25 g/1 oz coriander seeds |
| 225 g/8 oz fat bacon | 50 g/2 oz pork dripping or lard |
| 1 teaspoon salt | salt |
| black pepper | pepper |
| 900 ml/1½ pints dry red wine | |

Cut the pork in approximately 2·5-cm/1-inch cubes. Put the meat in a deep bowl. Cut the bacon in small dice and add to the bowl with the salt and freshly ground black pepper. Pour over the wine and leave the pork in a cool place to marinate for at least 24 hours. Marinating the pork for up to a week is not unusual and results in a flavour said in Cyprus to resemble wild boar.

Lift the meat from the marinade and pat it dry. Crush the coriander seeds. Melt the dripping or lard in a heavy frying pan and fry the pork, bacon and coriander seeds in small batches until well browned. Transfer the meat, seeds and pan juices to a deep casserole with a well-fitting lid.

Pour in the marinade, adjust the seasoning, and cook in a cool oven for about $3\frac{1}{2}$ hours, or until the meat is tender. Skim off any excess fat before serving with boiled rice or potatoes.

Stuffed cabbage is a dish which brings tears of nostalgia to the eyes of expatriate Hungarians, Bulgarians and Transylvanians. Variations on the theme of pork, bacon, smoked sausage and cabbage in a rich sauce of soured cream and paprika are apparently limitless. It is served with bread dumplings, or boiled potatoes, or both, and made well in advance for lunch on Christmas day. As the Hungarian explains: 'Only the cabbage is good reheated, not friendship or love.'

### Stuffed Cabbage – Toltott Kaposzta – Hungary

*Serves 8*

*Cabbage rolls*
8 large fresh white cabbage leaves
100 g/4 oz smoked bacon
1 small onion
450 g/1 lb lean minced pork
75 g/3 oz cooked white rice
1 egg
1 tablespoon paprika
$\frac{1}{2}$ teaspoon salt
black pepper
*Casserole*
3 tablespoons pork dripping or
   lard

450 g/1 lb belly of pork
1 small onion
2 tablespoons paprika
1 kg/2 lb sauerkraut
salt
black pepper
1 tablespoon plain flour
250 ml/8 fl oz stock
250 ml/8 fl oz soured cream
450 g/1 lb smoked sausage
8 pork chops

To make the cabbage rolls, blanch the cabbage leaves in boiling water for about 5 minutes. They should be flexible but not too tender. Drain and set them aside.

Chop the bacon in fine dice and cook it in a heavy frying pan over a low heat until the fat runs. Add the onion, peeled and finely chopped, and cook together until the onion is soft, but not brown. Raise the heat and add the minced pork. Turn it for a minute or two with the bacon and onion. Transfer the mixture to a bowl and add the cooked rice, beaten egg, paprika, salt and a generous seasoning of freshly ground black pepper. Mix together thoroughly.

Divide the pork between the cabbage leaves and roll them up from the stalk end, tucking in the sides to make neat parcels. Lay the rolls seam side down on a plate and set aside.

To prepare the casserole, melt 2 tablespoons of the pork dripping or lard in a large, heavy casserole. Cut the belly of pork into 16 pieces and fry them gently until the fat in the meat begins to run. Take out the pork and set aside. Add the onion, peeled and finely chopped, to the casserole and fry gently until soft, but not brown. Take the casserole off the heat and stir in the paprika. When it is thoroughly blended, add the drained sauerkraut, reserved fried pork, salt and pepper. Set aside.

Melt the remaining pork dripping or lard in a small saucepan and stir in the flour. Cook the roux for a minute before gradually adding the stock, stirring constantly. Cook the sauce for another two minutes before stirring in the soured cream.

Pour half the soured cream sauce into the casserole and mix it well with the sauerkraut and pork. Arrange the cabbage rolls on top of the sauerkraut and cover them with the rest of the soured cream sauce. Return the casserole to the stove and bring slowly to the boil. Lower the heat, cover tightly, and simmer gently for about 1½ hours.

To finish the casserole cut the smoked sausage into 8 pieces. Grill or fry the sausage and pork chops until tender. Arrange them on top of the cabbage rolls and serve very hot. More soured cream may be added at the end of the cooking time. Dill and caraway seeds are often used in this dish.

In Polish homes the substantial winter casserole is *bigos*, a hunters' stew of venison, beef, pork and smoked sausage cooked slowly on a bed of sauerkraut with dried mushrooms, onions, apples and tomatoes in a rich wine gravy. On New Year's Eve bigos is washed down with vodka. Danish housewives make *kraseragout*, a ragout of goose giblets and onions seasoned with a hint of curry powder and paprika. Madeira or sherry is added towards the end of the cooking time.

*Cassoulet*, one of the triumphs of French country cooking, is a peasant dish so good that gourmets make long detours to sample a recommended one. For, like the chef's stockpot, a fine restaurant's cassoulet is a living thing, topped up and added to, always the same and always subtly different. Save the dripping and pieces of Christmas goose for this recipe. Turkey, duck, ham – all find their way to new life through the cassoulet pot.

## Poultry and Beans – Cassoulet – France

*Oven temperature Cool 150° C, 300° F, Gas Mark 2*

*Serves 8*

| | |
|---|---|
| 1 kg/2 lb white haricot beans | salt |
| 225 g/8 oz fat bacon | black pepper |
| 2 large onions | 675-900 g/1½-2 lb cooked goose, |
| 5 cloves garlic | duck, turkey or chicken |
| 2 large tomatoes | 450 g/1 lb fresh coarse pork |
| 1 tablespoon chopped parsley | sausages |
| ½ teaspoon thyme | 100 g/4 oz goose or other dripping |
| ¼ teaspoon chopped sage | 75 g/3 oz fresh white breadcrumbs |
| 1·1 litres/2 pints stock, beef or | |
| chicken | |

Soak the beans overnight. Next day bring them to the boil in at least double their volume of fresh water and cook them, covered, until just tender, about 2½ hours. Cook the beans gently so that most remain whole. Drain and reserve.

Chop the bacon coarsely and cook it slowly in a heavy pot until the fat begins to run. Add the onions, garlic and tomatoes, peeled and finely chopped. When the onions are soft, but not browned, add the herbs and stock. Season to taste with salt and freshly ground black pepper. Cover and simmer the stock for about half an hour.

To assemble the dish, rub the inside of a deep casserole with a cut clove of garlic. Put the goose or other poultry, cut in large pieces, in the base with the sausages and the dripping. Spread the beans over the meat and pour in the stock. Bring the cassoulet slowly to the boil on top of the stove, then spread the crumbs over the top and finish cooking, uncovered, in a cool oven. After about 1½ hours most of the stock will have been absorbed and the breadcrumbs will have formed a crust over the beans.

Serve the cassoulet just as it is in bowls or deep soup plates.

*Guaiolote con molé poblano*, turkey with a chilli and chocolate sauce, is Mexico's most celebrated and celebrative dish. As is the way with such successful combinations of ingredients, the number of recipes to choose from is great. Authenticity is claimed for a recipe given in a pamphlet sold by the Convent of Santa Rosa in Puebla where the dish is said to have been invented in the eighteenth century for a visiting bishop. Its proportions are heroic compared with the timid versions usually given, but the quantities of chillies called for, 1 kg/2 lb mulato chillies, and 1·25 kg/2½ lb each of pasilla and ancho chillies, are quite unobtainable for most cooks and make a truly enormous quantity of sauce.

Tins of this complicated sauce are widely available in speciality food shops. In Mexico where all these chillies are sold from heaped market stalls, and packaged in supermarkets, city dwellers can buy freshly ground chilli blends, dark dry pastes, from scuttles labelled with the names of the dishes they are to be used for. A good shop will have several mole poblano pastes to choose from and you will be asked whether you would like a hot or a sweet mixture. The recipe which follows produces a sauce which is pungent and has heat without hell fire.

### Turkey with Chilli Sauce – Guajolote con Molé Poblano – Mexico

*Serves 10–12*

1 (3·5-4-kg/8-9-lb) turkey
100 g/4 oz butter or lard
*Sauce*
6 ancho chillies
6 mulato chillies
4 pasilla chillies
450 g/1 lb tomatoes
150 g/5 oz blanched almonds
50 g/2 oz seedless raisins
150 g/5 oz sesame seeds
6 cloves garlic

100 g/4 oz lard
1 teaspoon powdered aniseed
1 teaspoon powdered cinnamon
½ teaspoon powdered cloves
black pepper
1 slice fried tortilla or white bread
250-500 ml/8-16 fl oz stock,
    turkey or chicken
salt
25 g/1 oz dark cooking chocolate

First prepare the chillies*. Remove the stalks and seeds and tear the flesh into small pieces. Cover the chillies with boiling water and leave them to soak for at least an hour and preferably overnight.

Put the turkey in a large, heavy pot and cover it with cold water.

*See note, page xv on preparing fresh chillies.

Bring to the boil, skim the stock, cover and simmer for about 1 hour. Take the turkey out of the pot. Strain and reserve the stock. Pat the bird dry, spread it with the butter or lard, and set it in a generously greased roasting tin. Roast in a preheated moderately hot oven (200° C, 400° F, Gas Mark 6) for a further 1 hour or until it is well browned and the meat cooked. Test with a sharp skewer inserted into the thickest part of the leg, near the body. The juices should run clear. The skin should be rather hard and brittle.

To make the sauce, peel and roughly chop the tomatoes. Chop the almonds and raisins coarsely. Toast the sesame seeds until golden in a heavy frying pan over a high heat, shaking the pan occasionally. Peel and chop the garlic. Drain the chillies.

Melt the lard in a large heavy pot and fry together the chillies, tomatoes, nuts, raisins, sesame seeds and garlic. Use a low heat and sauté the mixture gently until the chillies and garlic are soft.

Purée the mixture in an electric blender, or put it through a mechanical food mill using the finest mesh disc.

Transfer the purée to a large, wide pot and add the spices and fried bread or tortilla broken into small pieces. Add sufficient stock to make a thin sauce, and stir the mixture over a low heat until it thickens. Add salt to taste and the chocolate. Stir until the chocolate melts.

Transfer the turkey to a heated serving dish and pour the sauce over it.

*Note*: It is more usual now to joint and fry the parboiled turkey in serving pieces.


Hospitality in the Philippines is of legendary generosity. A Filipino will save for a fiesta the way others will save for a trip. Fiesta foods are much the same for Christmas as for other major festivals and they involve days, and often nights, of preparation. Everyone helps. Cooking the feast is part of the party. After midnight mass on Christmas Eve there are presents and sometimes a savoury snack. The main meal, an exotic spread of hot and cold foods, is eaten before church. *Arroz a la Cataláña*, a pilaf of chicken, pork, shrimp and clams, *chicken relleno*, a boned fowl stuffed with pork, ham, eggs, cheese and pickles, steamed and served hot, *paella*, roast suckling pig, and huge bowls of plain and fried rice and salads are just some of the fiesta dishes. *Callos con garbanzos*, tripe with chick peas, is another, and demonstrates again the influence of Spain on Filipino cuisine. *Chorizos de Bilbao* are Spanish sausages made from beef and pork seasoned with garlic and hot red pepper.

# Tripe with Chick Peas – Callos con Garbanzos – Philippines

*Serves 6–8*

| | |
|---|---|
| 1 kg/2 lb tripe | 2 chorizos de Bilbao |
| 1 cow heel | 1 medium red pepper |
| 4 tablespoons olive oil | 20 green olives |
| 6 cloves garlic | 175 g/6 oz chick peas, cooked |
| 1 large onion | salt |
| 3 tablespoons tomato purée | black pepper |

Thoroughly clean the tripe and cow heel. Put them in a large pot with just enough water to cover. Bring slowly to the boil, cover tightly, and simmer them together over a low heat until very tender. This will usually take about 3 hours but the cooking time can vary according to the type of tripe used. Drain, and cool the meat. Skim the stock of fat and reduce it to about 500 ml/16 fl oz by fast boiling. Cut the tripe into strips about 2·5 cm/1 inch by 1·2 cm/$\frac{1}{2}$ inch. Take the meat off the cow heel and cut it into pieces of approximately the same size.

Heat the oil in a casserole and sauté the onion and garlic, peeled and finely chopped, until golden. Add the reduced stock, tomato purée, the sausages, cut in 2·5-cm/1-inch slices, and the red pepper, de-seeded and chopped. Cook, covered, over a low heat for about 10 minutes or until the pepper is tender. Add the tripe, cow heel, olives and chick peas. Season to taste with salt and freshly ground black pepper. Bring the casserole to the boil and simmer for a further 5 minutes before serving very hot.

*L'estouffat de boeuf* is one of the traditional dishes served in Gascony on Christmas Eve. It is in this region of south-west France that Armagnac is made, hence its lavish use. Ask the butcher to tie the meat into a thick, sausage-shaped roll. Long slow cooking is the secret of this magnificent dish.

# Long-Cooked Beef – L'Estouffat de Boeuf – France

*Oven temperature Moderate 160° C, 325° F, Gas Mark 3; then*
*Cool 140° C, 275° F, Gas Mark 1*

*Serves 6*

350 g/12 oz fresh rind of pork
1·5 kg/3 lb topside of beef
salt
black pepper
4 shallots

1 large onion
2 small carrots
125 ml/4 fl oz Armagnac or
 brandy
500 ml/16 fl oz dry red wine

Put the fresh pork rind in an oval casserole which will hold the meat without too much space around it. Season the beef with salt and freshly ground black pepper, and lay it on the pork rind. Add the peeled shallots, the onion, peeled and quartered, and the scraped carrots. Arrange the vegetables round the meat and add the Armagnac or brandy and the wine. The liquid should just cover the meat. Cover, using kitchen foil to make a good seal if necessary, and put the casserole in a preheated moderate oven. After 1 hour reduce the oven heat to cool and continue cooking for about 6 hours.

To finish, skim the fat from the casserole and cut the pork rind, which is usually eaten with the meat, into serving pieces. Carve the beef in thick slices and lay them on a warmed serving dish. Pour over the gravy with its pork rind and vegetables. Serve with plenty of creamed potatoes.

The meatballs made for Sweden's Christmas *smörgåsbord* are walnut-sized or even smaller. Peru's Christmas meatballs, called *papa rellena*, stuffed potatoes, are indeed potato-sized. Each is a meal in itself. They are a hit with children who think it fun to find a meatball inside a golden jacket of fried potato.

## Stuffed Potatoes – Papa Rellena – Peru

*Serves 6*

1·5 kg/3 lb potatoes
2 tablespoons butter
1 large onion
1 clove garlic
675 g/1½ lb minced pork or beef
3 hard-boiled eggs

salt
black pepper
2 eggs, beaten
50 g/2 oz plain flour
100 g/4 oz lard

Peel the potatoes and boil them in salted water until quite tender. Drain, mash them very thoroughly, and set aside.

Melt the butter in a large heavy frying pan. Add the onion and garlic, peeled and finely chopped, and the pork or beef. Sauté them together over a low heat until the meat is slightly browned and cooked through. Transfer the meat to a bowl and add the hard-boiled eggs, finely chopped. Season the mixture to taste with salt and freshly ground black pepper.

Form the meat mixture into six balls. Divide the mashed potato into six portions and cover each meatball with an even layer of potato.

Roll the potato-covered balls in beaten egg and then in flour. Melt the lard and carefully fry them over a low heat, turning them gently until they are crisp and golden all over. Herbs may, of course, be added to the meat although the original recipe does not list any.

# SAVOURY PIES

Savoury pies is a loose description of the offerings in this chapter. It covers everything from *juustipiirakka*, the little rye crust cheese pies served with broth in Finland, to the banquet-sized Christmas pies of old England, the fiesta *tamales* of central and south America, and the Caribbean and African specialities cooked in a similar fashion. These are splendid recipes for hot or cold buffet parties.

> Little Jack Horner sat in a corner
> Eating a Christmas Pie.
> He put in his thumb
> And pulled out a plum
> And said – what a good boy am I.

The plum Jack Horner of the nursery rhyme found was not the fruit though it could be seen as a fruit of his labour. For Jack Horner was steward to the last Abbot of Glastonbury. He was entrusted with delivering a Christmas pie from the abbot to Henry VIII in London. During the journey he looked under the pie crust to find the deeds of several manor houses in the county of Somerset. He helped himself to the papers of the Manor of Mells which remained in the Horner family for some years afterwards.

The great Christmas pies were truly majestic constructions. For the best of them a coffin of strong pastry, which was not intended to be eaten, enclosed, say, a goose stuffed with a chicken, stuffed with a pheasant, stuffed with a partridge, stuffed with a pigeon. All the birds were boned, encased in strong paste, and the gaps filled with pieces of game, forcemeat, herbs and hard-boiled eggs. After baking, highly flavoured stock was poured in to fill every nook and cranny and when it had set to a jelly, melted butter was used to seal the pie. Effectively this made a terrine which would keep for some time and allowed the pies, the most famous of which were made in Yorkshire, to be sent as gifts all over the country in the days before fast trains.

Pies of this type were first made in the Middle Ages when a plain flour and water crust was wrapped round meat to prevent it drying out during baking. This method of baking or roasting meat is still used occasionally, especially for cured hams, but pastry now is usually made to be eaten.

Raised pies with a hot water crust are quite easy to make. The process is not a quick one, but the results are spectacular and delicious – so much crisper and tastier than bought pies that the effort is more than repaid. Once baked they keep fresh in a refrigerator for about a week, but the pastry loses its special crunch. Ideally these pies should be baked no more than a day before they are to be eaten. Freezing pies as soon as they are finished allows them to be made well in advance. Thaw them at room temperature for 12 to 24 hours, depending on size. Although jellies do sometimes lose their set when thawed, I have not found this to be so with raised pies.

## Raised Game Pie – England

*Oven temperature Hot 230° C, 450° F, Gas Mark 8; then*
*Moderate 160° C, 325° F, Gas Mark 3*

*Serves 8*

*Filling*
450 g/1 lb pheasant, grouse, partridge or hare, meat only
125 ml/4 fl oz port wine
salt
black pepper
350 g/12 oz lean pork
225 g/8 oz smoked bacon, lean and fat
1 medium onion
½ teaspoon chopped sage
1 tablespoon chopped parsley
½ lemon
225 g/8 oz fresh pork sausage meat

*Jellied stock*
1 kg/2 lb veal bones, chopped
game carcasses
1 medium onion
1 medium carrot
2 bay leaves
6 black peppercorns
*Pastry*
450 g/1 lb plain flour
1 teaspoon salt
1 egg yolk
225g/8 oz lard, or half lard and half butter
175 ml/6 fl oz water
1 egg, to glaze

First prepare the filling ingredients. Cut the meat off the game and reserve the carcasses for the stock. Slice the meat into slivers about 5 cm/2 inches long by 6 mm/¼ inch wide and thick. Reserve any trimmings. Marinate these in the port with a little salt and black pepper, and set aside.

Put the game meat trimmings, pork, bacon and peeled onion through the coarse blade of a mincer and mix the ground meats in a bowl with the sage and parsley. Season with salt, plenty of freshly ground black pepper and the finely grated rind of $\frac{1}{2}$ lemon. Mix well and set aside.

Roll teaspoonfuls of the sausage meat into balls and set aside.

To make the stock, put the veal bones and game carcasses in a large pot with the peeled onions and scraped carrot, roughly chopped. Cover with cold water and bring to the boil. Skim the stock, add the bay leaves and crushed peppercorns, cover and simmer for $2\frac{1}{2}$ hours. Strain the stock through a fine sieve lined with muslin and discard the bones. Reduce the stock to about 300 ml/$\frac{1}{2}$ pint by fast boiling. Set aside to cool.

To make the pastry, sift the flour and salt into a warmed mixing bowl. Make a well in the flour, drop in the egg yolk and cover it over with flour. Heat the lard, or lard and butter with the water in a small saucepan, and when the fat has melted, bring to the boil. Pour immediately over the flour and stir vigorously with a wooden spoon until the mixture is cool enough to handle.

Turn out the dough on to a lightly floured board and knead it until it is soft and pliable. Rest the dough, covered, in a warm place for about 20 minutes.

To assemble the pie, lightly grease an oval or rectangular pie mould, 1·5 litre/$2\frac{1}{2}$ pint capacity, or line an 18-cm/7-inch loose-bottomed cake tin with foil. Pat dry the strips of marinating game.

Roll out two-thirds of the pastry into a piece to line the mould. Fold the pastry in half and lower it carefully into the mould. Unfold it and ease it smoothly and evenly into the base and up the sides of the mould. Press the dough well into the join between the base and sides of the tin and into any indentations on a fancy mould. Ideally, the lining should be about 6 mm/$\frac{1}{4}$ inch thick. If it is too thin the pie will suffer a structural failure, and if it is too thick there will be a layer of cooked, but soggy dough between the meat and the crust.

Put half the ground pork and bacon mixture in the bottom of the lined tin. Cover with slivers of game, arranged lengthwise and interspersed with the sausage meat balls. Top with the remaining pork and bacon. Press the mixture in lightly and mould the top into a dome shape. Dampen the top edge of the pastry with beaten egg. Roll the remaining dough to a thickness of about 6 mm/$\frac{1}{4}$ inch. Lift it over a rolling pin and lay it gently on top of the pie. Press the lid on firmly and trim the pastry with a sharp knife. Decorate the edge and ensure a good seal by pressing firmly with the back of a fork. Cut a 2·5-cm/ 1-inch cross through the pastry in the centre of the lid and fold back the four points to make a good opening for escaping steam. Reroll the pastry trimmings and cut decorative flowers or leaves. Stick them to the pie lid with beaten egg glaze, then paint all the exposed pastry with the glaze.

Set the pie on a baking tin and bake in a preheated hot oven for 20 minutes to set the pastry. Reduce the heat to moderate, cover the pie loosely with foil, and bake for another 3 hours. Remove the foil for the last half hour of cooking time. Leave the pie in its mould until almost cool.

Remove the mould and when the pie is nearly cold, pour into it as much of the cool liquid stock as it will accept. Pour slowly through a small funnel or icing nozzle.

Leave the pie in a cool place for several hours before serving. The jelly will set to fill the gaps between the pastry and the meat which will have shrunk during baking. Serve the pie cold, cut into slices or wedges.

With so much work involved it is well worth doubling or trebling the quantities to make several pies in one session.

For a classic pork pie of the same size, fill with 1·25 kg/2¾ lb of fresh pork from the leg or shoulder. The meat should have a moderate amount of fat. Cut it in 6-mm/¼-inch dice and mix with 1 teaspoon salt, ½ teaspoon black pepper and 1 leaf of sage, very finely chopped. Season the stock with marjoram, sage, thyme and bay.

Queen Victoria's chef Francatelli explains how to raise a pie without a mould in his instructions for a capon pie with truffles. His own recipe for hot water crust is too hard and cardboard-like for modern tastes, so quadruple the pastry recipe for game pie if you are ambitious enough to construct his magnificent pie for a large party.

First, bone a capon, spread it out on the table, and season the inside with prepared spices and a little salt; then spread a layer of forcemeat of fat livers, and place upon this, in alternate rows, some square fillets or strips of fat bacon, tongue and truffles; cover these with a layer of the forcemeat, repeat the strips of bacon, then fold both sides of the skin over each other, so as to give the capon a plump appearance, and set it aside on a dish.

Next, pare off the sinewy skin from the mouse piece, or inner part of a leg of veal, daube it with seasoned lardons of fat bacon, then place this, and an equal quantity of dressed ham, with the capon.

Prepare 4 lbs of hot water paste; take two-thirds of this, mould it into a round ball on the slab with the palm of the hand, and then roll it out in the form of a band, about 2 feet long and 6 inches wide; trim the edges, and pare the ends square, taking care to cut them in a slanting direction; wet them with a paste brush dipped in water with a little flour, and wrap them over one another neatly and firmly, so as to show the join as little as possible. Next roll out half the remainder of the paste, either in a circular or oval form, about $\frac{1}{4}$ inch thick, to the size the pie is intended to be made; place this, with buttered paper, under it, on a baking sheet, wet it round the edge with a paste brush dipped in water, and stick a narrow band of the paste, about $\frac{1}{2}$ inch high, all round it, to within an inch of the edge. The wall or crust of the pie is to be raised up round this, and by pressing on it with the tips of the fingers, it should be made to adhere effectually to the foundation. Then, by pressing the upper part of the pie with the fingers and thumbs of both hands, it will acquire a more elegant appearance, somewhat resembling the curved lip of a vase. The vase must be spread out in proportion to the top, by pressing on it with the thumb. The bottom and sides of the pie should now be lined with a coating of forcemeat of fat livers, or, if preferred, with veal and fat bacon, in equal proportions, well-seasoned, chopped fine and pounded. Next place in the veal and ham, previously cut up in thick slices and well seasoned, and fill up the cavity with some of the forcemeat. Then add the capon and cover it over, and round, with the remainder of the forcemeat, placing some truffles in with it, and cover the whole with thin layers of fat bacon. Roll out the remainder of the paste, and after wetting this, and the pie round the edges, use it to cover in the pie, pressing the edges tightly with the fingers and thumb, in order to make them adhere closely together. Trim the edge neatly and pinch it round with the pastry pincers. The pie should then be egged over, and decorated, for which latter purpose a similar kind of paste must be used, being first rolled out thin, then cut out in the form of leaves, half moons, rings, etc., and arranged according to the designs required : or, if preferred, a moulding raised from decorating boards with some of the paste may be used instead.

The pie must be placed in the oven, and baked for about 4 hours, and when done, should be withdrawn, and about a pint of strongly reduced consommé (made from the carcasses of the capons, two calves' feet and the usual seasoning), should be introduced within it through a funnel. It must then be kept in a cold place until wanted for use; when the cover should be carefully removed without breaking it, and after the top of the pie has been decorated with some bright aspic jelly, it may be put on again and sent to table.

Note : for making pies of turkeys, fowls, pheasants, grouse, partridges etc., follow the above directions.

The Filipino fish pastries *pastelitos de pescado* are a simple fiesta dish which translates well into canapés. Use any cooked white fish for these pastries.

## Fish Pastries – Pastelitos de Pescado – Philippines

*Oven temperature Moderately hot 200° C, 400° F, Gas Mark 6*

*Makes 20–24 pieces*

| | |
|---|---|
| *Pastry* | 2 medium tomatoes |
| 450 g/1 lb plain flour | 25 g/1 oz butter |
| 1 teaspoon sugar | 450 g/1 lb cooked fish, flaked |
| 1 teaspoon salt | 100 g/4 oz frankfurter sausages |
| 175 g/6 oz butter | 4 tablespoons grated cheese |
| 6 egg yolks, beaten | salt |
| *Filling* | black pepper |
| 1 medium onion | |

To make the pastry, sift the flour, sugar and salt into a mixing bowl. Dice the butter into the bowl and work it lightly into the flour with your fingertips or a pastry blender. When the mixture has the texture of fine breadcrumbs mix in 4 of the beaten egg yolks. Sprinkle the mixture with just enough cold water to bring the dough together. Gather the dough into a ball and rest it in the refrigerator.

To make the filling, peel and finely chop the onion, and peel, de-seed and finely chop the tomatoes. Melt the butter in a large frying pan and sauté the onion and tomatoes together until the onion softens. Add the flaked fish, the frankfurters, finely chopped, and cheese. Season the mixture to taste with salt and freshly ground black pepper, and cook the ingredients together for another three minutes.

Roll the pastry dough into a large rectangle about 3-4 mm/ $\frac{1}{8}$ inch thick. Divide in two and trim the pieces to matching size. Cover one piece of pastry with the filling, spread in an even layer, and top with the second piece of pastry. Run the rolling pin lightly over the top. Cut the filled pastry into neat rectangles and arrange them on a greased and floured baking sheet. Brush each piece with beaten egg yolk and bake in a preheated moderately hot oven for about 20 minutes or until the pastry is golden brown. Serve hot or cold.

# Cheese Piirakkaa – Juustipiirakkaa – Finland

*Oven temperature Hot 230° C, 450° F, Gas Mark 8*

*Makes 24*

| Crust | Filling |
|---|---|
| 125 ml/4 fl oz water | 175 g/6 oz Cheddar or Gruyère |
| ½ teaspoon salt |   cheese, grated |
| 1 tablespoon melted butter or oil | 2 tablespoons plain flour |
| 75 g/3 oz plain flour | *To baste* |
| 75 g/3 oz rye flour | 4 tablespoons hot milk |
| | 1 tablespoon melted butter |

To make the pastry, mix the water, salt and butter or oil in a bowl and beat in the white flour to make a smooth paste. Add the rye flour and stir until well blended, then turn the dough out on to a floured board and knead it until smooth. Roll the dough, with your hands, into a 2·5-cm/1-inch diameter sausage shape, and cut it into 24 pieces. Roll each piece of dough into a thin circle 7·5-10 cm/3-4 inches in diameter.

To make the filling, simply mix the grated cheese with the flour.

Place about 2 tablespoons of filling on each piece of pastry and spread it to within 1·2 cm/½ inch of the edge of each circle. Fold two sides of the pastry towards the centre, leaving a 1·2 cm/½ inch band of filling exposed in the middle. Crimp the edges of the now oval pastries and arrange the piirakkaa on a greased baking sheet. Bake in a preheated hot oven for about 15 minutes, or until the pastries are lightly browned. Baste twice during baking, and again as soon as they are out of the oven.

Serve the piirakkaa hot, covered with a napkin, to soften the rye crust a little, with soup. If they are to be eaten cold, wrap them in foil while still hot to prevent the pastry from hardening too much.


*Tamales* have been the fiesta food of Mexican Indians since the Aztec priests made them as offerings to the gods. In the wake of the Spanish explorers came missionaries, and the place of tamales as a sacred food was transferred to the Christian festivals. Mexican tamales vary from region to region as well as with the skill of the cook. The most celebrated are made with blue Mexican corn shortened with lard.

Tamales are akin to stuffed pasta inasmuch as morsels of meat and vegetables in a well-seasoned sauce are enclosed in cooked dough. But there the similarity ends. Tamale fillings are usually highly spiced with chilli and they are always cooked in individual wrappers by steaming. The main difficulty facing Mexicans far from home is the dough itself. In the old days dried corn was soaked in a mixture of water and wood-ash, a lye in other words, and cooked before being scraped for hours on a slab of volcanic rock. Now cornmeal flour called *masa-harina* does away with the backbreaking work, but its availability is very limited outside central and northern America. (Mexican embassies always know if there is any to be bought locally.) Masa harina is an off-white flour and has a distinctive taste which comes from treating the corn with lye. Fine yellow cornmeal is widely available and makes nutty flavoured dough often served in the Yucatan. Corn shucks, or husks, the proper wrappers for tamales in many parts of Mexico, and banana leaves, used in the Yucatan, are seldom obtainable either. Baking parchment and kitchen foil are less colourful substitutes which work well. Cut rectangles of baking parchment or foil 23 cm by 10 cm/ 9 inches by 4 inches. Pork and turkey are also traditional tamale fillings at fiesta time and any leftover turkey with chilli and chocolate sauce, guajolote con molé poblano (see page 71) may, of course, be used instead of the chicken and sauce given in the following recipe.

### Chicken Tamales – Tamales de Pollo – Mexico

*Makes 24*

24 corn husks
5 tablespoons lard
275 g/10 oz instant masa-harina
  or cornmeal flour
1½ teaspoons baking powder
½ teaspoon salt

350 ml/12 fl oz chicken stock or
  water
*Filling*
350 g/12 oz cooked chicken
Mexican chilli sauce (see page 182)

Soak the corn husks in hot water for about half an hour to soften them, then pat dry.

Cream the lard until very light and fluffy in a large bowl. Sift together the masa-harina, baking powder and salt. Gradually beat the flour mixture into the lard a little at a time. When all the flour has been incorporated add the hot stock a little at a time, beating constantly, to form a soft dough.

To prepare the filling cut the cooked chicken into fine dice and moisten it with the sauce.

To assemble the tamales put a rounded tablespoonful of the dough in the middle of each wrapper and spread it into a rectangle which extends almost the full width, but only about 7·5 cm/3 inches along the length. Put a rounded tablespoon of filling on the centre of each piece of dough. Fold one long side of the wrapper just past the centre of the filling, then fold in the opposite side to make an overlapping centre seam. Turn the ends in over the seam, overlapping them just enough to tuck into each other.

To cook the tamales, lay them, seam side down in a fish kettle, steamer, or colander, in as many layers as necessary. Steam them, tightly covered, over boiling water for about 1 hour, or until the dough is cooked. Serve tamales very hot, piled on a heated serving dish, in their wrappers.


Maybe it says more of national characteristics than of differing cuisines that Nigerians see the replacement of leaves with kitchen foil as progress and happily use it for their festive dish *moyin-moyin*. A Nigerian cook uses foil if she can afford it and positively enjoys improvization. Blackeye beans are the basis of the dough for moyin-moyin, and fillings vary greatly with the whim of the cook and what is available in the market.

### Bean Dough Parcels – Moyin-Moyin – Nigeria

*Makes 18*

18 foil wrappers
450 g/1 lb blackeye beans
250 ml/8 fl oz palm oil or
   vegetable oil
2 small onions
4 medium tomatoes

1 tablespoon powdered chilli
salt
pepper
350 g/12 oz cooked pork sausage,
   kidney or liver

To make the foil wrappers cut kitchen foil into rectangles about 30 cm by 12 cm/12 inches by 4½ inches. Make each piece into a bag about 7·5 cm by 15 cm/3 inches by 6 inches by folding the strips in half and turning the edges over three times on either side.

Break up the beans in a coffee grinder to pieces the size of chopped nuts for a dessert topping. Put the broken beans in a bowl and cover them with cold water. After 5 minutes skim off the skins and eyes which have floated to the surface, drain the residue and pick out any remaining pieces of skin. Put the skinned beans in an electric blender and blend them to a smooth paste with sufficient water to produce the consistency of very thick cream. Set aside.

Heat the oil in a heavy pot and fry the onions and tomatoes, peeled and finely chopped, until the onions are golden. Add the chilli powder and stir. Now combine the bean and onion mixtures, add the seasonings to taste, and stir them thoroughly until well blended. Dice the cooked meat.

To assemble the moyin-moyin put a tablespoonful of the bean mixture in each bag, followed by a portion of the meat and another tablespoonful of beans. Turn over the tops of the bags three times to make a good seal, but allowing plenty of room for the mixture to swell.

Stack the packages upright in a fish kettle or steamer, or in a colander over a pot, and steam them, tightly covered, over boiling water for about 45 minutes. The contents are fully cooked when the bean dough has a solid consistency throughout. Uncooked centres are damp like undercooked cake.

Serve moyin-moyin in their wrappers on a warmed dish. Jollof rice (see page 97) is the usual accompaniment. Puddings and fruit are seldom served at mealtimes but are eaten as snacks. Drinking with meals is not customary either in Nigeria, but at Christmas, beer, mineral waters or the powerful local gin are offered after Christmas dinner.

# VEGETABLES AND SALADS

Vegetables are just about the last consideration when Christmas menus are being planned, often because their choice is assumed by the selection of the bird or joint. Roast goose calls for caramelized potatoes and red cabbage in Denmark, and distinctive casseroles of puréed potatoes, turnips or carrots are more or less mandatory with the baked Christmas hams of Finland. New Zealanders' choice of new potatoes and peas with joints of sweet new season's lamb might appear equally conservative but for their delightful custom of gathering the vegetables fresh from the garden on Christmas morning. With buttered asparagus or corn on the cob to begin the meal, weeks of skilful gardening are invested in bringing them all to the Christmas table at their peak.

Roast potatoes and boiled brussels sprouts turn up beside the Englishman's turkey with a regularity which would be less monotonous if either vegetable were generally more skilfully cooked. So as well as particular Christmas dishes this chapter includes some general guidance on cooking a few everyday vegetables plus some recipes which are especially useful because they can be prepared in advance.

First let's deal with roast potatoes. The raw materials should be old potatoes (or maincrop potatoes as the growers like to call them) and fresh fat or oil. Peel the potatoes, cut them into chunks of approximately equal size, and parboil them in salted water for 5 minutes. Drain and dry them, then put them in a roasting tin with hot lard or dripping and roast near the top of a hot oven (220° C, 425° F, Gas Mark 7) for about 40 minutes. If the potatoes are turned over at half time and served as soon as they are ready, this method produces roast potatoes which are crisp outside and creamy smooth inside. It works very well if you happen to be roasting a joint or poultry at such a high temperature.

To accompany slow roasted meat, using an oven temperature of about 180° C, 350° F, Gas Mark 4, put the parboiled potatoes in the roasting tin with the joint for the last hour of its cooking time. While this second method will certainly produce very tasty potatoes there is no guarantee they will be crisp as juices from the meat or poultry will soak into them.

So if, like me, you favour slow roasted meat and crisp roast potatoes, and do not have two ovens, try the pan method. Boil even-sized chunks of old potato in salted water until they are tender but not falling apart. Drain the potatoes well. Heat enough fresh vegetable oil to cover the potatoes in a pot on top of the stove. When the oil is really hot, about 190° C/375° F is ideal, drop in the cooked potatoes and cook them on a fairly high heat until they are crisp and golden. Lift them from the pan, drain them on kitchen paper and serve them immediately.

I particularly like peanut oil for frying, but corn oil or blended vegetable oils are fine. Olive oil is too distinctively flavoured for this job. The oil is hot enough when it browns a cube of day-old bread in 40 to 50 seconds. Lard or dripping can also be used for pan-roasting potatoes.

### Sugar-Browned Potatoes – Brunede Kartofler – Denmark

*Serves 4–6*

| | |
|---|---|
| 1 kg/2 lb small new potatoes | 50 g/2 oz granulated sugar |
| salt | 50 g/2 oz unsalted butter |

Wash the potatoes and cook them in their skins in boiling salted water until they are tender right through but not falling apart. Drain them and when they are cool enough to handle, peel off the skins with a pointed knife.

Put the sugar in a heavy frying pan and melt it over a low heat. Stir the sugar occasionally until it is a deep golden colour and gives off a rich caramel smell. Be careful not to let it turn too dark or it will have a bitter, burned taste. Add the butter and mix it thoroughly with the caramel.

Now add the potatoes to the caramel and cook them over a very low heat, jiggling the pan until each potato has a glossy brown coat.

Some recipes recommend rinsing the potatoes in cold water to make them take an even coating of caramel. A more reliable tip is to have patience and cook the potatoes very gently.

Heap the caramelized potatoes on a warmed serving dish and serve immediately, or use them to garnish roast pork, duck, goose or baked ham.

If you use tinned new potatoes for this recipe try to find a variety packed in salt water with no added mint flavouring, and dry them thoroughly.


Finland's special potato casserole must have originated with one of those happy accidents which sometimes happen in the kitchen. Its originality is due to a 'malting' process during which starch in the potato mixture turns into a simple sugar. In modern kitchens this chemistry takes place in a very slow oven. But it is not hard to imagine a farmer's wife of long ago leaving a dish of mashed potato near her big wood-burning stove while she busied herself with Christmas bread making, and discovering that in the meantime the potato had turned yellow, sweet and unexpectedly delicious. Its taste is reminiscent of chestnuts.

### Potato Casserole –Imellettyperunasoselaatikko – Finland

*Oven temperature Very cool 110° C, 225° F, Gas Mark ¼; then Moderately hot 190° C, 375° F, Gas Mark 5*

*Serves 6–8*

| | |
|---|---|
| 1·5-2 kg/3-4 lb old potatoes | milk |
| 50 g/2 oz plain flour | salt |
| 4 tablespoons dark corn syrup (optional) | butter |

Peel the potatoes, boil them in salted water until tender, drain and mash them thoroughly. Beat the mashed potato, adding a little milk if it is too stiff to work, and mix in the flour, blending it thoroughly. Add the syrup if you are using it.

Butter a heavy casserole dish, one which has a well-fitting lid. Put the potato mixture into the dish, cover it tightly, and cook in a very cool oven for 5 hours. Check the mixture from time to time adding a little milk if it appears too dry. This very slow cooking will make the potato slightly yellow, and very soft and sweet.

To finish the dish add salt to taste and beat the mixture smooth. Dot the top of the purée with butter and bake it, uncovered, in a moderately hot oven for about 20 minutes or until browned on top. Serve the potato casserole piping hot with baked or boiled ham.

### Jansson's Temptation – Janssons Frestelse – Sweden

*Oven temperature Moderately hot 200° C, 400° F, Gas Mark 6*

*Serves 4–8*

| | |
|---|---|
| 2 kg/4 lb old potatoes | 350 ml/12 fl oz single cream |
| 450 g/1 lb onions | 25 g/1 oz butter |
| 12 anchovy fillets | |

Peel the potatoes and grate them coarsely. Peel the onions and slice them into thin rings. Chop the anchovy fillets into small pieces.

Butter a gratin or oven-to-table baking dish and cover the base with a layer of potato. Cover with a layer of onion rings and anchovies and another layer of potato. The number of layers will depend on the size of the dish, and the top layer should be potato. Pour over half the cream and dot the dish with the rest of the butter. Bake in a preheated moderately hot oven for 20 minutes. Now pour over the remaining cream and bake for another 30 minutes or until the potatoes are tender.

Serve Jansson's Temptation straight from the oven as a first course or supper dish, or as a hot buffet dish with some of the cold Scandinavian herring specialities.

Another unusual potato-based dish comes from South America and mixes whole boiled potatoes with a cheese and chilli sauce. Although garnished as a salad, it is served hot, or at least warm, and makes an interestingly different accompaniment to almost any cold meats or poultry.

### Potatoes Huancaina Fashion – Papas a la Huancaina – Peru

*Serves 6–8*

| | |
|---|---|
| 3 tablespoons lemon juice | 1 teaspoon ground turmeric |
| 1 dried hot red chilli, preferably *bontaka* | 2 fresh red or green chillies* |
| black pepper | salt |
| 1 large onion | 4 tablespoons olive oil |
| 8 medium potatoes | 4 hard-boiled eggs |
| 175 g/6 oz cheese, Queso Blanco or Mozzarella | 8 black olives |
| 150 ml/¼ pint double cream | 1 lettuce, preferably cabbage variety |

*See general note page xv, on preparation of fresh chillies.

Pour the lemon juice into a bowl. Remove any seeds from the dried red chilli, chop it very finely, and add it to the lemon juice with a generous seasoning of freshly ground black pepper. Peel the onion, slice it into thin rings and add them to the lemon juice. Stir the onion rings in the marinade, cover the bowl and set it aside.

Peel the potatoes and cook them whole in boiling salted water until they are tender but not dropping to pieces.

While the potatoes are cooking make the sauce. Crumble or coarsely grate the cheese and combine it with the cream, turmeric, one of the fresh chillies de-seeded and finely chopped, salt and pepper. Use a blender or beat by hand until the mixture is smooth and creamy.

Heat the olive oil over a moderate heat in a heavy frying pan. Pour in the sauce, reduce the heat, and, stirring constantly, cook it for 5 to 8 minutes, or until it thickens.

To assemble the dish, drain the potatoes and arrange them on a warmed serving dish. Pour the sauce over them. Drain the onion rings and scatter them over the dish. Garnish with the remaining fresh chilli de-seeded and cut into tiny slivers, quartered hard-boiled eggs, black olives, and the shredded heart of a crisp lettuce.

Another warming winter dish which makes magic of potatoes and cheese is the alpine favourite, *gratin Savoyard*. This version, rich, creamy, and tantalizingly flavoured with garlic, is the one served by Jacques Dandel of *Jacques Bar* in Val d'Isère to skiers ravenous and ruddy from days spent hurtling down the mountains of the Haute Savoie.

### Savoyard Potatoes — Gratin Savoyard – France

*Oven temperature Moderate 180° C, 350° F, Gas Mark 4*

*Serves 6–8*

| | |
|---|---|
| 1·5 kg/3 lb old potatoes | 1 egg yolk |
| 1 clove garlic | 50 g/2 oz cheese, Beaufort or |
| salt | Gruyère type |
| black pepper | 25 g/1 oz butter |
| nutmeg | |
| 600 ml/1 pint creamy milk or a | |
| mixture of milk and single | |
| cream | |

Peel the potatoes and cut them in thin slices. Rub a gratin or shallow oven-to-table dish with the peeled clove of garlic and arrange a layer of overlapping potato slices in the base. Season the potatoes with salt, freshly ground black pepper and grated nutmeg. Continue layering the potatoes and seasoning until all the slices are used up.

Mix the milk, or milk and cream, and egg yolk together and pour enough into the dish to come up to the level of the top layer of potatoes.

You may need more or less milk according to the size of the dish. Grate the cheese finely, sprinkle it over the potatoes and dot the top with butter. Bake uncovered in a preheated moderate oven for about 2 hours, or until the potatoes are tender and all the milk has been absorbed. It is almost impossible to overcook this dish which will keep warm for hours with occasional additions of milk to prevent it drying out.

Serve gratin Savoyard with plain roasts or cold meat or poultry. Leftovers are almost unheard of, but this dish does reheat well. If you are preparing it in advance, omit the cheese and cook the potatoes through; then reheat with the cheese topping.

Variations on the same theme are numerous and go under many names. Try stock, wine and cream in differing proportions as the cooking liquor. Tuck onion rings, pieces of ham or grated cheese betweeen the layers of potato. Use lots of garlic, or none at all.

In Puerto Rico where the Day of the Kings, Epiphany, on 6th January, is the principal feast day of the Christmas season, baked yams accompany stuffed banana leaves and chickens on tables laden with festive delicacies to sustain long hours of dancing and singing.

### Baked Yams – Batatas – Puerto Rico

*Oven temperature Moderately hot 190° C, 375° F, Gas Mark 5*

*Serves 6–8*

| | |
|---|---|
| 1·5 kg/3 lb yams | 100 g/4 oz butter |
| salt | 250 ml/8 fl oz milk |
| pepper | |

Peel the yams and cut them in slices about 3 mm/⅛ inch thick. Season the sliced yams with salt and freshly ground black pepper. Butter a gratin or shallow baking dish and arrange the slices of yam in overlapping layers, dotting each layer with small pieces of butter. Pour in the milk and bake the dish, uncovered, in a preheated moderately hot oven for about 1½ hours or until the yams are tender.

Cooking times for yams can vary greatly according to the type and maturity of the root. It is easier to keep the dish warm after it is cooked through than to risk spoiling trickier recipes while waiting for the yams.

Tiny new potatoes, whole chestnuts and baby onions tossed together in a butter glaze, make an attractive combination to serve with roast turkey, and offering them all in one dish saves time while serving, especially at big family gatherings.

## Glazed Potatoes, Chestnuts and Onions – United States

*Serves 8–10*

| | |
|---|---|
| 1 kg/2 lb fresh chestnuts | 1 kg/2 lb small white onions |
| 900 ml/1½ pints turkey or chicken | 100 g/4 oz butter |
|    stock or salted water | 25 g/1 oz castor sugar |
| 1 kg/2 lb new potatoes | |

Using a small sharp knife, slit the skin on the rounded side of each chestnut. Drop the chestnuts into rapidly boiling salted water and boil them vigorously for 10 minutes. Drain, and when they are cool enough to handle, peel off the skins, being careful to keep the chestnuts whole.

In a heavy pot heat the stock or salted water to boiling, drop in the peeled chestnuts, and simmer them gently for about 20 minutes or until they are just tender. Drain and keep warm.

Cook the new potatoes in briskly boiling salted water until they are tender. Drain, and as soon as they are cool enough to handle, peel off the skins. Keep warm.

Peel the onions. Heat the butter in a large heavy frying pan over a low heat. Add the onions and sugar and cook the onions, covered, shaking the pan frequently, until they are tender. Lift out the onions, leaving behind as much of the cooking liquor as possible, and combine them with the potatoes and chestnuts.

Turn up the heat under the frying pan and reduce the liquor by fast boiling to a syrupy glaze. Pour it over the vegetables and turn them in it gently until all are glistening. Serve hot immediately.

Another classic Finnish casserole of root vegetables is *lanttulaatikko*, a purée of turnips with cream. It is an essential Christmas dish which makes a real treat of the often scorned yellow turnip. Rutabagas are the variety chosen by Finnish cooks, but any yellow winter turnip works well in this dish as long as it is not too woody.

# Rutabaga (Turnip) Casserole – Lanttulaatikko – Finland

*Oven temperature Moderate 180° C, 350° F, Gas Mark 4*

*Serves 6–8*

2 kg/4 lb rutabagas or Swedish
  turnips
salt
20 g/¾ oz dry white breadcrumbs

4 tablespoons single cream
nutmeg
2 eggs, beaten
40 g/1½ oz butter

Peel the turnips, cut into large dice and cook in boiling salted water until tender, between 25 and 40 minutes depending on the type and age of turnips available. Drain and mash the flesh thoroughly. Soften the breadcrumbs in the cream and add to the mashed turnips. Season the mixture well with salt and nutmeg and mix in the beaten eggs.

Turn the mixture into a well-buttered casserole or soufflé dish big enough to allow room for it to rise a little, dot the top with butter, and bake in a moderate oven for about 1 hour or until lightly browned on top.

Almost as good, but less festive looking, is a purée of well-drained boiled swedes beaten with a generous knob of butter and plenty of freshly ground black pepper.

Young white turnips are the kind to choose for the next recipe, a sharply flavoured combination of turnips and oranges which is particularly good with rich meats like pork and goose.

## Turnips with Oranges – England

*Serves 4–6*

12 young white turnips
2 medium oranges
salt

50 g/2 oz butter
black pepper

Peel the turnips carefully to retain their attractive shape. Finely grate the rind of 1 orange and reserve it. Squeeze the juice from both oranges. Put the whole turnips and orange juice in a pot, add a little salt, and simmer them, covered, over a low heat for about 25 minutes, or until they are tender. Drain the turnips and discard the cooking liquor.

Put the turnips in one layer in a well buttered oven-to-table dish. Dot each turnip with butter and sprinkle them with the grated orange peel and a generous seasoning of freshly ground black pepper.

Pop the dish under a hot grill for a minute or two to melt the butter and crisp the orange peel. Serve immediately.

Parsnips, like turnips, are a neglected vegetable and seldom appear on restaurant menus although their place in country cooking wherever they are grown is long established. Their distinctive sweet taste and mealy texture go well with Christmas meats and poultry. Peeled and parboiled parsnips can be roasted round a joint or braised with butter or dripping. Boiled parsnips are very good puréed with cream and black pepper, and mixed purées of parsnips with potatoes, carrots or swedes are inexpensively delicious. Parsnip fritters look more festive if there is time for last minute frying.

### Parsnip Fritters – United States

*Serves 4*

| | |
|---|---|
| 450 g/1 lb parsnips | 2 tablespoons milk |
| 25 g/1 oz butter | 3 tablespoons plain flour |
| salt | 25 g/1 oz dripping or butter |
| black pepper | |

Peel the parsnips, cut into roughly equal-sized chunks and boil them, covered, in salted water for about 30 minutes or until they are tender. Drain and mash them thoroughly, or rub through a coarse sieve. Add butter and a generous seasoning of salt and pepper, and the milk. Mix together until well blended. Shape the parsnip mixture into eight small patties and coat each piece with flour.

Melt the dripping or butter in a heavy frying pan and fry the fritters slowly over a low heat until they are golden brown and crisp on the outside.

Lift them gently from the pan, drain on absorbent kitchen paper, and serve immediately. The parsnips will absorb quite a lot of fat which makes these fritters a rich accompaniment to lean meats like turkey and chicken.

Pickled beetroots are common enough in salads, but beetroots are seldom eaten fresh which is a sad waste of their magnificent colour and sweet, earthy taste. Whole baby beetroots are at their best served hot with lots of melted butter and freshly ground black pepper. They go well with roast game and roast beef. Fresh, pre-cooked, and even bottled beetroots (provided there is no vinegar in the recipe) are all suitable for reheating in butter. If you have been lucky enough to find fresh uncooked beetroots, boil them whole, in their skins, for about 1 hour, or until they are tender. Leave the tapering roots on the beetroots until they are boiled or their colour will bleed away in the water. When they are cool enough to handle, rub off the skins and trim away the roots and stalks. Reheat them in butter on top of the stove, shaking the pot from time to time to stop them sticking.

Braised red cabbage is a firmly established accompaniment to the roast Christmas goose of Denmark, where, no doubt, its festive colour as well as its seasonal availability have contributed to the tradition.

### Braised Red Cabbage – Rødkaal – Denmark

*Oven temperature Moderate 160° C, 325° F, Gas Mark 3*

*Serves 6*

| | |
|---|---|
| 1 kg/2 lb red cabbage, fresh | 6 tablespoons water |
| 50 g/2 oz butter | 6 tablespoons white wine vinegar |
| 25 g/1 oz castor sugar | 4 tablespoons redcurrant jelly |
| 1 teaspoon salt | 1 small eating apple |

Remove any damaged or floppy outer leaves from the cabbage and quarter it. Cut away the tough central stalk and slice the cabbage finely.

Combine the butter, sugar, salt, water and vinegar in a heavy casserole and bring them to the boil on top of the stove. Toss in the shredded cabbage and bring to the boil again, stirring to make sure that all the cabbage is coated with the cooking liquid. Cover the casserole tightly and bake in a preheated moderate oven for about 2 hours. Check occasionally to make sure the cabbage is not drying out, and add a little water if necessary.

Add the redcurrant jelly and the apple, peeled and grated, and return the casserole to the oven for another 10 minutes.

Braised red cabbage reheats well. It is often prepared a day or two before it is eaten to improve the sweet-sour taste.

A less sweet and more subtly flavoured version of oven-braised red cabbage omits the vinegar and redcurrant jelly, and uses belly of pork, juniper berries and dry white wine to flavour the dish. Variations of the recipe, with or without the apple, are popular throughout north-east Europe.

Still with the cabbage family we come to brussels sprouts. Commercially frozen sprouts are better than limp 'fresh' sprouts from the green-grocer or supermarket. If you can buy or pick good fresh brussels sprouts, strip off the outer leaves and cut away the tough stalks. Drop them into boiling salted water and cook them briskly until they are still a little crisp inside, or just tender right through if you prefer. Rinse them quickly in cold water. Melt a generous knob of butter in the pan you cooked them in, and turn the cooked sprouts in the melted butter. Serve them quickly in a heated dish with a liberal seasoning of freshly ground black pepper.

If you are using frozen sprouts follow the instructions on the bag or packet. Overcooking is the most usual reason for soggy, yellowing sprouts and they do not take kindly to being kept warm.

Big creamy butter beans are traditionally served with roast goose or pork in parts of northern England. Tinned butter beans are easier to find than dried ones, and if well drained, just as good in the next recipe.

### Baked Butter Beans – England

*Oven temperature Moderate 180° C, 350° F, Gas Mark 4*

*Serves 4–6*

| | |
|---|---|
| 450 g / 1 lb cooked butter beans | fresh parsley |
| 1 medium onion | fresh or dried thyme |
| 2 medium tomatoes | fresh or dried rosemary |
| 2 stalks celery | salt |
| 75 g / 3 oz butter | pepper |

Drain the tinned beans and rinse them in cold running water. Peel and chop the onion finely. Peel and de-seed the tomatoes and chop them roughly. Chop the celery finely.

Melt two-thirds of the butter in a pot over a medium heat. Add the onion, tomatoes and celery and sauté them together until they are just soft. Stir in one sprig of parsley, finely chopped, and a pinch of thyme and rosemary. Season the mixture generously with salt and freshly ground black pepper, and stir in the beans.

Butter an oven-to-table dish and turn the beans into it. Dot the beans with the remaining butter and bake in a preheated moderate oven for about 20 minutes. Serve hot from the baking dish.

Jollof rice and moyin-moyin (see page 84) are Nigeria's favourite festive dishes and they are made for all kinds of celebrations, including Christmas. At its simplest jollof rice is no more than brown rice coloured red and flavoured with chilli and tomato. But that is seen as poor fare for a feast and meat is added 'to make it a little bit fascinating' as an enthusiastic Nigerian cook put it. Pieces of bacon, chicken and kidney, simmered in stock and then fried in oil, are the most popular additions. Herbs too, thyme and bay, are added according to taste and availability. The finished dish is dry, rather like an Indian pilau, with each grain of rice separate and any fried meat added at the last moment.

## Jollof Rice – Nigeria

*Serves 6–8*

| | |
|---|---|
| 125 ml/4 fl oz ground nut or other vegetable oil | 4 tablespoons tomato purée |
| 6 medium onions | 1·5 litres/2½ pints stock, meat or chicken |
| 4 hot Nigerian peppers or fresh red chillies* | 675 g/1½ lb brown rice |
| | salt |

* See note on preparation of chillies on p. xv.

Put the oil in a large pot, one which has a tightly fitting lid, and heat it over a low heat. Sauté gently together the onions, peeled and roughly chopped, the peppers or chillies, de-seeded and finely chopped, and the tomato purée. When the onions have softened a little add the stock and simmer the mixture for about 10 minutes.

Wash the rice and add it to the cooking liquor. Stir to blend the ingredients well, bring the rice to the boil, lower the heat to a simmer, clamp on the lid firmly and cook gently for about 35 minutes or until the rice is tender. All the liquid should have been absorbed and each grain should be separate. The exact cooking time varies greatly according to the variety of brown rice used. If the rice becomes too dry before it is fully cooked, add water by sprinkling it, a little at a time, into the pot. Season to taste with salt.

Serve jollof rice piled on to a warmed dish or bowl. If you wish, fry bite-sized pieces of cooked meat or poultry and heap them on top of the rice.

In the farmhouses of Cumberland and Northumberland savoury pudding has been made for generations as an accompaniment to roast goose or pork. Prunes or raisins can also be included in the dish which must have been a welcome winter warmer for men coming in from a night's lambing on the snow-covered hills of the Border country. The oatmeal in this recipe is a pointer to the area's affinity with Scotland.

### Savoury Pudding – England

*Oven temperature Moderately hot 190° C, 375° F, Gas Mark 5*

*Serves 8–10*

| | |
|---|---|
| 100 g/4 oz fine oatmeal | 1 tablespoon chopped sage, thyme |
| 100 g/4 oz fresh breadcrumbs | and parsley, mixed |
| 600-750 ml/1-1¼ pints milk | pepper |
| 2 large eggs | salt |
| 75 g/3 oz plain flour | 3 medium onions |
| 100 g/4 oz suet | |

Put the oatmeal and breadcrumbs into a large bowl. Heat 600 ml/1 pint milk to boiling point and pour it into the bowl. Let the mixture stand for about 10 minutes, then beat in the eggs.

In another bowl mix the flour with the shredded or grated suet, the herbs, pepper and salt. Peel and chop the onions and add them to this mixture.

Now combine the oatmeal and flour mixtures and beat well. Add a little more milk if the pudding is too stiff to beat.

Turn the mixture into a well-buttered cake tin or soufflé dish and bake in a preheated moderately hot oven for about 1 hour. Serve savoury pudding hot in thick slices or wedges with roast goose or pork.

The Scottish connections of the next recipe, for the Christmas speciality of Barbados, *jug jug*, are well documented – which is just as well because it would take a detective of some gastronomic distinction to divine such a metamorphosis. Folklore has it that jug jug started life as an attempt by Scots exiled to Barbados in the seventeenth century to recreate the haggis of their homeland. This would have been for the celebration of Hogmanay, or New Year's Eve, of course, but somewhere down the centuries jug jug has become a Christmas speciality and is served as an accompaniment to ham or roast chicken.

Pigeon peas are an important ingredient of this odd delicacy and go by many names. Jamaicans call them *gungo, gunga* or *goon-goo* peas. In Trinidad they are known among other names, as *arhar dahl*, and in the Spanish speaking islands as *gandules*. They are sold dried or in tins. To prepare dried pigeon peas soak them over night and boil them next day in salted water for about 15 minutes.

## A Caribbean Haggis – Jug Jug – Barbados

*Serves 8–10*

| | |
|---|---|
| 100 g/4 oz lean pork | pinch thyme |
| 100 g/4 oz corned beef | 2 spring onions |
| 450 g/1 lb cooked pigeon peas | 50 g/2 oz ground millet |
| 2 medium onions | salt |
| 1 sprig parsley | black pepper |
| 3 stalks celery, with leaves | 40 g/1½ oz unsalted butter |

Put the pork in a heavy pot, add enough water to cover it, and bring the liquid slowly to the boil. Reduce the heat and simmer the pork, covered, for about 40 minutes. Chop the corned beef into large cubes and add it to the pork. Simmer the meats for another 20 minutes before adding the pigeon peas. Cook them together for a minute or two, then strain the mixture, reserving the stock, and set aside.

Return the stock to the pot and add the onions, peeled and roughly chopped, the parsley, the celery, roughly chopped, the thyme, the spring onions, chopped, and the millet. Season the mixture to taste with salt and freshly ground black pepper, and bring it to the boil. Lower the heat, and cook it, stirring constantly, for about 15 minutes.

Put the meat and pea mixture through a mincer and add it to the millet mixture. Cook them gently together for another 25 minutes, by which time the jug jug should be fairly dry and stiff.

Add one-third of the butter and mix it in thoroughly before heaping the jug jug on a warmed serving dish. Spread it with the rest of the butter and serve it, like a vegetable, with a large spoon.

The tart flavour of cooking apples is a popular contrast with rich Christmas roasts, and many stuffing recipes include it. The Danes traditionally serve the apples separately with roast goose or duck as a garnish appreciated by the eye as well as the stomach.

## Apples with Port and Prunes – Aebler med Svedsker – Denmark

*Oven temperature Moderate 180° C, 350° F, Gas Mark 4; then Moderately hot 200° C, 400° F, Gas Mark 6*

*Serves 8*

16 prunes
225 g/8 oz castor sugar
250 ml/8 fl oz port wine

8 cooking apples
900 ml/1½ pints water

Marinate the prunes in an ovenproof dish with 1 tablespoon of the sugar and the port wine for six hours or overnight. Then bake the prunes uncovered in the marinade in a preheated moderate oven for about half an hour, or until the prunes are plump and tender but not falling apart.

Peel the apples carefully to preserve their shape and cut them in halves vertically. Hollow out the cores neatly. Heat the water with the rest of the sugar in a large, preferably shallow pot, and boil the syrup for a minute or two before adding the apples. Simmer the apples gently for about 10 minutes, or until they are tender but not breaking up.

Drain the apples and the prunes. (The syrup and the port marinade can be boiled down together for a really good fresh fruit salad dressing.)

Place a prune in the hollow of each apple and arrange the apples on a generously buttered baking dish. Cover the dish with foil and bake in a preheated moderately hot oven for 10 minutes. Serve immediately arranged round the bird or joint.

Salads are usually associated with summer so it is a surprise to find that the strongest traditions for Christmas salads are found north of the equator and call for winter vegetables. In Naples the eel or carp of Christmas Eve is accompanied by this delicious cauliflower salad.

# Cauliflower Salad – Insalata di Rinforz – Italy

*Serves 4–6*

| | |
|---|---|
| 1 large cauliflower | 1 tablespoon lemon juice |
| 2 cloves garlic | 1 teaspoon castor sugar |
| 18 black olives | 1 teaspoon made mustard |
| 1 tablespoon capers | salt |
| 4 tablespoons olive oil | pepper |

Cut off the leaves and tough central stalk of the cauliflower and break the head into florets. Bring a large pot of salted water to the boil and drop the florets into it. Cook the cauliflower until it is just tender, but still has a bite of crispness, and drain it.

Rub the serving bowl or dish with a cut clove of garlic. Put the cooked cauliflower into the bowl and sprinkle it with olives and capers.

To make the dressing, blend or shake together the olive oil, lemon juice, sugar, mustard, salt, freshly ground black pepper, and pressed or finely chopped garlic to taste. Pour it over the cauliflower and mix well.

If chopped or crushed garlic in any salad dressing is too much of a good thing, use oil flavoured subtly with garlic. Soak three bruised cloves of garlic in about a cup of olive oil. Keep the oil in a stoppered jar for several days, then discard the garlic and use the oil for salad dressings.

Greek salad, from Poland, calls for parsley root which is seldom available, in England at least. Grated parsnip or celeriac are suitable substitutes in this sweet-sour salad.

## Greek Salad – Saładka Grecka – Poland

*Serves 6*

| | |
|---|---|
| 2 large carrots | salt |
| 1 medium parsley root | sugar |
| 1 large onion | lemon juice |
| 4 tablespoons vegetable oil | black pepper |
| 4 tablespoons tomato purée | paprika |

Scrape the carrots and parsley root and grate them coarsely. Peel and finely chop the onion.

Heat the oil in a heavy pot over a medium heat. Drop in the vegetables and fry them quickly for about 2 minutes. Add the tomato purée and about 4 tablespoons water, lower the heat, and cook the vegetables, uncovered, for about 10 minutes or until they are tender. Season to taste with salt, sugar, lemon juice, coarsely ground black pepper and paprika.

Arrange the salad on a dish and serve it very cold. Its sweet-sour taste goes well with the cold herring dishes at the beginning of the fish chapter.

Beetroot salads are popular throughout Scandinavia. They invariably turn out pink which makes them an eye-catching choice for any cold table.

### Beetroot Salad – Punajuurisalaatti – Finland

*Serves 6–8*

| | |
|---|---|
| 2 medium potatoes | 2 tablespoons lemon juice |
| 2 medium carrots | 2 tablespoons beetroot juice |
| 2 medium tart apples | (optional) |
| 1 small onion | salt |
| 2 medium dill pickles | white pepper |
| 450 g/1 lb cooked fresh beetroots | sugar |
| *Dressing* | *Garnish* |
| 250 ml/8 fl oz double cream | 1 lettuce |

Peel the potatoes and cook them in boiling salted water until they are tender but not breaking up. Scrape the carrots and cook them in boiling salted water until they are tender. Cut the cooked vegetables in neat dice.

Peel and core the apples and cut them in dice. Peel the onion and grate it coarsely. Dice the dill pickles. Peel and dice the beetroots.

To make the dressing, whip the cream until it is thick but not stiff. Add the lemon juice and beetroot juice and season it to taste with salt, freshly ground white pepper and sugar.

Combine the dressing with the diced vegetables and fruit and pile the mixture into a bowl lined with crisp lettuce leaves.

Red cabbage and apple salad sharpened with horseradish is a Swedish speciality. It makes an interesting change from the ubiquitous coleslaw.

Use plain preserved horseradish or one of the creamed varieties if fresh is not obtainable.

## Red Cabbage Salad – Rodkålssallad – Sweden

*Serves 4–6*

fresh red cabbage         salt
unsweetened apple purée    pepper
fresh horseradish

Shred the cabbage very finely. Blend the apple purée with the horse-radish and combine this with the shredded cabbage. Season to taste with salt and pepper. Chill for about 3 hours before serving.

# PUDDINGS

The puddings of Christmas are many, varied, and, with a few exceptions, wonderfully rich. The most splendid of them all is England's Christmas or plum pudding. Who invented it and when? Historians of the kitchen do not all agree, so let us start with the entry on plum pudding given by Theodora Fitzgibbon in *The Food of the Western World*, her astoundingly comprehensive and thoroughly readable encyclopaedia of European and North American food.

Its innovation at the English court was the occasion for one of the presentations with which William the Conqueror frequently favoured members of his domestic staff, in this case Robert Argyllon, who received a manor at Addington in Surrey. He received it, according to the *Cook's Oracle* (fourth edition, 1822), 'by the service of making one mess in an earthen pot in the kitchen of our Lord the King, on the day of his coronation*, called De la Groute, ie, a kind of Plum porridge or Water gruel with plums in it. This dish is still served up at the Royal Table, at Coronations†, by the Lord of the said Manor of Addington.' The present-day Christmas pudding evolves from the substitution of prunes, and later still dried fruits, for plums, with the addition of spices, eggs, etc.

The likeliest explanation for how the sloppy eleventh century concoction evolved into the rich pudding we know now is given by F. Marian McNeill in *The Scots Kitchen, Its Lore and Recipes*. In a lengthy footnote she writes:

From the earliest times, our Celtic forefathers celebrated with winter solstice and the return of the fructifying sun from the farthest point in its circuit with a ceremonial cutting of the mistletoe, the bringing in of evergreens, and the supping of a festive gruel which was the symbol of the inexhaustible Cauldron of Keridwen – a sort of Celtic cornucopia – and the portent of future abundance. In the Highlands, this gruel has always been a special kind of sowans; in the Lowlands, they used more commonly a rich brose, known as the Yule Brose. In the Middle Ages (and long after), when sugar, spices and dried fruits were increasingly imported from foreign

* William the Conqueror was crowned on Christmas Day 1066.
† It was last served at the coronation of George IV in 1820.

lands, the more prosperous classes celebrated the festival with plum pottage or porridge.

In the early years of the eighteenth century, plum porridge mysteriously solidified into plum pudding. Nobody knows just how, when, or where it happened. Possibly in some household the porridge was accidentally allowed to boil dry, but was removed before it got burned, and the participants decided that it tasted better that way – and the idea caught on.

History aside, the traditions surrounding Christmas pudding are as rich as the pudding itself. First there is the sprig of holly on top – to keep away witches as some authorities would have it, and the silver coins or charms inside – for luck. There is the mixing ceremony when every member of the family takes a turn or two with the wooden spoon on Stir up Sunday (the Sunday which falls closest to St Andrew's Day in November), and the serving ritual of taking it to the table with blue flames of burning brandy licking over it.

In Cornwall, where Christmas puddings are given as presents, the worth of the gift is judged by the weight of the pudding and the amount of fruit packed into it. This is one way of looking at a good pudding, but there are others. For one of my grandmothers the best Christmas pudding was the blackest Christmas pudding she could make. Some people like them heavy, others light. The one point on which almost everybody agrees is that Christmas pudding should be as fruity as possible.

A fine, home-made Christmas pudding puts commercially made varieties to shame. It takes a fair amount of time and no great amount of skill to make one and the following tips apply to all the recipes. Dried fruit should always be of the best quality you can find. Whole candied caps of orange, lemon and citron peel usually have a much better flavour than the mixed peel sold in small dice. The easiest way to prepare either type for those recipes which include peel, is to put it through a mincer using the coarse blade.

Many recipes use dark beer, such as Guinness, instead of milk or brandy. Any bitterness in the taste of the beer is more than offset by the sweetness of the fruit and some cooks insist that beer brings out the flavour of the fruit better than spirits.

Long steaming helps to make Christmas pudding dark and the second steaming will make it darker than the first. It is important not to let water get into the puddings while they are steaming. Fill the pudding basins to within 2·5 cm/1 inch of the rim, and cover the basins with buttered greaseproof paper and kitchen foil. Cut circles of paper and foil about 2·5 cm/1 inch larger all round than the diameter of the basins.

Lay the foil on top of the paper and put both on together and press the overlap down the sides of the basins so that the foil holds the paper in place while both are tied on firmly with string.

To store the puddings after the first steaming allow them to cool before taking off the buttered papers and foil and re-covering the basins with fresh paper, not buttered this time.

Before steaming the puddings a second time, for serving, cover them the same way as for the initial cooking.

To steam the puddings, place the basins in one or more large pots with tightly fitting lids and pour in boiling water until it comes about one-third of the way up the sides of the basins. Bring the water back to the boil over a high heat, then clamp on the lid, and reduce the heat until the water is bubbling gently. Be careful not to let the pot boil dry and top up the water level with boiling water as required.

To serve the puddings, turn them out on to heated serving plates and pour about two tablespoons of heated brandy over each. Light the warm spirit immediately.

Brandy butter, wine sauces or custards, or cream are the traditional accompaniments to serve with Christmas pudding. Choose from the recipes in the chapter on sauces.

Christmas puddings mature and improve in flavour if stored in a cool, dry place for several months. Adding extra brandy after the first steaming when the puddings are completely cold, and again before they are reheated on Christmas Day, is an optional refinement. I recommend it.

My idea of a perfect Christmas pudding is dark coloured, light textured, and fragrant with fruit, spice and brandy. The following recipe, dating from around 1700, combines these virtues. The quantities listed make two large puddings, each big enough to serve ten to twelve people. If you have the ingredients to make one large or two small puddings there is no need to vary the cooking times.

### Christmas Pudding – England – Circa 1700

*Serves 20–24*

| | |
|---|---|
| 350 g / 12 oz currants | 50 g / 2 oz blanched almonds |
| 350 g / 12 oz seedless raisins | 1 teaspoon grated nutmeg |
| 225 g / 8 oz sultanas | 100 g / 4 oz dark brown sugar |
| 1 fresh lemon | 4 large eggs |
| 225 g / 8 oz shredded suet | 175 ml / 6 fl oz brandy, or brandy |
| 350 g / 12 oz fresh white | and rum |
| breadcrumbs | 150 ml / ¼ pint milk |

Put the dried fruit in a large mixing bowl. Finely grate the peel of the lemon over the fruit. Add the suet, breadcrumbs, finely chopped almonds, nutmeg and sugar and mix all the dry ingredients thoroughly.

In a separate bowl beat together the eggs, brandy or brandy and rum, and the milk, and stir the liquid into the fruit mixture. Mix well.

Let the mixture, which is a fairly dry one, stand in a cool place for about 12 hours before dividing it between two or more buttered pudding basins. Cover the basins with paper and foil and steam the puddings for 6 hours (see page 106).

On Christmas Day steam the puddings for at least another 2 hours before serving.

The next recipe makes a pudding which is lighter in colour than the last. King George I was known as the 'Pudding King' – a comment on his taste for the food of his homeland and English prejudice on the subject of German food – and this is the recipe served to him on his first Christmas in England in 1714.

## King George I's Christmas Pudding – England

*Serves 25–30*

225 g/8 oz stoned prunes
225 g/8 oz raisins
225 g/8 oz sultanas
225 g/8 oz currants
100 g/4 oz stoned dates
100 g/4 oz glacé cherries
225 g/8 oz mixed candied peel
225 g/8 oz self-raising flour
350 g/12 oz shredded suet

225 g/8 oz fresh brown
  breadcrumbs
225 g/8 oz demerara sugar
1 teaspoon mixed spice
1 teaspoon salt
½ nutmeg
6 large eggs
150 ml/¼ pint milk
1 tablespoon lemon juice
150 ml/¼ pint brandy

In a large bowl mix together the prunes, chopped, raisins, sultanas, currants, and the dates and cherries, chopped, with the peel, chopped or coarsely minced. Add the flour and mix it with the fruit using your hands. Add the suet, breadcrumbs, sugar, mixed spice and salt. Grate half a nutmeg into the bowl and mix these dry ingredients together thoroughly.

In a separate bowl beat together the eggs, milk, lemon juice and brandy. Pour this mixture into the big bowl and stir until all the ingredients are well blended..

Leave the pudding mixture to stand in a cool place for about 12 hours before dividing it between two or more buttered pudding basins. Cover the basins with paper and foil and steam the puddings for about 6 hours (see page 106).

On Christmas Day steam the pudding for at least another 2 hours before serving.

The plum pudding recipe used by Charles Elmé Francatelli, chef to Queen Victoria, is more heavily spiced. It also makes a more solid pudding. This recipe calls for only one boiling so the pudding is not a dark one.

# Queen Victoria's Plum Pudding – England

*Serves 16–20*

| | |
|---|---|
| 350 g/12 oz raisins | 2 tablespoons ground cinnamon, |
| 350 g/12 oz currants | cloves and nutmeg, mixed |
| 225 g/8 oz candied orange, lemon | ½ teaspoon salt |
| and citron peel | 2 lemons |
| 575 g/1¼ lb shredded beef suet | 4 large eggs |
| 450 g/1 lb plain flour | 450 ml/¾ pint milk |
| 350 g/12 oz moist dark brown | 125 ml/4 fl oz brandy |
| sugar | |

Put the raisins, currants, chopped or minced peel into a large mixing bowl with the shredded suet, sifted flour, sugar, spices and salt. Grate the rinds of two lemons over the bowl and mix the ingredients thoroughly together.

In a separate bowl beat the eggs with the milk and brandy. Pour this mixture into the big bowl and stir until all the mixture is well blended.

Leave the pudding mixture to stand in a cool place for about 12 hours before turning it into one large or two, or more, smaller basins. Cover the paper and foil and steam for 4½ hours (see page 106). Francatelli's serving instructions are: 'Dish it up with a German custard sauce over it.'


Leftover Christmas pudding can be sliced and fried in butter, sprinkled with sugar and served with whipped cream or brandy butter. Another delicious way of serving it is Eliza Acton's 'The Elegant Economist's Pudding'. She speaks for herself.

Butter thickly a plain mould or basin, and line it entirely with slices of cold plum or raisin pudding, cut so as to join closely and neatly together; fill it quite with a good custard; lay, first a buttered paper, and then a floured cloth over it, tie them securely, and boil the pudding gently for an hour; let it stand for ten minutes after it is taken up before it is turned out of the mould. This is a more taste-ful mode of serving the remains of a plum-pudding than the usual one of boiling them in slices, or converting them into fritters. The German sauce, well milled or frothed, is generally much relished with sweet boiled puddings, and adds greatly to their good appear-ance; but common wine or punch sauce, may be sent to table with the above quite as appropriately.

Mould or basin holding 1½ pints, lined with thin slices of plum-pudding; ¾ pint new milk boiled gently 5 minutes with grain of salt, 5 bitter almonds, bruised; sugar in lumps, 2½ oz; thin rind of ½ lemon, strained and mixed directly with 4 large well-beaten eggs; poured into mould while just warm: boiled gently 1 hour.

Metric equivalents are slices of cold plum pudding to line a 900-ml basin; milk, 450 ml boiled gently 5 minutes with a grain of salt and 5 bruised bitter almonds; sugar in lumps, 65 g; thin rind of ½ lemon; large eggs, 4. You can use kitchen foil over the buttered paper instead of the floured cloth.

New Zealanders are much attached to English Christmas tradition, but Christmas pudding can be just too much when the festivities come at the height of summer. This New Zealand recipe for a rich ice-cream bombe is probably just as fattening as the traditional plum pudding, but at least it is cold and needs no last minute attention or precious cooker space on Christmas Day.

### Christmas Ice-Cream – New Zealand

*Serves 10–12*

| | |
|---|---|
| 175 g/6 oz fine shortcake biscuit crumbs | 275 g/10 oz mincemeat |
| | 600 ml/1 pint vanilla ice cream |
| 65 g/2½ oz butter | 175 g/6 oz glacé cherries |
| 450 ml/¾ pint double cream | 40 g/1½ oz blanched almonds |
| 1 tablespoon brandy | ½ teaspoon almond essence |
| ½ teaspoon vanilla essence | |

Butter a 1·5-litre/2½-pint bombe mould or bowl. Combine the shortcake crumbs with the melted butter and line the mould with this mixture, pressing it evenly round the sides. Chill until this crust is firm.

Whip the cream and stir in the brandy and vanilla essence. Combine the cream with the mincemeat. Spoon this mixture into the lined mould, spreading it in an even layer and leaving a deep hollow for the ice cream. Freeze until the cream is firm.

Soften the ice-cream slightly. Stir in the cherries, whole or chopped, the nuts, roughly chopped, and almond essence. Pack this mixture into the mould and smooth it over evenly. Cover and freeze for at least 12 hours.

Unmould the bombe straight from the freezer. Dip the mould *briefly* in hot water and turn the bombe out on to a flat plate. Return it to the main compartment of the refrigerator for about an hour before serving.

Port wine jelly was a smart pudding to serve at festive gatherings in the nineteenth century. Expense is no doubt one reason it is so seldom made now. Set in an elaborate mould it looks lovely and tastes even better. Serve it on its own, or with whipped cream and tiny almond biscuits. You could even go wild and decorate it with gold leaf (from artists' suppliers) as was the custom for jellies served at fifteenth-century feasts. This is not a jelly to serve to children. Only half the wine is subjected to heat so the flavour of the jelly is superb and so is its effect.

### Port Wine Jelly – England

*Serves 4–6*

3 tablespoons gelatine  
600 ml / 1 pint port wine (red not  
   tawny)  
2 teaspoons lemon juice  

100 g / 4 oz castor sugar  
$\frac{1}{4}$ teaspoon grated nutmeg  
$\frac{1}{4}$ teaspoon powdered cinnamon  

Soak the gelatine in a quarter of the port and all the lemon juice for a few minutes. When it has softened add another quarter of the port, the sugar and the spices, and bring the mixture almost, but not quite to the boil, stirring constantly. When the gelatine has completely dissolved, strain the mixture through a fine sieve, or better still, through a sieve lined with muslin. Allow the jelly to cool right down before adding the rest of the port.

Pour the jelly into a wetted mould and leave it to set in a cool place.

To unmould the jelly, dip the mould *briefly* in hot water, and turn it out on a flat plate.

Another heady pudding is the delicious and quickly made eighteenth-century trifle called a whim-wham. Trifles are traditional Boxing Day and Christmas party puddings in England.

### Whim-Wham – England

*Serves 6*

| | |
|---|---|
| 25 g/1 oz butter | 2 oranges |
| 100 g/4 oz blanched almonds | 150 ml/¼ pint sweet sherry |
| 1 tablespoon castor sugar | 125 ml/4 fl oz brandy |
| 18 sponge finger biscuits | 450 ml/¾ pint double cream |

Melt the butter in a heavy frying pan and fry the almonds over a medium heat until they are golden. Sprinkle them with the sugar and shake the pan over a low heat until it melts. Spread the almonds on a lightly greased plate to cool. The sugar and butter harden to form a brittle toffee coating.

An hour or two before serving, put the sponge fingers, broken in halves, into a large serving bowl. Squeeze the juice from the oranges, mix it with the sherry and brandy, and pour into the bowl. (The alcohol evaporates and the sponge fingers become soggy if the liquid is added too long before serving.)

Just before serving, whip the cream until it will hold a peak. Pour it over the sponge fingers which should have absorbed all the liquid. Sprinkle the top with toffee coated almonds and serve at once.

### Old-fashioned Trifle – Scotland

*Serves 8–10*

| | |
|---|---|
| 2 eggs | 175 g/6 oz strawberry jam |
| 2 egg yolks | 100 g/4 oz macaroons or ratafias* |
| 25 g/1 oz castor sugar | 175 ml/6 fl oz sweet sherry or |
| 1 teaspoon cornflour | sherry and brandy mixed |
| 600 ml/1 pint milk | 450 ml/¾ pint double cream |
| ½ vanilla pod | 40 g/1½ oz flaked almonds |
| 8 trifle sponges or stale sponge | |
| cake | |

* See recipe page 172.

Mix together in a bowl the eggs, egg yolks, sugar and cornflour. Heat the milk and vanilla pod slowly together until almost at boiling point. Take off the heat, remove the vanilla pod, and pour the milk over the egg mixture stirring briskly. Cook the custard very gently, stirring constantly, until it has thickened. (Egg custard burns easily so it is best cooked in a double boiler or in a bowl over a pot of hot water. The water should be just simmering.) Cover and cool the custard.

Spread the trifle sponges, split in halves, or the pieces of stale sponge cake, with the jam, and arrange them in the bottom of the serving bowl. Sprinkle them with broken macaroons or ratafias, and the sherry, or sherry and brandy mixed. Spoon the cold custard into the bowl and cover it with the cream, whipped until it will hold a peak.

Toast the almond flakes until they are golden, and when they are cool, sprinkle them over the trifle.

There are endless variations on the trifle theme. The essential ingredients are a good egg custard and plenty of lightly whipped cream. The jam can be strawberry, apricot or cherry, or the fruits themselves. Sherry almost always plays a part in trifle, but any of the fruit flavoured liqueurs can be used, diluted with sherry or fruit syrup or juice. The top of the trifle may be left plain, or piped and decorated with glacé fruits, small ratafias, or crystallized flowers.

Another choice for ending Poland's elaborate Christmas Eve feast is a refreshing cranberry pudding. Cornflour or arrowroot can be substituted for potato flour as a thickener for this simple dessert.

### Cranberry Dessert – Kisiel Żurawinowi – Poland

*Serves 4–6*

450 g / 1 lb fresh cranberries          50 g / 2 oz potato flour
100 g / 4 oz granulated sugar

Boil the cranberries briskly in 450 ml / ¾ pint water until the skins burst. Rub the cooked berries through a sieve. Return the purée to the cooking pot and add the sugar. Mix the potato flour with a little water and stir it into the purée. Bring the mixture to the boil, reduce the heat, and cook gently until it thickens.

Pour the thickened purée into a pretty bowl and serve it chilled with whipped cream.

A compote of stewed dried fruits – figs, prunes, apples, apricots, peaches and pears – generously laced with gin or rum is another traditional choice offered for the dessert course in Poland. Allow the cooked fruit to cool before adding the spirits.

In Chile, sliced custard apples in an uncooked syrup of orange juice and icing sugar are a popular seasonal choice.

A rich egg custard and semolina cream encased in delicate phyllo pastry and soaked in spiced syrup is a festive dessert served in Greek homes. Phyllo pastry is sold ready made in specialist food stores where it often goes under the name of strudel pastry.

### Custard Pastry – Galactobouriko – Greece

*Oven temperature Moderately hot 190° C, 375° F, Gas Mark 5*

*Serves 12–16*

| | |
|---|---|
| 12 sheets phyllo pastry | 5 large eggs |
| 100 g/4 oz butter, melted | ¼ teaspoon salt |
| *Filling* | vanilla essence |
| 950 ml/32 fl oz milk | 1 teaspoon powdered cinnamon |
| 75 g/3 oz semolina | *Syrup* |
| 1 teaspoon cornflour | 450 g/1 lb granulated sugar |
| 1 piece lemon rind | 350 ml/12 fl oz water |
| 225 g/8 oz granulated sugar | 5 cm/2 inches cinnamon stick |
| 50 g/2 oz butter | |

To make the filling, heat the milk to just below boiling point in a heavy-based pot. Add the semolina, cornflour and lemon rind and stir briskly over a medium heat until the mixture thickens. Cool to lukewarm then beat in half the sugar and the butter.

In a separate bowl beat the eggs with the remaining sugar. Combine the egg and semolina mixtures, adding salt and vanilla essence to taste.

Generously butter a baking tin about 30 cm by 20 cm/ 12 inches by 8 inches and at least 3 cm/1¼ inches deep. Lay a sheet of phyllo pastry in the base, trimming it if necessary, and paint it with melted butter. Top with five more sheets of pastry, painting each with butter before adding the next. Pour in the filling and cover it with six more sheets of buttered phyllo. Score the top layers of pastry with a diamond pattern. Bake in a preheated moderately hot oven for about 1 hour.

To make the syrup put the sugar and water into a pot with the piece of cinnamon. Heat gently until the sugar has dissolved, then boil briskly for about 5 minutes. Pour the syrup over the pastry while it is still warm from the oven. Serve galactobouriko warm or cold. It keeps for over a week in a refrigerator.

Another very sweet pudding made for Christmas is *natillas piuranas* from Peru.

### Caramelized Milk Pudding – Natillas Piuranas – Peru

*Serves 6–8*

1 (475-ml/16-fl oz) tin sweetened,   ½ teaspoon bicarbonate of soda
  condensed milk                    200 g/7 oz dark brown sugar
600 ml/1 pint milk                  3 tablespoons water

Put the condensed milk, fresh milk and bicarbonate in a pot and bring them to the boil over a high heat, stirring constantly. Set aside.

Combine the sugar and water in a large heavy-based pot and cook over a low heat until the sugar dissolves. Pour in the hot milk mixture and cook over a very low heat, stirring constantly, for about 1¼ hours. The mixture will become a thick amber-coloured pudding.

Pour the pudding into one large or several individual serving dishes. Eat it at room temperature or chilled.

A less sweet milk pudding is eaten at Christmas in the Philippines where the festive version of *leche flan* includes small coins for luck.

### Caramel Custard – Leche Flan – Philippines

*Oven temperature Cool 140° C, 275° F, Gas Mark 1*

*Serves 4–6*

*Custard*                    1 lemon
475 ml/16 fl oz milk         *Caramel*
8 egg yolks                  175 g/6 oz brown sugar
175 g/6 oz castor sugar      4 tablespoons water

115

Scald the milk. Beat egg yolks and sugar together and gradually beat in the milk. Add the grated lemon rind and mis thoroughly. Set aside.

To make the caramel dissolve the sugar in the water in a small saucepan over a low heat, then boil the syrup briskly until it caramelizes. Do not let the caramel become too dark or it will taste bitter. Pour the caramel into a well-buttered shallow oven-proof dish.

Pour the custard over the caramel. Stand the custard dish in a larger baking tray, and pour water into the outer container until it comes about half way up the sides of the custard dish. Bake in a preheated cool oven for about 1 hour or until the custard has set.

Cool the custard before turning it out of the mould, caramel side up. Lucky coins wrapped in kitchen foil can be pressed into the cold custard before it is unmoulded.

Norway's national festive dessert, *eggedosis*, is served after church on Christmas Day.

### Egg Flip – Eggedosis – Norway

*Serves 6–8*

| | |
|---|---|
| 10 eggs yolks | 100 g/4 oz castor sugar |
| 1 egg white | 175-250 ml/6-8 fl oz brandy |
| 2 teaspoons cold water | or Madeira wine |

Beat the egg yolks and white in a large bowl. Add the water and sugar and beat the mixture over a pan of hot, but not boiling, water until it is pale and fluffy.

Pour about 2 tablespoons brandy or Madeira wine into each of 6 to 8 large wine glasses and pour over the warm egg mixture.

Serve immediately with macaroons or meringues. If the alcohol is omitted from the recipe a glass of Madeira should be served separately with this pudding.

The macaroons and meringues served with eggedosis have undoubtedly become customary because so many egg whites are needed to make them. So here are two more pudding recipes using lots of egg white. Both have excellent Christmas credentials.

# Soft Meringue – Pavlova – Australia

*Oven temperature Very cool 120° C, 250° F, Gas Mark ½*

*Serves 6*

*Meringue*
2 egg whites
1 teaspoon white wine vinegar
3 tablespoons hot water
350 g/ 12 oz castor sugar
1 teaspoon cornflour

½ teaspoon vanilla essence
*Decoration*
300 ml/½ pint double cream
2 kiwi fruit (Chinese gooseberries),
    fresh or tinned, or passion fruit

Put all the meringue ingredients in a large bowl and beat them together until the mixture holds a firm peak (about 3 minutes with an electric beater).

Mark a circle about 20 cm/8 inches in diameter on a piece of kitchen foil and anchor the foil to a heavy oven tray with dabs of fat. Pile the meringue on to the foil and spread it as evenly as possible within the circle. Bake in a preheated very cool oven for 1¼ hours.

When the meringue is cool transfer it to a flat serving plate. Mask the whole creation with whipped cream and decorate it with slices of peeled kiwi fruit. Serve well chilled.

*Salzburger nockerln* brings drama to the table with bright flames of rum dancing over a mountain-shaped hot soufflé. It is well worth the last minute preparation which gives the diners time to recover their appetites.

# Salzburger Soufflé – Salzburger Nockerln – Austria

*Oven temperature Moderately hot 200° C, 400° F, Gas Mark 6*

*Serves 4–6*

1 tablespoon honey
2 tablespoons double cream
8 egg whites
100 g/4 oz granulated sugar
4 egg yolks

½ teaspoon vanilla essence
1 orange
1 lemon
2 tablespoons plain flour
3 tablespoons rum

117

Put the honey and cream in a 20-cm/8-inch soufflé dish in the bottom of a moderately hot oven while you make the soufflé.

In a large bowl whisk the egg whites until they will hold a stiff peak. Slowly whisk in the granulated sugar and whisk until the sugar has dissolved.

In a smaller bowl whisk together the egg yolks and vanilla essence. Grate the orange and lemon rind over the bowl and stir gently. Carefully fold the egg yolk mixture into the meringue, then the flour.

Take the soufflé dish from the oven and spoon the mixture over the melted honey and cream. Heap it up into a mountain shape. Return the dish to the oven for about 20 minutes on a middle shelf, or until the soufflé is firm and golden brown.

While it is in the oven, clear space at the dining table for the finale. Warm the rum in a long-handled soup ladle, set it alight, and pour the flaming liquid over the soufflé. Serve immediately.


Rice puddings enriched with eggs, nuts, spice and sometimes sherry have an honoured, if mobile, place in Scandinavian Christmas meals. In Denmark *grød* is sometimes served before the meat course, and a portion set aside for the *julenisse*, the little gnome who guards the family and lives in a barn or attic. Sweden's *julgröt* has a single whole almond baked in a plain rice pudding and whoever finds it will be the next person to marry. General good luck for the following year is assured to the Finn who finds the whole almond in the traditional baked rice pudding.

### Baked Rice Pudding – Unni Riisipuuro – Finland

*Oven temperature Moderate 180° C, 350° F, Gas Mark 4*

*Serves 6–8*

| | |
|---|---|
| 225 g/8 oz long-grain white rice | ½ teaspoon salt |
| 725 ml/24 fl oz milk | 65 g/2½ oz unblanched almonds |
| 50 g/2 oz butter, melted | 1 teaspoon powdered cinnamon |
| 100 g/4 oz granulated sugar | 1 blanched almond |
| 3 large eggs | |

Cook the rice, uncovered, in rapidly boiling water until it is tender but not mushy. Drain and rinse in cold water.

Beat together the milk, melted butter, sugar, eggs and salt. Combine with the rice and pour into a well-buttered 1·75-litre/3-pint oven-to-table dish. Slice the unblanched almonds, mix them with the cinnamon and sprinkle them over the pudding. Bake in a moderate oven for about 1 hour or until the pudding is as firm as desired. Press the whole almond into the pudding and cover the hole.

Serve the pudding hot or chilled. Hand round a jug of single cream.

Butter and cinnamon top the baked rice pudding served before roast goose in Denmark. One dessert version of rice pudding is enriched with cream instead of eggs. A spoonful of cherry liqueur, or a cold raspberry or cherry sauce, tops each portion.

### Rice and Almond Pudding – Ris à l'Amande – Denmark

*Serves 8–10*

900 ml/1½ pints milk
50 g/2 oz castor sugar
225 g/8 oz long-grain white rice
50 g/2 oz blanched chopped
  almonds

125 ml/4 fl oz sweet sherry
1 teaspoon vanilla essence
250 ml/8 fl oz double cream

Put the milk in a large heavy-based pot and bring it to the boil. Add the rice and sugar, lower the heat, and simmer the rice, uncovered, for about 25 minutes, or until it is tender but not mushy. Remove from the heat and when the rice is cool, stir in the chopped almonds, sherry and vanilla essence.

Whisk the cream until it holds a peak and fold it into the rice mixture. Turn the pudding into a pretty bowl and chill well before serving.

In Malta a hot chestnut 'stew' flavoured with chocolate and tangerine completes the Christmas meal.

### Chestnut Pudding – Mbuljuta – Malta

*Serves 4–6*

450 g/1 lb dried chestnuts
2 tablespoons cocoa

175 g/6 oz castor sugar
1 tangerine

Put the chestnuts in a bowl, cover them with cold water, and leave them to soak for at least 12 hours.

Skim the soaking liquid, strain the chestnuts and reserve the liquid. Pick any loose pieces of skin from the chestnuts.

Put the chestnuts and reserved liquid in a heavy-based pot, bring to the boil and cook, covered, for about 30 minutes, or until they are tender. Add the cocoa, sugar, and tangerine rind, finely grated. Continue cooking, partially covered, for another 30 minutes, stirring frequently. By this time some of the chestnuts will be whole or in large pieces and some will have broken down to form a sauce.

Finally, check the flavour and add cocoa or sugar to taste. Serve hot.

Drinks tinted a violent pink with pomegranate juice are one of Mexico's colourful fiesta customs. Corn husks too are dyed pink for the sweet tamales served at Christmas. To colour the corn husks add red food colouring to hot water and soak them for about half an hour. Pat them dry and grease the inside surface of the husks with lard or butter before assembling the tamales. Baking parchment or kitchen foil cut in sheets approximately 23 cm by 10 cm/9 inches by 4 inches can be substituted for the corn husks in which the pieces of stuffed dough are wrapped for steaming. Use any mixture of candied or glacé fruits for the filling, the more different kinds the better.

### Sweet Tamales – Tamales Dulces – Mexico

*Makes 24*

| | |
|---|---|
| 24 prepared corn husks | ½ teaspoon salt |
| *Dough* | 100 g/4 oz castor sugar |
| 65 g/2½ oz lard | ½ teaspoon powdered cinnamon |
| 215 g/7½ oz instant masa-harina | 300 ml/½ pint warm water |
| or cornmeal flour | *Filling* |
| 1½ teaspoons baking powder | 450 g/1 lb chopped candied fruits |

In a large bowl cream the lard until it is light and fluffy. Sift together the masa-harina, baking powder, salt, sugar and cinnamon. Gradually beat the flour mixture into the lard a little at a time. When all the flour has been thoroughly absorbed, add the water, a little at a time, beating constantly to form a soft dough.

To assemble the tamales divide the dough between the 24 wrappers (about 1 tablespoonful each). Spread the dough to a rectangle about

10 cm by 7·5 cm/4 inches by 3 inches. The dough should extend close to the long edge of the wrappers. Drop a heaped tablespoonful of filling in the centre of the dough. Fold one long side of the wrapper a little more than half way across the filling. Fold the second long side in the same way to make an overlapping centre seam. Now turn the ends to the middle to cover the seam, overlapping them enough to tuck one end into the other. (If you are using kitchen foil wrappers bring the long sides to the centre and fold over together before turning the ends to the middle.)

Stack the tamales, seam side down, in a large steamer, fish kettle, or in a colander which fits over a large pot. Steam them, covered, over boiling water for about 1 hour. Top up with boiling water during cooking if necessary.

To serve, arrange the tamales dulces on a heated serving dish. Eat them piping hot.


For unexpected guests Brazil's Christmas dessert is a quick and easy pudding to make. Coconut milk may be substituted for the port.

### French Toast – Rabanadas – Brazil

*Serves 4*

| | |
|---|---|
| 3 tablespoons castor sugar | 2 eggs |
| 175 ml/6 fl oz port wine | 50 g/2 oz butter |
| 8 slices French bread | 1 teaspoon powdered cinnamon |

Mix 1 tablespoon of the sugar with the port and pour it over the bread arranged on a plate. Beat the eggs on another plate and when the bread has soaked up the sweetened port, dip each slice carefully in beaten egg to coat on both sides.

Melt the butter in a large frying pan and fry the soaked bread on both sides until golden brown and crisp on the outside.

Arrange the rabanadas on a warmed serving plate and sprinkle with the rest of the sugar mixed with the cinnamon. Serve hot.

# BREADS

Mystic significance of one sort or another has so long been attached to bread that it is no surprise to find customs of decidedly pagan origin well mixed with the baking of special Christmas breads. In the Shetland Islands oatcakes called Yule-brunies are still baked with a hole in the centre and edges pinched into points, a relic of the ancient Scandinavian Yule which was a festival of sun-worship. Oatcakes impressed with a cross and called Yule-bannocks are baked at day-break on Christmas morning, in honour of the Virgin's delivery, in other parts of Scotland. The Yule-log, dragged home from the forest on Christmas Eve, and so big that it burned for several days, survives as a practice still in Britain, and, of course, cakes baked in Yule-log shapes are common to many countries. In Swedish homes another old custom still repeated today is the *Julhög*, a pyramid of different breads and biscuits set before each member of the family on Christmas morning.

Germany's festive breads have been a feast for the eyes as well as the stomach since medieval times. As well as sculptured breads there are the famous *Gedildbrote*, picture breads embossed with stars, wreaths, horses, deer, serpents and many more intricate patterns in most of which ancient symbolic meanings can be traced to their use as offerings to the gods of long ago when bread took the place of animals poor folk could not afford to sacrifice. Similarly, plaited loaves may once have stood for offerings of hair. Crescent-shaped moon breads were being baked long before the Turks threatened Vienna. St Nicholas loaves and plaited breads in the shape of stars are popular Christmas breads in Germany today and many of the old shapes are still repeated in the wealth of biscuits made at Christmas time.

When everyday bread was coarse stuff, festive baking called for lavish use of fine ingredients, and many Christmas breads are so rich in fruit, fat and spices that they are almost cakes. These special breads and the traditions of baking them survive in homes where breadmaking is no longer an essential skill.

Of the plain Christmas breads the Scandinavian rye loaves are the main survivors, and so outstandingly good that it is easy to see why they are still made each year. The first is Finland's potato rye bread, a moist dark bread with a chewy crust and superb flavour.

# Potato Rye Bread – Perunalimppu – Finland

*Oven temperature Very cool 110° C, 225° F, Gas Mark ¼; then Moderately hot 190° C, 375° F, Gas Mark 5*

*Makes 2 loaves*

2 tablespoons dried yeast
250 ml/8 fl oz potato water
250 g/9 oz rye flour
450 g/1 lb mashed potatoes
175 g/6 oz dark corn syrup or
   light molasses (treacle)
1-2 teaspoons salt

2 teaspoons caraway seeds
400-450 g/14-16 oz strong or plain
   flour
*Glaze*
1 tablespoon sugar
1 tablespoon water

Sprinkle the yeast on 250 ml/8 fl oz of the water in which the potatoes have cooked. The potato water should be lukewarm, about 43° C/ 110° F. Sift half the rye flour into a fairly large bowl and stir in the dissolved yeast mixture. Blend well together and set aside in a warm place.

In another bowl combine the warmed mashed potatoes with the syrup or molasses, salt and caraway seeds. Add the remaining rye flour, beat the mixture smooth, cover the bowl and set it in a very cool oven for 1½ hours. The potato mixture will soften in the oven as starches in the potato convert to simple sugars in what the Finns call a 'malting' process.

Combine the yeast and potato mixtures in a large mixing bowl and blend them well together. Gradually add the sifted white flour, beating in each addition to make a stiff dough. The exact amount will depend on the consistency of the potato. Rest the dough in the mixing bowl for about 15 minutes before turning it out on to a floured surface and kneading it until smooth. This dough does not develop the elasticity of conventional mixtures.

Put the dough in a lightly oiled mixing bowl, rolling it to grease the mixture on all sides, and cover with a damp cloth or greased plastic bag. Set the bowl in a warm place for about 1 hour or until the dough has doubled its bulk. Punch down and leave the dough to rise again until it has doubled a second time.

Divide the dough in halves and form each piece into a ball. Place the balls well apart on a greased and floured baking sheet and leave them to rise in a warm place for about 25 minutes or until they appear puffy but have not quite doubled in size.

Bake the potato rye bread in a preheated moderately hot oven for 40 to 45 minutes or until the loaves sound hollow when tapped on the bottom.

Cool the loaves on a wire rack and while still warm from the oven brush the tops with the glaze of sugar dissolved in warm water.

For Finland's Christmas rye bread, *Joululimppu*, the loaves are shaped in dented, lopsided rounds.

### Christmas Rye Bread – Joululimppu – Finland

*Oven temperature Moderately hot 190° C, 375° F, Gas Mark 5*

*Makes 2 loaves*

175 g/6 oz dark molasses (black treacle)
500 g/18 oz rye flour
2 teaspoons salt
2 tablespoons dried yeast

450-575 g/1-1¼ lb strong or plain flour
*Glaze*
1 tablespoon dark molasses (black treacle)
1 tablespoon warm water

Mix the molasses in a large bowl with 350 ml/12 fl oz boiling water. Stir in 125 g/4½ oz of the rye flour, beat well, and set the mixture aside for about half an hour.

Now beat in another 125 g/4½ oz of rye flour and 350 ml/12 fl oz of boiling water. Set aside for about 1 hour.

Beat in 125 ml/4 fl oz more boiling water and cool the mixture until lukewarm, then add the salt.

Sprinkle the yeast on 4 tablespoons warm water, about 43° C/110° F, and whisk well. When it has completely dissolved stir it into the molasses and rye flour mixture. Gradually add the remaining rye flour and the white flour beating in each addition thoroughly, until a stiff dough is formed. Rest the dough for 15 minutes before turning it out on to a floured surface and kneading it until smooth.

Put the dough in a lightly oiled mixing bowl, rolling it to grease the mixture on all sides, and cover with a damp cloth or greased plastic bag. Leave it to rise in a warm place for about 1 hour or until it has doubled in bulk.

Turn out on to a lightly floured surface and divide the dough in halves. Shape each piece into a ball and pull it gently into a peak on one side. Arrange the loaves well apart on a greased baking sheet. Using your thumb punch the peaks down into the loaves, and leave them in a warm place to rise again until puffy, but not quite doubled in size.

Bake Joululimppu in a preheated moderately hot oven for about 50 minutes or until the loaves sound hollow when tapped on the bottom.

Cool the loaves on a wire rack, and while they are still warm from the oven, brush the tops with a glaze of molasses dissolved in warm water.

What the Scots call tea breads, the Scandinavians call coffee breads, and they are baked in large quantities for the Christmas tables of Sweden and Finland. They are offered to visitors throughout the holiday and served with fresh coffee. Coffee breads are invariably eaten before more elaborate biscuits and cakes, and may be baked in large, fancy loaves or small buns. There is a wealth of traditional shapes to choose from – plaits, stars, twists, pinwheels, and many more with names like Christmas wagon, bishops' wigs, Lucia buns, Christmas pigs, golden chariots and so on.

### Saffron Bread – Saffransbrod – Sweden

*Oven temperature Moderately hot 190° C, 375° F, Gas Mark 5*

*Makes 2 loaves or about 40 buns*

| | |
|---|---|
| 1 teaspoon saffron | 150 g/5 oz seedless raisins |
| 1 tablespoon brandy | 900 g/2 lb strong or plain flour |
| 600 ml/1 pint milk | *Decoration* |
| 4 tablespoons dried yeast | 1 egg |
| 175 g/6 oz castor sugar | chopped almonds |
| ¼ teaspoons salt | granulated sugar |
| 1 large egg | seedless raisins |
| 225 g/8 oz butter, melted | |

Dry the saffron for about 5 minutes in a cool oven (150° C, 300° F, Gas Mark 2) then dissolve it in the brandy. Heat the milk to lukewarm, about 43° C/110° F. Use about 125 ml/4 fl oz of the warm milk to dissolve the dried yeast. Sprinkle it over the milk, whisk well, and leave it for about 15 minutes.

In a large bowl mix the remaining warm milk with the saffron and

125

brandy, salt, egg, melted butter and 100 g/4 oz of the sifted flour. Add the yeast mixture, stirring constantly, and beat in the sugar, raisins and remaining flour, a little at a time, until a smooth, firm dough is formed.

Put the dough in a lightly oiled bowl, rolling it to grease the mixture on all sides, and cover with a damp cloth or greased plastic bag. Leave it to rise in a warm place for about 2 hours or until doubled in bulk.

Turn out the dough on to a floured surface and knead it until smooth and elastic. The dough is now ready to shape.

To make two large plaited loaves divide the mixture in halves. Divide one half into three equal pieces and roll them into three long strips. Plait the strips evenly, tucking the ends underneath, and carefully set the plait on a well-buttered baking sheet. Repeat with the second ball of dough. Set the loaves in a warm place to rise until the dough is puffy but not quite doubled in bulk. Brush the loaves with beaten egg glaze and sprinkle sugar and chopped almonds down the centre of each plait. Bake in a preheated moderately hot oven for 20 to 25 minutes or until the loaves are golden brown. Cool on a wire rack and serve warm.

To make saffron buns roll small pieces of dough into 'snakes' about 30 cm/12 inches long. To make a simple S-shaped bun coil the dough loosely from each end in opposite directions, and put a raisin in the centre of each curl. Two or three of these S-shaped pieces of dough may be set across each other to make larger more ornate buns. Lay the buns well apart on a generously buttered baking sheet and leave them in a warm place to rise until the dough is puffy but not quite doubled in bulk. Brush the buns with beaten egg glaze and bake them in a preheated hot oven (220° C, 425° F, Gas Mark 7) for 10 to 12 minutes or until the buns are golden brown. Cool on a wire rack and serve warm.

Finland's coffee bread, *pulla*, is a moist, rich bread, eaten hot without butter. It is baked throughout the year, often for Sunday morning callers, but at Christmas it is made into special shapes. Cardamom seeds give pulla its distinctive flavour.

# Coffee Bread – Pulla – Finland

*Oven temperature Moderately hot 200° C, 400° F, Gas Mark 6*

*Makes 2 or 3 loaves*

2 tablespoons dried yeast
475 ml/16 fl oz milk
175 g/6 oz castor sugar
1 teaspoon salt
1 teaspoon powdered cardamom
4 eggs

900 g-1 kg/2-2¼ lb strong or plain
   flour
100 g/4 oz butter, melted
*Decoration*
glacé cherries or raisins

Sprinkle the yeast on about 125 ml/4 fil oz warm water, about 43° C/ 110° F, in a large bowl. Whisk well and set aside in a warm place for about 15 minutes or until the yeast has completely dissolved. Scald the milk and cool it to lukewarm.

Add to the yeast mixture the milk, sugar, salt, cardamom, and beaten eggs with about 225 g/8 oz of the sifted flour. Beat to a smooth thick batter. Gradually add about another 350 g/12 oz of the flour, beating continuously to form a smooth, glossy dough. Beat in the melted butter before adding enough of the remaining flour to make a firm dough. Rest the dough, covered, for about 15 minutes before turning it out on a floured surface and kneading it until smooth and elastic.

Place the dough in a lightly oiled bowl, rolling it to grease the mixture on all sides, and cover with a damp cloth or greased plastic bag. Leave it to rise in a warm place for about 1 hour or until doubled in bulk. Punch down the dough, cover, and let it rise again until almost doubled in bulk. Chilling the dough at this stage will make it easier to form into fancy shapes.

To make two fancy Christmas cake loaves, *Joulukakut*, divide the dough into four equal pieces. Shape one piece into a flat, circular loaf about 30 cm/12 inches in diameter and place it on a lightly greased baking sheet. Divide the second piece of dough into three equal portions and roll each portion into a long, thin strand about 120 cm/48 inches in length. Cut a 10-cm/4-inch piece off each strand and reserve. Plait the strands and lay the plait in a circle on top of the loaf about 2·5 cm/1 inch inside the edge. Form the reserved short lengths into S-shaped curls and arrange them in a radial pattern from the centre of the loaf. Make a second loaf with the remaining two pieces of dough. Set the loaves to rise in a warm place until they are puffy but not quite doubled in bulk. Brush the loaves with beaten egg to glaze, and bake in a preheated moderately hot oven for 25 to 30 minutes or until golden brown. Do not overbake or the loaves will be too dry. Cool on a wire rack and serve warm.

To make three bishops' wig loaves, *papintukka*, divide the dough into nine equal pieces and roll each piece into a strand about 45 cm/18 inches long. Fold the first strand in half and place it on a lightly greased baking sheet. Curl the ends outwards and upwards into small coils. Place a second strand of dough beside and above the first and curl its ends in the same way. Repeat with a third strand. The finished pattern looks like an inverted U with a row of three curls down each side. Repeat the pattern twice with the remaining six pieces of dough, and set the loaves to rise in a warm place until they are puffy but not quite doubled in bulk. Place a glacé cherry half or a raisin on each curl and glaze the loaves with beaten egg. Bake in a preheated moderately hot oven for 20 to 25 minutes or until the loaves are golden brown. Cool on a wire rack and serve warm.

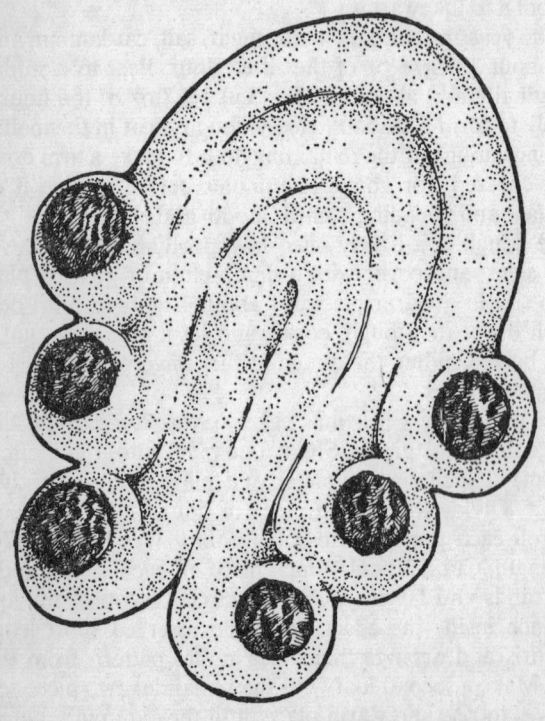

**Coffee Bread – bishop's wig**

Germany's favourite Christmas fruit bread *Dresdner stollen* should be stored for at least three days after it is baked. It is a dry, cake-like bread which keeps well for several weeks and is often gift-wrapped in clear cellophane tied with a bow of red ribbon.

## Christmas Bread – Weihnachts Stollen – Germany

*Oven temperature Moderately hot 190° C, 375° F, Gas Mark 5*

*Makes 2 loaves*

| | |
|---|---|
| 6 tablespoons rum | 675 g/1½ lb plain flour |
| 65 g/2½ oz seedless raisins | 250 ml/8 fl oz milk |
| 65 g/2½ oz currants | ½ teaspoon salt |
| 175 g/6 oz candied orange, lemon and citron peel, chopped | ½ teaspoon almond essence |
| | 2 eggs |
| 75 g/3 oz glacé cherries | 275 g/10 oz unsalted butter |
| 1½ tablespoons dried yeast | 75 g/3 oz chopped almonds |
| 175 g/6 oz castor sugar | 4 tablespoons icing sugar |

Put the rum in a small bowl with the raisins, currants, candied peel and quartered glacé cherries. Set aside to soak.

Sprinkle the yeast on about 3 tablespoons of warm water, 43° C/ 110° F, mixed with 1 tablespoon of the sugar, whisk well and set aside in a warm place until the yeast dissolves completely.

Drain the dried fruit, reserving the rum, and pat it dry. Toss the fruit in about 2 tablespoons of the flour and set it aside.

Dissolve 100 g/4 oz of the sugar with the milk in a saucepan over a very low heat. When the mixture is lukewarm remove from the heat and add the reserved rum, salt, almond essence, and the yeast mixture.

Sift 575 g/1¼ lb of the flour into a mixing bowl and add the yeast mixture, stirring constantly. Whisk the eggs until frothy and stir them into the dough followed by about 175 g/6 oz of softened butter. When the ingredients are thoroughly blended, turn out the dough on to a well-floured surface and knead it, sprinkling the dough with the remaining flour and kneading until it has all been incorporated. When the dough becomes smooth and elastic press in the dried fruits and chopped almonds a handful at a time. Continue kneading lightly until these are well distributed in the dough. Place the dough in a lightly oiled bowl, rolling it to grease the mixture on all sides, and cover it with a damp cloth or greased plastic bag. Leave it to rise in a warm place for about 2 hours or until the dough doubles in bulk.

Punch down the dough, divide it in halves, and leave it to rest for about 10 minutes. On a lightly floured surface roll out the dough into 1·2-cm/½-inch thick rectangles about 30 cm by 20 cm/12 inches by 8 inches. Melt the remaining butter. Brush each strip generously with butter and sprinkle liberally with sugar. To shape the loaves fold one long edge to the centre, and the opposite edge to overlap the centre in a 2·5-cm/1-inch seam. Press lightly to seal the edges and arrange the loaves, well apart, on a generously buttered baking sheet. Brush the dough with melted butter and set it aside to rise in a warm place until doubled in bulk.

Bake the bread in a preheated moderately hot oven for about 45 minutes or until the loaves are golden brown. Cool on a wire rack. While still warm from the oven brush the loaves with the remaining melted butter and dust generously with icing sugar. When completely cold, store the stollen in an airtight container and leave them to mature for at least 3 days before cutting.


*Christópsomo*, the Christmas bread of Greece, is flavoured with chopped orange peel and the dough rolled in sesame seeds before being formed into the shape of a cross and sprinkled with chopped almonds. Denmark's *Julekage* is flavoured with cardamom like the Finnish *pulla*. The dough includes generous quantities of candied pineapple as well as the usual glacé cherries and candied citrus peel, and it is baked in a standard loaf tin. Austria's *stritzel* is the most elaborately plaited of the Christmas loaves with a four strand plait, covered by a three strand plait topped with a two strand twist. Nutmeg and cumin spice its well-egged dough. Norway's *Julekake* is even more richly filled, with spiced apples or dried fruit, candied peel and almond paste, and is often baked in fancy shapes. Tricornes, half moons and figures of eight are three traditional forms which may well have their roots in pre-Christian festivities but are merrily continued today. This version, which has a centre of almond paste, is best baked in a rectangular loaf tin.

# Christmas Bread –Julekake – Norway

*Oven temperature Moderately hot 190° C, 375° F, Gas Mark 5*

*Makes 1 loaf*

1 tablespoon dried yeast
3½ tablespoons castor sugar
1 large egg
450 g/1 lb strong or plain flour
¼ teaspoon salt
75 g/3 oz butter
65 g/2½ oz seedless raisins

75 g/3 oz currants
75 g/3 oz mixed candied peel,
 chopped
1 teaspoon powdered cardamom
175 g/6 oz almond paste
 (see page 189)

Sprinkle the yeast on about 125 ml/4 fl oz warm water, 43° C/110° F, mixed with a teaspoon of the sugar. Whisk the mixture and set it in a warm place. When the yeast has completely dissolved, whisk in the egg and set the mixture aside.

Sift the flour, salt and remaining sugar into a mixing bowl. Dice the butter into the bowl and using your fingertips or a pastry blender, rub it lightly into the flour until the mixture resembles fine breadcrumbs. Make a well in the centre, and pour in the yeast mixture. Sprinkle a little flour over the liquid, cover the bowl and set it in a warm place for about half an hour or until the yeast has bubbled through. Stir the flour into the liquid, drawing it in gradually. Turn out the dough on to a lightly floured surface and knead it lightly until it is smooth and elastic. Mix the dried and candied fruits with the cardamom and press them into the dough a handful at a time.

Put the dough in a lightly oiled bowl, rolling it to grease the mixture on all sides, and cover it with a damp cloth or greased plastic bag. Leave it to rise in a warm place for about 1 hour or until it doubles its bulk. Punch down, knead again lightly, and divide the dough in halves. Place the first half in a well-greased and floured 1-kg/2-lb loaf tin. Roll the almond paste into a thick sausage about 3·7 cm/1½ inches shorter than the length of the tin and lay it on the dough. Put the remaining dough on top of the almond paste and tuck it in lightly. Set the tin aside in a warm place until the dough is puffy but not quite doubled in bulk.

Bake it in a preheated moderately hot oven for 50 to 60 minutes. Cool on a wire rack. When completely cold store the Julekake in an airtight container for at least 24 hours before slicing it.

# CAKES

Honey and dried fruits were the sweeteners used throughout Europe before cane sugar from the Caribbean plantations became an import which has grown steadily since the seventeenth century. Neolithic man knew the taste of honey and by the Bronze Age it had become more plentiful as greater areas of forest were cleared for grazing. The proverbial land flowing with milk and honey was no dream but a direct result of agriculture.

Oriental spices played an important role in Roman cooking though honey was still the universal sweetener. Pliny said of cane sugar from India that it was 'a kind of honey that collects in reeds' and added that its uses were only medicinal.

Raisins and currants and most of the spices we know today were lavishly employed by cooks to the medieval nobility. A form of gingerbread was already an established favourite in the thirteenth century when squares of the cake made in England were decorated with box leaves spiked with cloves. These decorations were sometimes gilded.

Travel played an important role in the growth of cake-making. Traders and crusaders returned home to northern lands with recipes from the far east and the Levant. Gradually, as the use of eggs and other raising agents was better understood and employed, cakes which had earlier been enriched breads evolved into the confections made today. Many of the cakes still made for Christmas are baked with recipes which have changed little for centuries. New kitchen equipment, and prepared and packaged ingredients have taken much of the labour out of baking. But the rich spicy smells and tastes are just the same, and their enjoyment all the greater for a pinch of sentiment.

Honey cakes and gingerbreads which are well spiced, though not always with ginger, were among the first cakes to be made for Christmas celebrations. Some of the earliest were no more than dry white breadcrumbs mixed with spice and honey to a stiff paste which could be moulded and decorated. Most of the recipes used today are simple ones, though the moulds and decorations may be very elaborate. Germany's many types of *Lebkuchen* and *Pfefferkuchen* are among the most lavishly ornamented gingerbreads and are fashioned into iced pictures as well as houses, figures and all kinds of fancy shapes. The

132

Swiss, Dutch, Austrians, Danes, Norwegians, Finns, Swedes, Scots and Silesians all make honey and spice cakes or biscuits for Christmas, and now there must be more varieties of honey and gingercake made in America than anywhere else. As each new wave of immigrants brought its treasured recipes and patterns to the New World, the repertoire of American cooks grew to embrace them. Nowhere in the world are such a variety of *Süssgebäck* or 'sweet bakings' as the German language best catches it, made at Christmas time. Here are just a few.

Edinburgh gingerbread is a rich, moist cake which improves with keeping for a week or two in an airtight container. The mixture includes dates and walnuts and is traditionally baked in a square or rectangular tin.

## Edinburgh Gingerbread – Scotland

*Oven temperature Moderate 180° C, 350° F, Gas Mark 4; then Cool 150° C, 300° F, Gas Mark 2*

*Makes 1 cake*

450 g/1 lb plain flour
¼ teaspoon salt
1½ teaspoons powdered ginger
1½ teaspoons powdered cinnamon
1½ teaspoons mixed spice
½ teaspoon powdered cloves
225 g/8 oz stoned dates
100 g/4 oz shelled walnuts

225 g/8 oz butter
350 g/12 oz molasses (black treacle)
200 g/7 oz dark brown sugar
4 large eggs, beaten
1 teaspoon bicarbonate of soda
warm milk

Sift the flour, salt and spices into a mixing bowl. Chop the dates and walnuts coarsely and add them to the flour.

In a small saucepan over a low heat melt together the butter, molasses and sugar. Pour this mixture gradually into the flour, stirring constantly. Add the beaten eggs, and the bicarbonate of soda dissolved in a tablespoon of warm milk. Stir the ingredients well with a wooden spoon so as not to mash the fruit, adding a little more warm milk if needed to make a mixture which will just drop from the spoon but is not too soft.

Spoon the mixture into a well greased baking tin about 20 cm/8 inches square and at least 6·5 cm/2½ inches deep, lined with baking parchment. Spread the mixture evenly, and bake in a preheated moderate oven. After 20 minutes lower the heat to cool and continue baking for another 2 hours or until a skewer inserted in the centre of the cake comes out clean. Cool the gingerbread on a wire rack, then strip off the papers and when completely cold, store in an airtight container.

Sweden's ginger cake is a lighter mixture, often baked in a ring mould. It is not usually decorated.

### Ginger Cake –Mjuk Pepparkaka – Sweden

*Oven temperature Moderate 160° C, 325° F, Gas Mark 3*

*Makes 1 cake*

| | |
|---|---|
| 100 g/4 oz butter | 1 teaspoon powdered cloves |
| 175 g/6 oz castor sugar | 200 g/7 oz plain flour |
| 3 large eggs | 1 teaspoon bicarbonate of soda |
| 1 teaspoon powdered ginger | 175 ml/6 fl oz soured cream |
| 1 teaspoon powdered cinnamon | dry breadcrumbs |

Cream the butter in a large bowl, add the sugar and beat the mixture until it is pale and very fluffy. Beat the eggs and add them, a little at a time to the butter and sugar, beating vigorously.

Sift together the spices, flour and bicarbonate of soda, and fold half into the creamed mixture, a little at a time. Fold in the soured cream, then incorporate the remaining flour.

Spoon the mixture into a ring mould, well greased and dusted with dry breadcrumbs. Bake the ginger cake in a preheated moderate oven for 50 to 60 minutes. Leave to cool in the tin for about 10 minutes, then turn out on to a wire rack. Store in an airtight container.

For a *lebkuchen häuschen*, the famous gingerbread house, a quite different recipe is used. It is for a cake which, if not eaten (and many such houses are brought out year after year) will dry out and keep from one season to the next. This kind of mixture is also used for other traditional fancy shapes. Lavish decoration is the rule for lebkuchen häuschen which is adorned with icing, small biscuits and sweets. If the cake is being made to last make sure the decorations will too and choose sweets and biscuits that will not crumble or slowly dissolve when in contact with the air. Icing made with icing sugar and egg white is very durable if kept dry.

For a 25-cm/10-inch high gingerbread house bake three batches of the next recipe. Cut the gingerbread as soon as it is baked with accurate card or baking parchment templates made according to the diagram (see page 136). Store the cut pieces in an airtight container until they are assembled with icing cement. If a large Swiss-roll tin about 45 cm by 30 cm/18 inches by 12 inches is not available, divide the mixture between smaller tins, calculating with the templates the number of pieces needed.

### Gingerbread House – Lebkuchen Häuschen – Germany

*Oven temperature Moderate 160° C, 325° F, Gas Mark 3*

*Make 3 times*

| | |
|---|---|
| 675 g/1½ lb plain flour | 450 g/1 lb castor sugar |
| 2½ teaspoons baking powder | 50 g/2 oz butter |
| ¼ teaspoon salt | 1 lemon |
| 1 teaspoon powdered ginger | 1 large egg |
| 1 teaspoon powdered cinnamon | 1 egg yolk |
| 1 teaspoon powdered cloves | *Icing* |
| ½ teaspoon grated nutmeg | 2 eggs whites |
| 350 g/12 oz honey | 350 g/12 oz icing sugar |

Sift the flour, baking powder, salt and spices into a large mixing bowl. Put the honey, sugar and butter in a large heavy saucepan and heat them gently together until the sugar has dissolved. Bring the mixture to the boil. Cool to room temperature, and add the juice and finely grated rind of the lemon. Beat about one-third of the flour and spice into the cool honey mixture, add the whole egg and the egg yolk, and incorporate them thoroughly before adding the remaining flour and spice.

Turn the dough into the mixing bowl and knead it lightly with floured hands until it is smooth and pliable. This dough will be a little sticky, but if it is too soft to handle, knead in a little more flour.

Press the dough evenly into a well-buttered and floured Swiss-roll tin about 45 cm by 30 cm/18 inches by 12 inches, and bake in a pre-heated moderate oven for about 40 minutes or until the cake feels firm when pressed lightly with the fingertips. Cool the cake in the tin for about 10 minutes before turning it on to a flat surface. Cut the required shapes using prepared templates (see page 136), then cool the pieces on a wire rack before storing.

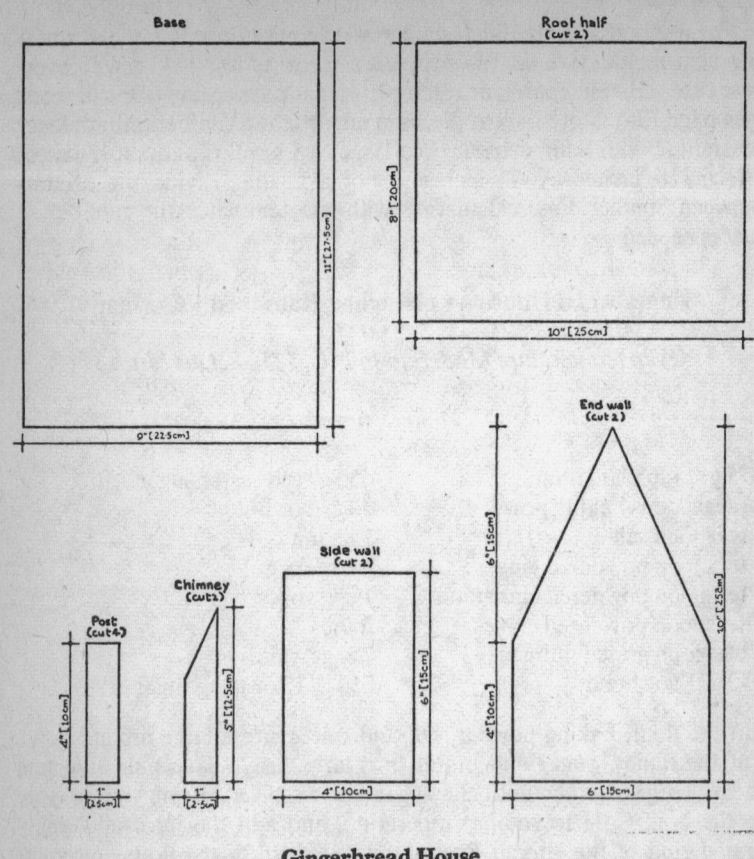

**Gingerbread House**

To make the icing, whisk the egg whites until they hold a soft peak then beat in the sifted icing sugar, about 4 tablespoons at a time, beating in each addition thoroughly. Beat continuously until a stiff icing is formed.

To assemble the lebkuchen häuschen, pipe icing doors, windows and shutters on the front, back and sides of the house. When these decorations have dried, lay the base on a tray or board and build up the house with icing cement. Allow the walls to dry before adding the roof and chimney, and leave these to set before completing the decorations with a fresh batch of icing if needed. Sprinkle icing sugar on the base for snow.

136

In Sweden a harder biscuit dough cut before baking makes the traditional *Pepparkaksstuga*. The recipe is a mixture used for Lucia gingersnaps too, the biscuits made in the shapes of people, animals and trees. The quantities given in the following recipe make the house and plenty of extra biscuits – the number will depend on the size of cutters used. Use the tiny fancy cutters for *petits fours* to make miniature decorations.

This dough is very well-behaved in the oven, hardly shrinking or spreading at all. Make accurate card or baking parchment templates according to the diagram on page 138. The windows may be cut out, or applied as decoration.

### Gingersnap House – Pepparkaksstuga – Sweden

*Oven temperature Moderate 180° C, 350° F, Gas Mark 4*

*Makes 1 house and biscuits*

*Dough*
175 ml/6 fl oz double cream
225 g/8 oz dark brown sugar
250 ml/8 fl oz molasses (black treacle)
2 teaspoons powdered ginger
2 teaspoons grated lemon rind

1 teaspoon bicarbonate of soda
575 g/1¼ lb plain flour
*Cement*
100 g/4 oz castor sugar
*Icing*
1 egg white
225 g/8 oz icing sugar

To make the dough, whip the cream in a large bowl until it is thick, but not stiff. Add the sugar, molasses, ginger, lemon rind and bicarbonate of soda and beat well. Add the sifted flour, all at once. Stir the mixture with a wooden spoon until it becomes too stiff to manage, then use your hands to blend it until it forms a firm dough.

Roll out the dough thinly on a lightly floured surface. Lay the templates on the dough (see page 138). Place a ruler on the template, lining it up with one edge, and pressing gently, cut along the edge with a sharp knife. Move the ruler to the next edge, cut, and so on.

Arrange the cut-out dough on buttered greaseproof paper on heavy baking tins. Brush the dough with water and bake in a preheated moderate oven for 20 to 25 minutes. Leave the pieces on the baking tins for about 5 minutes before laying them carefully on a wire rack to cool. Make sure that each piece is quite flat during cooling as the dough sets hard. When cold store the pieces in an airtight container until the house is assembled. Use the remaining dough to make tiny baked decorations, or plain or fancy biscuits.

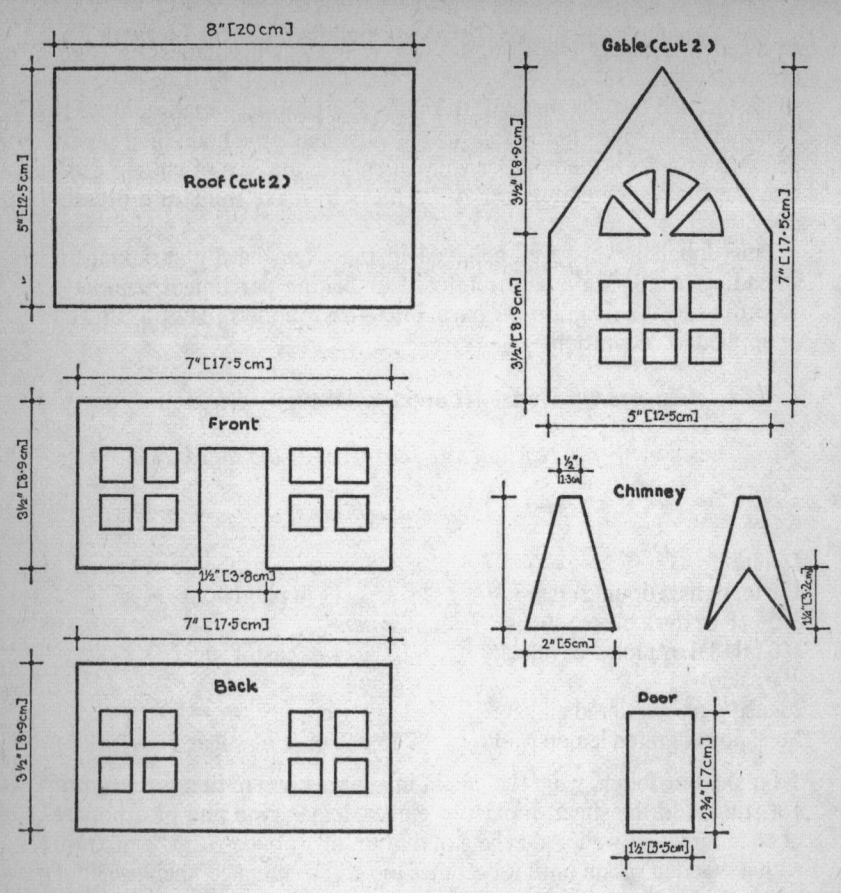

**Gingersnap House**

To assemble the house, melt the sugar over a low heat in a 23-cm/ 9-inch saucepan. Dip the edges of the biscuit pieces in the melted sugar and stick them together. The caramelized sugar sets in an instant, but it is dangerous stuff, so work carefully to avoid nasty burns.

To decorate the pepparkaksstuga, beat the egg white until it just holds a peak, then beat in the sifted icing sugar a little at a time until a stiff icing is formed. Pipe decorations on to the house and stick on any other decorations with small blobs of icing.

English Christmas cake, like Christmas pudding, should be made in September or October if it is to mature to its full richness. About 10 days before it is needed, the top and sides are covered with almond paste which is left to dry for about three days before the cake is frosted with royal icing. Alternatively, the top only may be covered with almond paste, decorated with closely packed lines of nuts and glacé fruits, and glazed. The sides of the cake are then covered with a paper frill.

## Christmas Cake – England

*Oven temperature Cool 150° C, 300° F, Gas Mark 2; then 140° C, 275° F, Gas Mark 1*

*Makes 1 cake*

275 g/10 oz plain flour
1 teaspoon salt
1 teaspoon mixed spice
225 g/8 oz butter
225 g/8 oz soft brown sugar
4 large eggs
1 tablespoon molasses (black treacle)
1 tablespoon grated lemon rind
225 g/8 oz sultanas
225 g/8 oz currants
225 g/8 oz seedless raisins

100 g/4 oz candied peel, finely chopped
100 g/4 oz glacé cherries, halved
50 g/2 oz ground almonds
125 ml/4 fl oz brandy
*Decoration*
6 tablespoons apricot jam
575 g/1¼ lb almond paste (see page 189)
3 egg whites
675 g/1½ lb icing sugar
2 teaspoons lemon juice
1½ teaspoons glycerine

Sift together the flour, salt, and mixed spice and set aside. In a large mixing bowl cream together the butter and sugar until very light and fluffy. In another bowl lightly beat together the eggs, molasses and lemon rind. Gradually beat the egg mixture into the fat adding a little flour with the last few additions of egg to stop the mixture separating.

Sift a few tablespoons of flour over the prepared fruit, candied peel and almonds and toss them all together.

Fold the remaining sifted flour into the creamed mixture, then the fruit and nuts, and lastly the brandy. Mix all these very thoroughly together.

Turn the mixture into a well-greased 20-cm/8-inch round cake tin, at least 7·5 cm/3 inches deep, which has been neatly lined with baking parchment. Make a shallow depression in the centre of the cake so that when the mixture rises in the oven the top will be level.

Bake in a preheated cool oven for 1½ hours, then lower the heat and continue baking for another 2½ hours. The cake is cooked when a warmed skewer plunged into the centre comes out clean.

Cool the cake in its tin for 24 hours before stripping off the paper. You may 'feed' the cake with 2 or 3 more tablespoons of brandy dribbled over the base before storing it in an airtight container. If the cake is baked well ahead of Christmas it may be 'fed' again about 4 weeks before it is decorated, and returned to an airtight container.

To apply the almond paste first measure round the outer edge of the cake with a piece of string. Take two-thirds of the almond paste and roll it out, on a surface dredged with icing sugar, to a rectangle half the length of the string and twice the depth of the cake in width. Trim and cut in halves lengthwise. Knead the trimmings into the remaining paste and roll it out to fit the cake top.

Brush the sides of the cake with an apricot glaze made by heating the jam with a tablespoon or two of water and sieving it. Put the two strips of almond paste round the cake and smooth over the joins. Brush the top of the cake with glaze and cover with the remaining almond paste, cut to fit with the cake tin and a sharp knife. Roll lightly with a sugar-dusted rolling pin and make sure the joins are neat and well sealed. Cover the cake with a clean cloth and leave it in a cool place for about 3 days to dry the paste a little before icing.

To make the icing whisk the egg whites until frothy. Stir in the sifted sugar, a spoonful at a time, with a wooden spoon. When half the sugar is incorporated, add the lemon juice. Continue adding more sugar, beating well after each addition, until the mixture almost holds a peak. Lastly stir in the glycerine which helps to prevent the icing becoming too hard.

To ice the cake smoothly as a base for piped decorations coat the top and sides on consecutive days so that a clean edge can harden after the first application. A second coat of thinner icing may be applied after 48 hours drying time. (Royal icing remains workable for several days if stored in an airtight container.)

Alternatively, the icing may be used to cover the whole cake with a fluffed, peaky frosting. Traditional decorations include holly, and small sugar or plaster robins, Yule logs, and Christmas trees.

When the icing has hardened sufficiently, the cake should be covered with a clean cloth until it is cut. After cutting it will still keep for months stored in an airtight container.

Twelfth cake is seldom made now in England for the last day of the

Christmas feast, which is a pity, if only because it is a very good cake. Traditionally it was not iced, but decorated with glacé cherries, angelica and other crystallized fruits. Twelfth Night used to be celebrated, often with a play or a masque, before the work of the New Year started in earnest. In the eighteenth and nineteenth centuries a single bean was baked into the cake and whoever found it was called King of the Bean and was assured of good luck in the coming year. Earlier still, the customs associated with Twelfth cake appear to have been more elaborate. Samuel Pepys, writing on 6 January 1666 said. :

> My wife to fetch away my things from Woolwich, and I back to cards to choose King and Queene, and a good cake there was, but no marks found; but I privately found the clove, the mark of the knave, and privately put it into Captain Cooke's piece, which made some mirthe, because of his lately being knowne by his buying of clove and mace of the East India prizes.

The good cake of Samuel Pepys' age would almost certainly have been a heavily spiced yeast raised mixture. The following nineteenth-century recipe makes a rich, buttery cake which is lighter in colour than Christmas cake.

### Twelfth Cake – England

*Oven temperature Cool 150° C, 300° F, Gas Mark 2*

*Makes 1 cake*

| | |
|---|---|
| 225 g/8 oz butter | 225 g/8 oz currants |
| 225 g/8 oz castor sugar | 225 g/8 oz seedless raisins |
| 4 eggs | 225 g/8 oz sultanas |
| 3 tablespoons brandy | 50 g/2 oz blanched almonds, |
| 225 g/8 oz plain flour | chopped |
| ¼ teaspoon grated nutmeg | 1 dried bean |
| ¼ teaspoon powdered cinnamon | |

Cream together the butter and sugar in a large bowl until pale and fluffy. Mix the eggs with the brandy and gradually beat them into the creamed fat, adding a little of the flour with the last few additions of egg to prevent the mixture from separating. Sift together the flour and spices and fold them gradually into the creamed mixture. Mix in the fruit and nuts and stir the mixture until all the ingredients are well distributed.

Spoon the mixture into a 30-cm/12-inch round cake tin which has been well greased and lined with baking parchment. Press the bean into the mixture. Bake in a preheated cool oven for 3 hours. Rest the cooked cake in its tin for about half an hour then turn it out on to a wire rack. When quite cold strip off the papers and store it in an airtight container.

'A black substance inimical to life' was Robert Louis Stevenson's description of black bun, an invention peculiar to the Scots. It is a fatless, highly spiced fruit cake baked in a rather hard pastry crust, and it should be made well in advance to allow the flavour to mature. Black bun was originally the Scots' Twelfth cake, but was transferred to Hogmanay, New Year's Eve, after the banning of Christmas festivities by the sixteenth-century church reformers. In the early nineteenth century huge cakes weighing sixteen pounds or more were exported to England and the colonies. The following recipe is faithful to the tradition but moderate in scale.

### Black Bun – New Year Cake – Scotland

*Oven temperature Moderate 180° C, 350° F, Gas Mark 4*

*Makes 1 cake*

*Pastry*
250 g/9 oz plain flour
2½ teaspoons baking powder
¼ teaspoon salt
75 g/3 oz butter
cold water
*Filling*
450 g/1 lb muscatel raisins
450 g/1 lb currants
50 g/2 oz candied peel, chopped
50 g/2 oz slivered almonds
100 g/4 oz demerara sugar

225 g/8 oz plain flour
2½ teaspoons baking powder
1 teaspoon powdered ginger
1 teaspoon powdered cinnamon
¼ teaspoon powdered allspice
¼ teaspoon black pepper, freshly
    ground
5 tablespoons whisky
5 tablespoons buttermilk or fresh
    milk
*Glaze*
1 egg, beaten

To make the pastry sift together twice the flour, baking powder and salt, and put them in a bowl with the butter cut in dice. Using your fingertips or a pastry blender lightly rub in the fat until the mixture resembles fine breadcrumbs. Add sufficient water to make a soft dough.

On a lightly floured surface roll out two-thirds of the dough and use

142

it to line a lightly greased and floured 20-cm/8-inch round, preferably loose-bottomed cake tin.

Stone the muscatel raisins. Put all the fruit and nuts for the filling in a large mixing bowl. Sift together twice the flour, baking powder and spices before adding them to the fruit. Toss the fruit and flour well together before moistening the mixture with the whisky and buttermilk.

Spoon the filling into the pastry lined tin and press the mixture to pack it neatly. Turn the top edge of the pastry lining down over the filling and brush the exposed pastry with water. Roll out the remaining pastry and cut it in a circle which exactly fits the top. Lower the pastry lid on to the cake and press the edges well to seal. With a skewer make four holes right down to the bottom of the cake. Prick the pastry top all over with a fork and brush it with beaten egg to glaze.

Bake black bun in a preheated moderate oven for 2 hours. If the pastry lid shows signs of burning before the cake is cooked, cover the top loosely with baking parchment or foil, removing the cover for the last 10 minutes of cooking time.

Allow the cake to cool in the tin. When completely cold store it in an airtight container.

Unusual crystallized fruits, pears, water melon, plums, apricots and figs as well as candied citrus peel are included in Chile's Christmas cake *pán de Pascua* which is served with coffee at the end of dinner on Christmas Eve.

## Christmas Cake – Pán de Pascua – Chile

*Oven temperature Moderately hot 190° C, 375° F, Gas Mark 5; then Moderate 160° C, 325° F, Gas Mark 3*

*Make 1 cake*

25 g/4½ oz butter
1½ tablespoons warm water
250 g/9 oz icing sugar
6 large eggs
125 /4½ oz seedless raisins
125 g/4½ oz mixed crystallized fruits, chopped
50 g/2 oz walnuts, broken

550 g/19 oz plain flour
2 tablespoons baking powder
1 teaspoon powdered cinnamon
¼ teaspoon grated nutmeg
2 or 3 whole cloves
2 tablespoons Pisco or rum
1 tablespoon white wine vinegar
250 ml/8 fl oz milk

143

In a large bowl cream the butter and warm water until light and fluffy. Gradually beat in the sifted icing sugar, a little at a time. Separate the eggs. Reserve the whites and beat the yolks into the creamed mixture. Fold in the raisins, candied fruits, and the walnuts, coarsely chopped.

Sift together twice the flour, baking powder and ground spices. Fold the flour into the mixture. Add the cloves, Pisco or rum, and vinegar, and mix well together. Whisk the egg whites until they hold a peak and fold them gently into the cake. Finally add enough of the milk to make a mixture which will just drop from the spoon but is not too soft.

Spoon the mixture into a well-buttered 20-cm/8-inch round cake tin at least 7·5 cm/3 inches deep, which has been lined with baking parchment. Bake in a preheated moderately hot oven for 15 minutes, then lower the heat to moderate and bake for a further 45 minutes. The cake is fully cooked when a warmed skewer plunged into the centre comes out clean.

Rest the cake in its tin for about 10 minutes before turning it on to a wire rack to cool. Dust with icing sugar before serving.

A popular Christmas season fruit cake in Finland is *viikunakakku*, a fig butter cake, aptly named as these are flavours which give this particularly good cake its distinctive taste.

### Fig Butter Cake – Viikunakakku – Finland

*Oven temperature Moderate 180° C, 350° F, Gas Mark 4*

*Makes 1 cake*

175 g/6 oz butter
100 g/4 oz brown sugar
3 large eggs
2 tablespoons grated orange rind
175 g/6 oz plain flour
1 teaspoon baking powder
65 g/2½ oz dried figs, chopped

65 g/2½ oz seedless raisins, chopped
25 g/1 oz walnuts, finely chopped
ground almonds or castor sugar
icing sugar

In a large bowl cream together the butter and sugar until pale and fluffy. Beat together the eggs and orange rind and beat them gradually into the creamed fat, adding a little of the flour with the last few additions of egg to stop the mixture separating.

Sift together twice the flour and baking powder. Toss the figs, raisins and nuts in about 2 tablespoons of flour. Stir in the fruit, nuts and flour mix until they are well distributed.

Spoon the mixture into a ring mould, well buttered and dusted with ground almonds or castor sugar. Bake in a preheated moderate oven for 40 to 45 minutes. The cake is fully cooked when a warmed skewer plunged into the centre comes out clean.

Rest the cake in its tin for about 10 minutes before turning it on to a wire rack to cool. When completely cold, dust the cake with icing sugar. Serve in thin slices.

*Pannettone* is literally part and parcel of Christmas in Italy. In December every year about 200 million of the familiar blue or gold packages of Pannettone made by the Motta and Alemagna companies are sold within the country, and that is not counting the millions more exported all over the world. Pannettone is seldom made at home. In this case the real thing is the commercially baked product. Italian folklore has it that the recipe is a secret. Nevertheless it appears in numerous books where details of its production involve directions of extraordinarily disparate degrees of complication. The following recipe is one of the simplest.

### Milanese Cake – Pannettone Milanese – Italy

*Oven temperature Moderate 180° C, 350° F, Gas Mark 4*

*Makes 1 cake*

| | |
|---|---|
| 1 tablespoon dried yeast | 50 g/2 oz butter |
| 350 g/12 oz plain flour | 3 tablespoons seedless raisins |
| 50 g/2 oz castor sugar | 90 g/3½ oz candied citron peel, |
| ¼ teaspoon salt | chopped |
| 3 egg yolks | 1 tablespoon melted butter |
| 150 ml/¼ pint warm milk. | |

Start Pannettone the day before you plan to bake it, and do not hurry the dough.

In a small bowl sprinkle the yeast on 5 tablespoons of lukewarm water, about 43° C/110° F, whisk well, and set aside until the yeast has completely dissolved.

Sift the flour, sugar and salt into a large, warmed bowl, and make a hollow in the centre. Beat the egg yolks with the lukewarm milk. Add the egg and yeast mixtures to the flour and stir the mixture, drawing in flour from the sides of the bowl. Beat in the butter, which should be slightly softened, and continue beating until the dough is smooth. Cover the bowl with a damp cloth or a greased plastic bag, and set it to rise in a warm place until it has doubled in bulk, about $1\frac{1}{2}$ hours.

Punch down the dough, and using your hand, beat it until it no longer sticks to the sides of the bowl. Cover the bowl tightly with plastic wrap or foil and refrigerate it overnight.

Next day turn out the dough on to a lightly floured surface and knead it until smooth. Flatten the dough and scatter over it the raisins and chopped citron peel. Knead these lightly into the mixture until they are well distributed. Gather the dough into a ball and place it in a 20-cm/8-inch round cake tin well buttered and fitted with a foil or baking parchment cuff in the fashion of a soufflé dish. Set the dough to rise in a warm place until it has again doubled in bulk. The dough is considered just right when little air bubbles appear on the surface.

Cut a shallow cross in the top of the dough and brush the cake with melted butter. Bake it in a preheated moderate oven for about 35 minutes, or until it is firm to touch and a rich golden colour. Cool on a wire rack.

At Christmas and New Year few people like to visit friends empty-handed. Home-made cakes have long been appropriate calling gifts, especially in those places where the art of baking is highly esteemed and skilfully practised. Nowhere has the custom of exchanging cakes been better kept than in the countries which once formed the Austro-Hungarian Empire. When all the sumptuous *tortes* concocted by rival chefs of those far off days in Vienna are recreated in domestic kitchens, time, trouble, and expense as well as the artistry of the cook must be weighed in assessing the worth of the resulting offerings. A well-made *dobostorte*, with its many layers of sponge, chocolate butter cream and glistening caramel, ranks highly on all counts.

### Chocolate Layer Cake – Dobostorte – Czechoslovakia

*Oven temperature Moderate 180° C, 350° F, Gas Mark 4*

*Makes 1 cake*

*Cake*
225 g/8 oz unsalted butter
225 g/8 oz castor sugar

4 large eggs
1 teaspoon vanilla essence
175 g/6 oz plain flour

146

*Filling*
275 g/10 oz castor sugar
¼ teaspoon cream of tartar
8 egg yolks
50 g/2 oz cocoa powder

1 teaspoon vanilla essence
450 g/1 lb unsalted butter
*Topping*
175 g/6 oz castor sugar
6 tablespoons water

To make the sponge layers, cream together the butter and sugar in a large bowl until light and fluffy. Whisk the eggs with the vanilla essence and beat them into the creamed mixture, a little at a time, adding a small amount of the sifted flour with the last few additions of egg to stop the mixture separating. Fold in the remaining sifted flour.

To bake the sponge in thin layers, generously butter and flour the underside of a 23-cm/9-inch round cake tin. Spread a layer of the cake mixture about 3 mm/⅛ inch thick over the upside down base and bake it in a preheated moderate oven for about 8 minutes. Transfer the cooked sponge layer to a wire rack and repeat the baking procedure to make seven layers in all.

To make the filling, put the sugar and cream of tartar in a small saucepan with 175 ml/6 fl oz of water and stir over a low heat. When the sugar has dissolved completely, increase the heat and boil the syrup without stirring to 115° C/240° F, on a sugar thermometer, or it forms a soft ball when dropped in cold water. Remove from the heat immediately. Whisk the egg yolks until pale and thick and gradually add the syrup, whisking continuously. Continue to whisk until the mixture is cool and has formed a smooth, thick cream. Beat in the cocoa and vanilla essence, then add the softened butter, a little at a time, beating in each addition before adding the next. Chill the filling.

Before making the caramel topping put the best looking sponge layer on a wire rack. Heat the sugar and water in a small saucepan over a low heat and when the sugar has dissolved completely, boil it rapidly, without stirring, until a rich, golden caramel is formed. Pour it immediately over the sponge and using a buttered knife mark it quickly into 12 or 16 equal portions. Do not cut right through the caramel.

To assemble the cake, spread all but the glazed layer of sponge with about 3 mm/⅛ inch of the filling. Stack them neatly, ending up with the caramelized top. Coat the sides with the remaining chocolate butter cream and chill the cake before serving.

Finland's Christmas prune cake has a moist topping of puréed prunes and whipped cream.

## Christmas Prune Cake – Joululuumukakku – Finland

*Oven temperature Moderately hot 190° C, 375° F, Gas Mark 5*

*Makes 1 cake*

*Cake*
175 g/6 oz butter
75 g/3 oz castor sugar
2 large eggs
175 g/6 oz plain flour
1 teaspoon baking powder

*Topping*
250 ml/8 fl oz cooked puréed prunes
1 teaspoon grated lemon rind
2 tablespoons castor sugar
250 ml/8 fl oz double cream

Cream together the butter and sugar until pale and fluffy. Whisk the eggs and add them, a little at a time, beating constantly until the mixture is thick and creamy. Sift together twice the flour and baking powder and stir them into the creamed mixture. Butter and dust with sugar a 20-cm/8-inch round flan tin with a raised base. Spoon in the cake mixture, level it lightly, and bake in a preheated moderately hot oven for about 45 minutes or until it is a light, golden brown. When cooked, a warmed skewer plunged into the thickest part of the cake will come out clean. Turn it on to a wire rack to cool.

To make the topping combine the prune purée with the grated lemon rind and sugar.

Fill the hollow in the centre of the cake with the prune mixture. Whip the cream until it holds a peak and pipe it round the exposed rim of the cake. Chill well before serving.


Yule log cakes do not appear to have much of a history, but they are certainly popular now in North America, Britain, and especially in France. A roll of plain or chocolate sponge cake filled with butter cream and decorated with melted chocolate or chocolate butter cream ridged to look like bark is the usual formula. There is a French dessert version made with chestnut purée mixed with melted chocolate and butter which is shaped into a log, ridged with a fork and then chilled. It may be covered with a simple dusting of icing sugar or coated with melted chocolate. I have to confess that having tried several recipes for this sickly confection there is none I would recommend. All were unmanageably tacky. The sponge based *Bûche de Noël* is another matter. The filling may be well laced with liqueur, or mixed with chestnut purée, or hazelnut paste or chocolate. The possibilities are legion and practical, so the recipe which follows is a basic one which may be elaborated as much as you fancy.

### Yule Log Cake – Bûche de Noël – France

*Oven temperature Hot 220° C, 425° F, Gas Mark 7*

*Makes 1 cake*

*Cake*
100 g/4 oz plain flour
1¼ teaspoons baking powder
¼ teaspoon salt
1 tablespoon cocoa
4 large eggs
100 g/4 oz castor sugar

1 tablespoon hot water
*Filling and topping*
100 g/4 oz unsalted butter
275 g/10 oz icing sugar
2 tablespoons cocoa
2-3 tablespoons brandy, rum or
    Grand Marnier

To make the cake, sift together twice the flour, baking powder, salt and cocoa. Put the eggs and sugar in a large bowl over a pan of hot water and whisk them together until pale and thick. Remove the bowl from the heat and lightly fold in half the flour. Fold in the remaining flour, add one tablespoon of hot water and mix lightly. Pour the mixture into a shallow Swiss-roll tin 33 cm by 23 cm/13 inches by 9 inches lined with baking parchment. Bake in a preheated hot oven for about 10 minutes.

Turn out the sponge on to a sheet of non-stick paper cut to the size of the baking tin. Remove the baking parchment and trim off the cake's crusty edges. While it is still hot, roll up the sponge with the paper inside, cover, and set aside until cold.

To make the filling, cream together the butter and icing sugar. Blend in the cocoa and liqueur, and beat the mixture until it is light and fluffy.

To assemble the cake, unroll the sponge and discard the paper. Spread one side with about a quarter of the filling and roll it up neatly. Spread the remaining butter cream over the log. Use a fork to make a ridged pattern, like tree bark, on the top and sides of the log and circular swirls on the ends like tree rings. Leave the log plain or decorate it with icing sugar snow and a sprig of holly.

# SWEET PASTRIES

Almonds appear in an extraordinary number of the pastries, puddings, breads, biscuits, cakes and candies made for Christmas. The nut's fine flavour, versatile flesh and naturally long shelf life are explanation enough for its universal popularity.

One of the best known almond pastries is *baklava* with its layers of finely chopped spiced almonds sandwiched between buttery sheets of tissue-fine phyllo pastry. Before the advent of machine rolled pastry, baklava was for big occasions only, Christmas and Easter particularly. Commercial phyllo pastry should not be despised. Much better baklava can be made at home with ready-made pastry and fresh almonds than coffee shops usually sell.

### Almond Pastry – Baklava – Greece

*Oven temperature Moderate 160° C, 325° F, Gas Mark 3*

*Makes about 20 pieces*

| | |
|---|---|
| 450 g/1 lb blanched almonds | 225 g/8 oz butter, melted |
| 75 g/3 oz castor sugar | cloves |
| 1 orange | *Syrup* |
| 1 teaspoon powdered cloves | 450 g/1 lb granulated sugar |
| 1 teaspoon powdered cinnamon | 350 ml/12 fl oz water |
| 450 g/1 lb prepared phyllo or | 10 cm/4 inches cinnamon stick |
| strudel pastry | 4 cloves |

To prepare the filling, chop the almonds very finely and mix them in a bowl with the sugar. Grate the rind of an orange over the bowl, add the spices and toss together until well mixed.

Choose a large rectangular baking tin, at least 2·5 cm/1 inch deep, which is roughly the size of the pastry leaves – or trim the pastry to fit an available tin. Grease the tin generously with butter and lay a sheet of phyllo in the base. Paint it with melted butter and add another sheet.

When there are five sheets of buttered phyllo in the base, spread a layer of the nut mixture over them. Top with five more sheets of buttered phyllo, another layer of filling, 2 sheets of buttered phyllo, and more filling. Continue placing the pastry and filling in alternate layers, leaving 5 sheets of phyllo for the top. Cut right through the pastry and filling, making intersecting diagonal cuts. Spike each diamond-shaped piece of pastry with a clove. Place the tin on a baking sheet and bake the baklava in a moderate oven for about 1 hour, or until the pastry is crisp and golden brown.

To make the syrup, put the sugar and water in a saucepan with the cinnamon and cloves. Melt the sugar over a low heat, and when it has completely dissolved, bring the syrup to the boil and cook it for about 3 minutes until slightly thickened but not coloured. Strain the syrup over the pastry straight from the oven, and cool it in the tin. When completely cold, store the baklava in an airtight container. It keeps well for a number of weeks.

French Twelfth Night cake, *galette des rois*, cake of the kings, is traditionally eaten on the Feast of the Epiphany. There are numerous versions. A plain circle of flaky pastry with a criss-cross diamond pattern scored on top is common in northern France, a simple crown of yeast dough south of the Loire. Elsewhere two circles of melting puff pastry enclose a rich filling of almond paste, in a version called *Pithiviers* after the town just south of Paris. Pastry shop windows, a picture at any time in France, glitter with shelves of galettes des rois and Pithiviers topped with golden paper crowns. For what each of the pastries conceals is a single bean. Whoever finds the bean wears the crown as king for the day and all the family has to fulfil the monarch's wishes. The custom, which in former times led to excesses frowned upon by clerics, is said to be a relic of a pagan feast called the *Basilinda*.

## Twelfth Night Cake – Pithiviers – France

*Oven temperature Moderately hot 190° C, 375° F, Gas Mark 5*

*Serves 6–8*

65 g/2½ oz butter
65 g/2½ oz castor sugar
2 eggs
65 g/2½ oz ground almonds

4 tablespoons rum
450 g/1 lb prepared puff pastry
  (see page 163)
1 tablespoon icing sugar

To prepare the filling, cream the butter, add the sugar and beat together until light and fluffy. Whisk in one beaten egg and the ground almonds. When these are well blended, beat in the rum. Set aside.

Roll out half the puff pastry to make a circle about 20 cm/8 inches in diameter and place it on a greased baking tin. Heap the filling on the pastry and spread it, keeping a domed shape, to within 2·5 cm/1 inch of the edge.

Roll out the second piece of dough to make a matching circle. Dampen the rim of the pastry base with the remaining egg, beaten, and carefully cover with the second circle of dough. Brush the top only, not the edges, with egg glaze, and chill the assembled pastry for at least 30 minutes.

Decorate the top of the pithiviers with a pattern of curved cuts radiating from the centre to within 2·5 cm/1 inch of the edge, cutting about half way through the top layer of pastry. Decorate the edge by making small cuts right through both layers of pastry from the edge for a distance of about 1·3 cm/½ inch towards the centre. Brush the top again with egg glaze and bake the pastry in a preheated moderately hot oven for about 30 minutes, or until golden brown. Dust the top with icing sugar and brown under a very hot grill. Cool on a wire rack and serve cold.

Holland's Christmas pastry also calls for puff paste and almonds, and is made twice during the festivities, for Sinterklaas Eve on 5 December when St Nicholas arrives with Black Peter and gifts for the children, and again for Christmas Eve. For the Sinterklaas feast it is shaped in the initial letter of the family name and called *letterbanket* or *boter-letter*, and for Christmas Eve into a wreath or ring, the *Kerstkrans*.

### Christmas Ring – Kerstkrans – Holland

*Oven temperature Hot 220° C, 425° F, Gas Mark 7*

*Serves 4–6*

100 g/4 oz ground almonds
75 g/3 oz castor sugar
1 lemon
salt
2 eggs
225 g/8 oz prepared puff pastry
  (see page 163)

*Decoration*
2 tablespoons apricot jam
glacé cherries
candied citron or angelica
toasted almond flakes

To make the filling, mix together the ground almonds and sugar in a small bowl. Grate the rind of a lemon over the bowl, add a pinch of salt and mix these ingredients thoroughly before binding the mixture with a beaten egg. On a floured surface roll the almond paste into sausage-shaped pieces about 2·5 cm/1 inch thick. Wrap them in grease-proof paper and chill well.

Roll out the pastry on a floured surface to make a strip about 9 cm/ 3½ inches wide and about 3 mm/⅛ inch thick. Place the rolls of almond paste end to end along the middle of the pastry strip, damp one side of the strip with water, and fold the dough up over the paste in an overlapping seam. Press along the seam with your fingertips to seal it.

Arrange the filled roll in a ring, seam side down on a floured baking sheet, and join the ends securely. Brush the ring with beaten egg diluted with a little water, and bake in a preheated hot oven for about 30 minutes or until the pastry is golden brown.

Cool the kerstkrans on a wire rack. While the pastry is still warm, glaze it with warm, sieved apricot jam and decorate it lavishly with halved glacé cherries, leaves cut from candied citron or angelica, and flakes of toasted almond. Eat warm or cold.

*Mandelformar* are little fluted tarts made of almond pastry for Christmas in Sweden. They are baked blind and served plain, as shells, or filled with whipped cream topped with raspberry jam. This pastry can also be used as a change from shortcrust mixtures for large flans.

## Almond Tarts – Mandelformar – Sweden

*Oven temperature Moderately hot 190° C, 375° F, Gas Mark 5*

*Makes about 45 tarts*

| | |
|---|---|
| 175 g/6 oz unsalted butter | 1 teaspoon almond essence |
| 100 g/4 oz castor sugar | 1 large egg |
| 150 g/5 oz ground almonds | 275 g/10 oz plain flour |

Cream the butter and sugar in a mixing bowl until light and fluffy. Add the ground almonds, almond essence and beaten egg and mix well. Sift the flour and work it into the creamed mixture.

Turn the dough on to a lightly floured surface and knead it lightly until smooth, adding a little more flour if necessary. Wrap the dough in greaseproof paper or foil and chill well..

Butter small fluted tart tins generously. Use your thumbs to line the tins by pressing small lumps of dough over the bases and up the sides. Trim away any excess dough with a sharp knife. Arrange the tins on a baking sheet and bake in a preheated moderately hot oven for about 15 minutes or until the pastry is a light golden colour. The exact timing will depend on the thickness of the crust and the number of tarts in the oven.

Invert the tarts on a wire cooling tray and tap the tins to release them. When quite cold store mandelformar in an airtight container. If they are to be filled, top with whipped cream and a small blob of jam just before serving.

Mince pies are eaten throughout the Christmas season in many parts of the English-speaking world. The earliest mince pies were boat-shaped cribs, sometimes iced, and by the reign of Elizabeth I had become traditional Christmas fare. The Reformation church banned them as 'popish' since their form symbolized the nativity cradle, and their spices the gifts of the Kings. Minced meat is still included in the filling of home-made pies in parts of England and the United States, but is seldom seen now in the products of commercial bakeries. All that remains of what was once a means of preserving meat is a little shredded suet. Mince pies are made with puff or shortcrust pastry in tart tins with shallow cups approximately 6·5 cm/2½ inches in diameter.

## Mince Pies – England

*Oven temperature Moderately hot 200° C, 400° F, Gas Mark 6*

*Makes about 24 pies*

450 g/1 lb prepared puff pastry (see page 163) or 450-675 g/1-1½ lb prepared shortcrust pastry (see page 165)

450 g/1 lb mincemeat (see page 187)
4 tablespoons milk
1-2 eggs

Roll out the pastry on a light floured surface to about 3 mm/⅛ inch thick. Shortcrust pastry may be used a little thicker if liked. Using a pastry cutter, or rim of a drinking glass, cut 24 circles of dough about 1·2 cm/½ inch larger than the diameter of the finished pies. (The exact size will depend on the depth of the moulds.) Then cut 24 lids exactly the diameter of the moulds.

Grease the moulds and line them with the larger pastry circles. Put 1 rounded tablespoonful of filling in each pie. Do not over-fill or the mincemeat will bubble out during baking. Dampen the edges of the pastry linings with milk and top them with the smaller circles of dough. Seal the two pastry edges firmly together with your fingertips or a pastry crimper.

Brush the lids with beaten egg and bake in a preheated moderately hot oven for about 15 minutes, or until the pastry is golden brown. When cooked, allow the pies to settle for about 5 minutes before sliding them out of the tins. Dust the tops with castor or icing sugar.

Serve mince pies hot or warm, on their own with tea or coffee, or with whipped cream or brandy butter (see page 188) as a dessert. Cold mince pies will keep for several days in an airtight container and can be reheated in a warm oven.

Finland's Christmas pies, *Joulutortut*, are the subject of much competitive baking. These prune-filled pastries use a very simply made dough.

## Christmas Tarts – Joulutortut – Finland

*Oven temperature Moderately hot 200° C, 400° F, Gas Mark 6*

*Makes about 24 tarts*

| Pastry | Filling |
|---|---|
| 350 ml/12 fl oz double cream | 450 g/1 lb prunes |
| 1 teaspoon baking powder | 725 ml/24 fl oz water |
| ¼ teaspoon salt | 75 g/3 oz castor sugar |
| 375 g/13 oz plain flour | 2 tablespoons lemon juice |
| 225 g/8 oz butter, softened | |

To make the pastry, whip the cream until stiff in a large bowl. Sift the baking powder, salt and flour into the cream and mix thoroughly. Add the softened butter and stir until the dough is well blended. Wrap the pastry in greaseproof paper or foil and chill it well.

To make the filling, cook the prunes in the water over a low heat until they are soft. Drain them and discard the cooking liquor. Remove the stones and purée the flesh by pressing it through a sieve or whirling it in an electric blender. Add the sugar and lemon juice and mix well.

Roll out the pastry to a thickness of about 6 mm/¼ inch and cut it into 7·5-cm/3-inch squares. Divide the filling between the squares, placing a small mound of purée in the centre of each one. With a sharp knife cut from each corner to within 1·2 cm/½ inch of the centre of the squares. Fold one half of each corner to the centre to form a pinwheel or star.

Arrange the pastries on ungreased baking tins and rest at room temperature for about 10 minutes. Bake Joulutortut in a preheated moderately hot oven for about 10 minutes, or until the pastry is pale golden brown. Cool on a wire rack and serve warm or cold.

Coconut cream pie is a Christmas favourite in Puerto Rico.

## Coconut Cream Pie – Torta de Crema de Coco – Puerto Rico

*Serves 6–8*

23-cm/9-inch baked shortcrust
  pie case
600 ml/1 pint milk
2 tablespoons cornflour
225 g/8 oz castor sugar

¼ teaspoon salt
2 large eggs
225 g/8 oz coconut, freshly grated
1 teaspoon vanilla essence
100 g/4 oz icing sugar

Scald ¾ of the milk in the top of a double boiler, or in a bowl over a pot of boiling water. Mix the remaining cold milk with the cornflour, sugar and salt. Stir it into the hot milk and cook, stirring, until the mixture is thick and smooth. Cover and continue cooking for another 10 minutes. Separate the eggs, reserving the whites for the meringue, and beat the yolks lightly. Add ¾ of the coconut to the egg yolks and stir into this mixture a little of the hot custard. Add the coconut mixture to the hot custard and cook together, stirring constantly, for about 3 minutes. Remove from the heat and add the vanilla. Pour the coconut cream into the pastry case.

When the custard is quite cold, whisk the reserved egg whites until light and foamy. Add half of the icing sugar and whisk until stiff. Add the remaining sugar and whisk until the meringue will hold a peak. Pile the meringue on top of the coconut cream and sprinkle with the remaining grated coconut. Serve chilled in wedges.

An unusual apple pie of whole apples moistened with mulled ale is traditionally made at Christmas in England from this eighteenth-century recipe.

## Bedfordshire Apple Florentine Pie – England

*Oven temperature Hot 230° C, 450° F, Gas Mark 8*

*Serves 4*

4 large cooking apples
3 tablespoons demerara sugar
1 tablespoon finely grated lemon
  rind
450 g/1 lb prepared shortcrust
  pastry (see page 165)

600 ml/1 pint pale ale or good
  lager
¼ teaspoon grated nutmeg
¼ teaspoon powdered cinnamon
3 cloves

Peel and core the apples and arrange them in a deep buttered 1·8-litre/ 3-pint pie dish. Sprinkle the apples with 2 tablespoons of the sugar mixed with the grated lemon rind.

Roll out the pastry to make a thick crust for the dish and lay it over the apples. Make a hole in the top to allow the steam to escape and bake the pie in a preheated hot oven for about 30 minutes.

Heat the ale, but do not boil, with the nutmeg, cinnamon, cloves and remaining sugar. Carefully lift the pie crust and pour the warm, spiced ale on to the apples. Divide the pastry in four and replace one piece on each apple. Serve very hot, in bowls, giving each person plenty of the mulled ale. Cold, whipped cream may be handed round in a separate bowl and nowadays creamy natural yoghurt would be a refreshing combination with this old-fashioned pie.

Poppy seed pastry rolls are synonymous with Christmas in Hungary, Poland, and in Vienna, the mecca of the Austrian pastry makers' art. *Beigli* is the popular Hungarian name for the poppy seed and walnut pastries which, whether baked at home or bought in a pastry shop or supermarket, are an essential part of the festivities. Beigli is served to everyone visiting Hungarian homes between Christmas and New Year, with morning coffee, lunch, and dinner too. The rite of baking and buying beigli, of comparing their respective merits, is a ceremony re- peated year after year.

### Poppy Seed Roll – Beigli – Hungary

*Oven temperature Moderate 180° C, 350° F, Gas Mark 4*

*Makes 1 roll*

| *Pastry* | *Filling* |
|---|---|
| 1 tablespoon dried yeast | 100 g/4 oz unsalted butter |
| 4 tablespoons castor sugar | 3 tablespoons honey |
| 4 tablespoons lukewarm water | 1 tablespoon double cream |
| 4 tablespoons milk | 100 g/4 oz ground poppy seeds |
| 1 teaspoon vanilla essence | 65 g/2½ oz seedless raisins |
| ½ teaspoon grated lemon rind | 2 tablespoons rum |
| ½ teaspoon salt | ½ teaspoon grated orange rind |
| 3 egg yolks | *Glaze* |
| 225 g/8 oz strong or plain flour | 1 egg, beaten |
| 50 g/2 oz unsalted butter, softened | 1 tablespoon milk |

158

To make the pastry, sprinkle the yeast and a pinch of sugar into the lukewarm water, about 43° C,/110° F. Let it stand for a few minutes, whisk, and set aside in a warm place until the mixture has almost doubled in volume.

In a large bowl combine the yeast solution with the milk, vanilla essence, grated lemon rind, the rest of the sugar, and salt. Stir in the egg yolks. Sift the flour and beat it into the yeast mixture a little at a time. Divide the butter in four, and beat it into the dough one piece at a time.

Turn out the dough on to a floured surface and knead it for about 10 minutes or until it is soft and pliable. Put the dough in a lightly buttered bowl, turn it in the butter and leave it to rise, covered, in a warm place.

To make the filling, cream together the butter and honey, then beat in the cream. Stir in the ground poppy seeds, raisins plumped in the rum and then finely chopped, and grated orange rind. Cook the mixture in a small saucepan over a low heat for about 10 minutes or until it is a stiff paste. Set aside to cool.

When the dough has doubled in bulk turn it out onto a floured surface and knead it lightly. Roll it out to a rectangle about 23 cm by 33 cm/9 inches by 13 inches. Spread the filling to within 2 cm/¾ inch of the edges of the dough. Turn over one long side of the rectangle and roll up the dough.

Carefully place the roll, seam side down, on a buttered baking tin. Brush the exposed dough with the beaten egg mixed with the 1 tablespoon of milk and leave it to stand in a warm, draught free place for about 20 minutes. Brush the roll again with egg glaze and bake it in a preheated moderate oven for about 45 minutes or until the pastry is a rich golden brown. The pastry should have a crackled surface. Cool on a wire rack and serve in slices like a Swiss roll.


A variety of fritters and doughnuts are also made for Christmas and New Year. Yeast raised doughs are the basis of *Berliner pfannkuchen* and *oliebollen*, the New Year doughnuts of Germany and Holland; cornmeal for Peruvian *picarones* and *buñuelos navideños* from Ecuador. Plum or apricot jam fills Berliner pfannkuchen which are usually served with hot punch.

# Berlin Doughnuts – Berliner Pfannkuchen – Germany

*Makes about 12*

| | |
|---|---|
| 1 tablespoon dried yeast | salt |
| 150 ml/¼ pint warm milk | 250 g/9 oz jam |
| 450 g/1 lb plain flour | lard for frying |
| 50 g/2 oz butter, melted | 75 g/3 oz castor sugar |
| 2 large eggs | |

Sprinkle the yeast on to the warm milk, about 43° C/110° F, in a large bowl. Whisk the mixture and leave it to stand in a warm place until the yeast has dissolved completely and the mixture is bubbling. Beat in a quarter of the sifted flour, cover, and leave the mixture to rise in a warm place for about 1 hour. Add the butter, eggs, a pinch of salt, and the remaining flour and beat the mixture to a smooth dough. Cover and set aside to rise in a warm place until it has doubled in bulk.

Turn the dough on to a floured surface and roll it out thinly. Using a circular pastry cutter, or the rim of a drinking glass, cut about 24 circles of dough. Put one tablespoon of jam in the centre of half the circles of dough and cover them with the remaining dough. Press the edges lightly with your fingertips to seal in the filling and leave the doughnuts to rise once more, covered, in a warm place.

Heat the lard in a deep fryer or large pot to about 190° C/375° F. At this temperature a 2·5-cm/1-inch cube of day-old bread will fry to a crisp golden brown in about 60 seconds. Fry the doughnuts, a few at a time so as not to lower the temperature of the fat too much, for about 4 minutes or until golden brown. Turn them over at half time. Drain on absorbent paper and roll the hot doughnuts in castor sugar. Serve warm.

The dough for Holland's New Year doughnuts is speckled with dried fruit and candied peel.

## New Year's Eve Fritters – Olieballen – Holland

*Makes about 18*

| | |
|---|---|
| ½ tablespoon dried yeast | 2 tablespoons granulated sugar |
| 350 ml/12 fl oz warm milk | ½ teaspoon salt |
| 225-275 g/8-10 oz plain flour | 3 tablespoons currants |

| | |
|---|---|
| 3 tablespoons raisins | 1 tablespoon grated lemon rind |
| 3 tablespoons chopped candied orange peel | vegetable oil for frying |
| | 90 g/3½ oz icing sugar |

Sprinkle the yeast over the warm milk in a small bowl. Whisk the mixture and let it stand in a warm place until the yeast has dissolved completely and the mixture has almost doubled its volume.

Sift 225 g/8 oz of the flour into a mixing bowl with the sugar and salt. Make a well in the flour and pour in the yeast mixture. Gradually draw in the flour with a wooden spoon. Drop in the eggs and beat the mixture until all the flour has been absorbed. The dough should just hold its shape. If it is too soft, beat in up to 50 g/2 oz more flour, adding it a little at a time. Cover the bowl with a damp cloth or plastic bag and leave it in a warm place for about 1 hour or until it has doubled in bulk.

Punch down the dough and gently mix in the currants, raisins, candied peel and lemon rind.

Pour the oil into a deep fryer or heavy pot to a depth of about 7·5 cm/3 inches and heat it to about 180° C/350° F. At this temperature a 2·5-cm/1-inch cube of day-old bread will fry to a crisp golden brown in about 90 seconds. Drop 3-tablespoonful balls of dough into the hot oil, a few at a time so as not to lower the heat of the oil too much, and fry for about 10 minutes, or until they are a crisp golden brown, turning them at half time. Drain the cooked oliebollen on absorbent paper. Eat them warm or cool, dusted with icing sugar just before serving.

Snowballs or *sneeuwballen*, deep fried balls of choux pastry filled with whipped cream and dusted thickly with icing sugar are another treat for New Year's Eve in Holland. More unusual are Ecuador's *buñuelos navideños*, cornmeal fritters soaked in a spiced syrup.

### Christmas Fritters – Buñuelos Navideños – Ecuador

*Serves 4*

| | |
|---|---|
| 475 ml/16 fl oz water | *Syrup* |
| ¼ teaspoon salt | 225 g/8 oz granulated sugar |
| 2 tablespoons butter | 250 ml/8 fl oz water |
| 4 tablespoons fine cornmeal | 10 cm/4 inches cinnamon stick |
| 75 g/3 oz plain flour | 1 teaspoon lemon juice |
| 5 large eggs | 1 teaspoon orange flower water |
| corn or soya oil for frying | |

161

Put the water, salt and butter in a heavy saucepan and bring to the boil. Sift together the cornmeal and flour, add them to the liquid in the pan and stir the mixture over a low heat until the dough forms a ball. Transfer the dough to a mixing bowl and beat it with a wooden spoon until it is lukewarm. Beat in the eggs one at a time.

Heat the oil in a deep fryer or heavy pot to about 190° C/375° F. At this temperature a 2·5-cm/1-inch cube of day-old bread will fry to a crisp golden brown in about 60 seconds. Drop tablespoons of the mixture into the hot oil, a few at a time so as not to cool the oil too much, and fry them till golden. Tap the fried balls to release any pockets of trapped oil and drain them on absorbent paper.

To make the syrup, put the sugar and water in a small saucepan with the cinnamon. Heat together gently until the sugar dissolves, then boil the syrup for a minute or two until it thickens slightly. Remove from the heat, extract the cinnamon, and stir in the lemon juice and orange flower water. Arrange the fried buñuelos on a deep plate and pour the syrup over them. Serve warm or cold.

Sweden's *klenäter* are fancy pastry strips deep fried and served with jam as a dessert or with coffee as a snack.

### Christmas Crullers – Klenäter – Sweden

*Makes about 50 pieces*

| | |
|---|---|
| 4 egg yolks | 1 tablespoon brandy |
| 50 g/2 oz castor sugar | 1 tablespoon grated lemon rind |
| 40 g/1½ oz butter | lard for frying |
| 175 g/6 oz plain flour | 100 g/4 oz granulated sugar |

Beat together in a small bowl the egg yolks and sugar. In a larger bowl cut the butter in small pieces over the sifted flour and using your fingertips, or a pastry blender, work them lightly together until the mixture resembles fine breadcrumbs. Add the egg and sugar mixture to the flour with the brandy and grated lemon rind. Mix well together. Form the dough into a ball, wrap it in greaseproof paper and chill well.

Turn the dough on to a floured surface and roll it out thinly. Using a pastry wheel and ruler, cut the dough into strips about 7·5 cm/3 inches long and 2 cm/¾ inch wide. The narrow ends may be square with the sides or at a diagonal angle to them. Make a long cut down the centre of each strip and pull one end through the hole so that when laid flat again each strip divides in the middle into two twists.

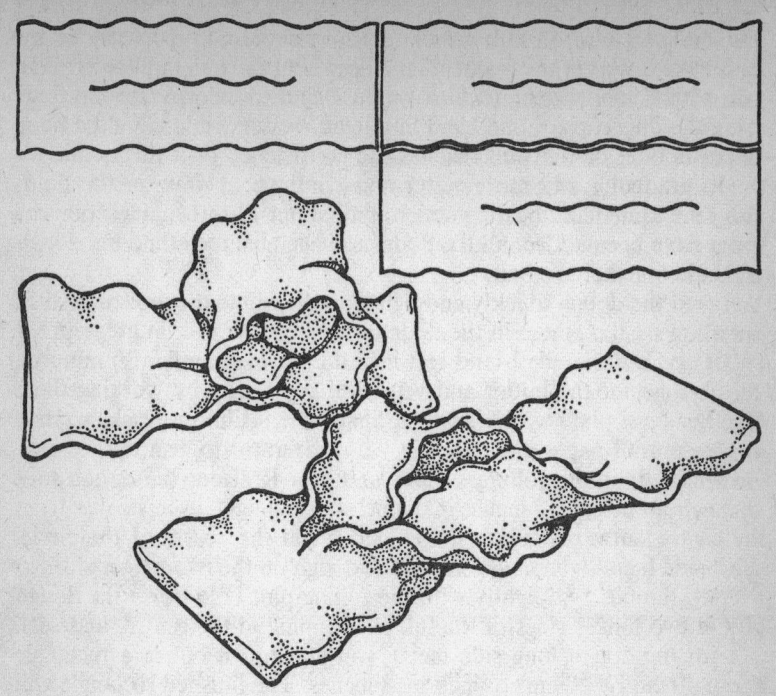

**Christmas Crullers – how to make the shape**

Heat the lard in a deep fryer or heavy pot to 190° C/375° F. At this temperature a 2·5-cm/1-inch cube of day-old bread will fry to a crisp golden brown in about 60 seconds. Fry the crullers, a few at a time, so as not to cool the fat too much, until light golden brown. Drain them on absorbent paper, sprinkle with granulated sugar and serve hot or cold.

## Puff Pastry – Basic Recipe

*Makes 900 g/2 lb*

| | |
|---|---|
| 450 g/1 lb plain flour | iced water |
| 1 teaspoon salt | 400 g/14 oz unsalted butter |
| 1 tablespoon lemon juice | 50 g/2 oz vegetable shortening |

163

Sift the flour and salt into a mound on a marble slab or pastry board and make a well in the centre of the heap. Put the lemon juice into the well with 6 tablespoons of iced water. Begin to incorporate the flour using the fingertips of one hand in a light, beating action. As the flour in the middle of the well reaches the consistency of a thick, smooth sauce, gradually add more water and continue to draw in the flour, using the same hand-beating action until about 12 to 14 tablespoons of water have been added, all the flour has been absorbed, and the dough will hold together in a ball.

Knead the dough quickly and lightly to distribute the moisture without allowing the gluten in the flour to develop. Wrap it in greaseproof paper and a damp cloth and rest it in the refrigerator for 30 minutes.

Mix together the butter and vegetable shortening by working them together on a plate with a spatula. Shape the fat into a brick, wrap it in greaseproof paper and put it in the refrigerator to firm up.

Lightly flour the rolling surface and pin. Roll out the dough to a circle about 30 cm/12 inches in diameter, using light, even strokes from the centre outwards. Place the chilled fat in the centre of the circle, short side facing you, and fold up the dough on the two longer sides to overlap the fat. Seal lightly with the rolling pin. Fold down the dough on the two longer sides of the fat, overlapping in the centre, and seal.

Turn the dough long side facing you and roll it out to a rectangle about 40 cm by 20 cm/16 inch by 8 inches. The finished rectangle will have a short side facing you.

Now make the *first turn*. Fold the bottom third of the dough up past the centre line and the upper third down on top of it. Lightly seal the edges with the rolling pin and make a shallow dent in the dough with one finger to denote that it has had one turn. Wrap it in greaseproof paper and a damp cloth and return the dough to the refrigerator for 15 minutes.

To make the *second turn*, lay the dough on a lightly floured surface – fold on your left and longest sealed edge on your right. Roll it out again to 40 cm by 20 cm/16 inches by 8 inches, fold in three as before, mark with two dents, wrap up and chill for another 15 minutes.

Repeat the rolling and folding four times, making two turns at each session. Wrap the finished pastry as before and chill until firm or, better still, overnight.

Use as directed. Wrapped pastry will keep for several days in the refrigerator, longer, of course, if frozen. Thaw frozen pastry slowly and thoroughly in the refrigerator before using.

# Basic Sweet Shortcrust Pastry

*Makes 900g/2 lb*

450 g/1 lb plain flour
4 tablespoons icing sugar
½ teaspoon salt

275 g/10 oz unsalted butter,
   softened
2 egg yolks
iced water

Sift the flour, sugar and salt into a large bowl. Add the butter in fairly large pieces and work it lightly into the flour with your fingertips or a pastry blender until the mixture resembles fine breadcrumbs.

In another bowl mix the egg yolks with 8 tablespoons of iced water. Sprinkle this over the flour mixture and work it in lightly with your fingertips or the blade of a knife until the dough just holds together. Gather it up and press it lightly into a ball. Wrap the dough in grease-proof paper and foil or a plastic bag and chill for at least 1 hour before rolling out. Chilled, wrapped dough will keep in the refrigerator for several days. Use as directed.

For a short savoury pastry increase the salt to 1 teaspoon and omit the sugar.

# BISCUITS

Christmas biscuits, or cookies, appear to have been made almost exclusively in Europe before settlers brought them to America. Here many have become such firm year-round favourites that their festive and regional origins are all but forgotten. The names may change from one continent and country to another but the ingredients are everywhere the same – sugar and spices and eager helpers to lick spoons and lap up crumbs.

The word cookie seems to derive from the Dutch *koekje*, the diminutive of *koek*, cake, and it was still a common term in nineteenth-century England. In Scotland its use continues but the meaning changes to a flat bun. The word biscuit derives from the Old French *bescoit*, a flat cake of unleavened bread. It still, in principle, applies to twice-baked goods, and now also to recipes which do not require double cooking, to produce crisp biscuits with good keeping qualities.

The Swedish recipe for Christmas gingersnaps, *Luciapepparkakor*, is the one to make for the gingersnap house on page 137 as well as plain and fancy biscuits. This Finnish variation is shortened with butter and cream.

### Finnish Gingersnaps – Suomalaiset Piparkakut – Finland

*Oven temperature Moderately hot 190° C, 375° F, Gas Mark 5*

*Makes about 60*

175 g/6 oz dark corn syrup or
  golden syrup
90 g/3½ oz dark brown sugar
100 g/4 oz butter
125 ml/4 fl oz double cream

1 tablespoon powdered ginger
1 tablespoon powdered cinnamon
350-400 g/12-14 oz plain flour
1 teaspoon baking powder
½ teaspoon salt

In a large bowl beat together the syrup, brown sugar and butter until the mixture is smooth, then beat in the cream. Sift together twice the spices, flour, baking powder and salt, and add them to the creamed mixture. Work the two together into a stiff dough. Chill the dough for several hours wrapped in greaseproof paper.

On a lightly floured surface roll out the dough to a thickness of 6 mm/¼ inch and using a pastry cutter, stamp out 7·5-cm/3-inch circles. Arrange them on well-greased and floured baking tins and bake in a preheated moderately hot oven for about 8 minutes. Rest the biscuits on the baking tins for two or three minutes before transferring them to a wire rack to cool. Store in an airtight container.

*Pfeffernüsse* are an almost essential part of Christmas in Germany where food and family ceremonial are inextricably bound together. The evocative smell of these spice biscuits baking is one of the first thrills of the festive season.

### Spice Biscuits – Pfeffernüsse – Germany

*Oven temperature Moderately hot 200° C, 400° F, Gas Mark 6*

*Makes about 70*

| | |
|---|---|
| 175 g/6 oz honey | 225 g/8 oz plain flour |
| 250 g/9 oz golden syrup | ½ teaspoon baking powder |
| 75 g/3 oz castor sugar | ½ teaspoon powdered cloves |
| 25 g/1 oz butter | ¼ teaspoon powdered allspice |

Put the honey and syrup in a large, heavy saucepan with the sugar and bring the mixture slowly to the boil. Stir until the sugar dissolves then simmer gently for about 5 minutes before stirring in the butter.

Sift together twice the flour, baking powder and spices. Gradually beat the flour into the honey mixture a little at a time and beating until the batter is thick and smooth.

Drop teaspoonfuls of the mixture well spaced on generously buttered baking tins. Bake in a preheated moderately hot oven for about 15 minutes or until the biscuits are light brown in colour and firm to touch. Rest them on the baking tins for two or three minutes before transferring to a wire rack to cool. Store in an airtight container.

Biscuits cut in fancy Christmas shapes – men, women, angels, pigs, reindeer, horses, cats, trees, stars and hearts – are made in all the nordic countries. Sometimes they are left plain, but often they are outlined and decorated with piped white icing. There are dozens of similar recipes to choose from, and small controversies rage over preferences for thin, crisp biscuits or thicker, softer ones. This recipe for bishop's pepper biscuits makes the softer kind.

### Bishop's Pepper Biscuits – Rovastinpipparkakut – Finland

*Oven temperature Moderately hot 190° C, 375° F, Gas Mark 5*

*Makes about 30*

| | |
|---|---|
| 1 large egg | 1 teaspoon bicarbonate of soda |
| 175 g/6 oz castor sugar | 1 teaspoon powdered cinnamon |
| 175 g/6 oz dark corn syrup or | 1 teaspoon powdered cardamom |
|   golden syrup | 1 teaspoon powdered ginger |
| 225 g/8 oz butter, melted | ½ teaspoon powdered allspice |
| 25 g/1 oz almonds, finely chopped | ½ teaspoon salt |
| 275 g/10 oz plain flour | |

In a large bowl beat the egg and stir in the sugar, syrup, melted butter and almonds. Beat until well mixed. Sift together twice the flour, bicarbonate of soda, spices and salt, and add them, a little at a time, to the syrup mixture, beating until a stiff dough is formed. Chill the dough well.

On a lightly floured surface roll the dough to a thickness of about 6 mm/¼ inch and using plain or fancy biscuit cutters, stamp out the biscuits. Arrange them on well-buttered baking tins and bake in a preheated moderately hot oven for about 10 minutes or until they are golden brown and firm to touch. The exact timing will depend on the size of the individual biscuits. Let them rest on the baking sheets for two or three minutes before transferring them to a wire cooling rack.

Use royal icing (see page 140) for piped decorations. Allow the icing to dry completely before storing the biscuits in an airtight container.

Dutch *speculaas* are another much-loved Christmas spice biscuit which are traditionally shaped in carved wooden moulds. They take their name from the method of moulding the dough – speculaas is a corruption of *speculum*, the Latin for mirror. Large cookies weighing up to 450 g/1 lb each, baked as figures of men and women known as 'lovers' are decorated with large slivers of blanched almonds. Smaller versions are also made in every size down to about 2·5 cm/1 inch. When no moulds are available, filled speculaas are baked in round cake tins with almond paste sandwiched between two layers of dough.

## Spice Cookies – Speculaas – Holland

*Oven temperature See recipe*

*Makes 1 large or 24 small cookies*

| | |
|---|---|
| 50 g/2 oz dark brown sugar | 1 tablespoon finely chopped |
| 1 tablespoon milk | candied fruits |
| 100 g/4 oz plain flour | 65 g/2½ oz butter |
| ¼ teaspoon baking powder | slivered, blanched almonds |
| ¼ teaspoon salt | (optional) |
| ½ teaspoon powdered cloves | 100 g/4 oz almond paste |
| ½ teaspoon powdered cinnamon | (optional) |
| ¼ teaspoon powdered ginger | 1 tablespoon single cream |
| ¼ teaspoon grated nutmeg | (optional) |
| 1 tablespoon finely chopped | |
| almonds | |

Put the sugar and milk in a small saucepan and heat gently until the sugar has dissolved.

Sift together twice the flour, baking powder, salt, and spices and put them in a mixing bowl with the chopped almonds and candied fruits. Add the melted sugar, and the butter cut in small pieces and mix well together. Knead the dough lightly until pliable. Chill well.

To make moulded speculaas dust the moulds thoroughly with corn-flour before pressing the dough evenly into them. Run a sharp knife along the edges of the design to trim off excess mixture, and tap out the moulded dough on to a greased baking tin. Press large slivers of blanched almonds into the design before baking. Large figures should be baked in a preheated cool oven (150° C, 300° F, Gas Mark 2) for 45 to 60 minutes. Bake small cookies in a preheated moderate oven (180° C, 350° F, Gas Mark 4) for 15 to 30 minutes depending on their size. Cooking is complete when the speculaas are golden brown and firm to touch. Cool on a wire rack and store in an airtight container.

To make filled speculaas divide the dough in halves. Press one half into a shallow round cake tin about 18 cm/7 inches in diameter. Pat it evenly over the base and a little way up the sides of the tin. Roll out the almond paste on a surface dusted with castor sugar to a circle about

16·5 cm/6½ inches in diameter, and lay it over the dough in the tin. Press the second piece of dough in an even layer on top of the almond paste. Brush the top with a little single cream and bake in a preheated moderate oven (160° C, 325° F, Gas Mark 3) for 35 to 40 minutes. Rest the baked speculaas in the tin for two or three minutes before turning it on to a wire rack to cool. Store in an airtight container.

Germany's prettiest moulded Christmas biscuits are *springerle*, made with a decorative board or rolling pin deeply patterned with a variety of festive symbols and pictures. The dough is deliciously flavoured with aniseed and these biscuits are best baked several weeks before Christmas because the flavour improves as they mature. Aniseed is not always easily obtainable. If using whole seeds, dust the baking sheets with them. If anise extract or powdered aniseed are available, incorporate one or other into the dough before baking. Prepare the biscuits a day before baking them.

### Christmas Aniseed Biscuits – Springerle – Germany

*Oven temperature Cool 150° C, 300° F, Gas Mark 2*

*Makes about 40*

4 large eggs
350 g/12 oz castor sugar
1 teaspoon anise extract or
  powdered aniseed

500 g/18 oz plain flour
1 teaspoon bicarbonate of soda

In a large bowl whisk the eggs until pale and fluffy before whisking in the sugar, a little at a time. Continue whisking until the mixture will fall back on itself in a slowly melting ribbon. Beat in the anise extract or powdered aniseed.

Sift together twice the flour and bicarbonate and beat them into the egg mixture a little at a time to form a firm dough. Knead the dough on a lightly floured surface until it is smooth and pliable, working in a little more flour if it is too sticky. Chill for about 2 hours.

On a well-floured surface, roll the chilled dough to about 1·2 cm/ ½ inch thick. Sprinkle the springerle mould or rolling pin generously with flour, tap out the excess, and press the mould or pin firmly into the dough. Cut the patterned dough into individual biscuits and arrange them on baking tins lined with baking parchment. Set the prepared biscuits aside to dry at room temperature before baking them in a pre-heated cool oven for about 30 minutes. They are cooked when the tops whiten and the bottoms of the biscuits are slightly golden. Cool on a wire rack and store in an airtight container.

If using whole aniseed, smear the baking parchment generously with butter and sprinkle it with whole aniseed before arranging the dough on it.

To make springerle without a carved mould or rolling pin, cut 1·2-cm/½-inch thick dough into a 3·5-cm/1½-inch squares and bake as directed.

Almond crescents are another Christmas biscuit popular in Germany. Czechoslovakia has a very similar almond biscuit flavoured with vanilla called *vanillekipfel*, vanilla crescents.

### Almond Crescents – Mandel-Halbmonde — Germany

*Oven temperature Moderate 160° C, 325° F, Gas Mark 3*

*Makes about 36*

| | |
|---|---|
| 225 g/8 oz unsalted butter | *Frosting* |
| 175 g/6 oz castor sugar | 1 egg white |
| 4 hard-boiled egg yolks | 40 g/1½ oz blanched almonds, |
| 2 egg yolks | finely chopped |
| 2 teaspoons grated lemon rind | 75 g/3 oz castor sugar |
| 350 g/12 oz plain flour | 1 teaspoon powdered cinnamon |

In a large bowl cream the butter, then beat in the sugar a little at a time. Cream together until the mixture is very pale and fluffy. Put the hard-boiled egg yolks into a sieve and press them through with the back of a spoon into the creamed mixture. Add the raw egg yolks and grated lemon rind and mix well. Gradually beat in the sifted flour to form a firm dough.

To prepare the frosting, whisk the egg white in a small bowl until it will hold a firm peak. In another bowl mix the finely chopped almonds with the sugar and cinnamon.

Shape small rolls of the dough about 6 cm/2½ inches long into crescents. Dip each one in the beaten egg white and then in the almond sugar. Arrange them, spaced well apart, on baking tins lined with baking parchment and bake them in a preheated moderate oven for about 12 minutes or until the biscuits are firm to touch. Transfer them carefully to a wire rack. When cold store mandel-halbmonde in an airtight container.

Ratafias are small almond macaroons which have been made in England since the sixteenth century, if not earlier. The Italian version, *amaretti*, may be even older. They are an essential ingredient of trifle and often served separately with creams or jellies. This recipe is based on the one given in *The Court and Country Confectioner*, an anonymous English publication of 1772.

## Ratafias – England

*Oven temperature Cool 150° C, 300° F, Gas Mark 2*

*Makes about 100*

5 egg whites                              450 g/1 lb castor sugar
225 g/8 oz ground almonds

In a large bowl whisk the egg whites until they hold a stiff peak. Fold in the ground almonds and castor sugar and mix well together to make a soft, sticky dough.

Line several baking tins with baking parchment and pipe small blobs of the mixture, about 1·2 cm/½ inch in diameter, on to the paper using a plain nozzle and spacing them well apart. Bake the ratafias in a pre-heated cool oven for about 40 minutes or until they are a pale, pinkish brown and crisp at the edges.

Leave the ratafias on the baking parchment to cool on a wire rack before peeling them off the paper. Allow them to become completely cold before storing in an airtight container.

A few drops of almond essence may be added to the mixture before baking.

*Spritskransar*, the famous Swedish spritz rings, are piped almond biscuits. These have a shortbread texture.

## Spritz Rings – Spritskransar – Sweden

*Oven temperature Moderately hot 200° C, 400° F, Gas Mark 6*

*Makes about 45*

| | |
|---|---|
| 225 g/8 oz butter | 1 teaspoon almond essence |
| 75 g/3 oz icing sugar | 25 g/1 oz ground almonds |
| 1 egg yolk | 225 g/8 oz plain flour |

Cream together the butter and sugar in a large bowl until light and fluffy. Add the egg yolk and almond essence and mix well. Sift together the ground almonds and flour and stir them gradually into the creamed mixture to form a smooth, soft dough.

Using a star nozzle, pipe the mixture into neat 5-cm/2-inch diameter rings on baking tins lined with baking parchment. Bake in a preheated moderately hot oven for about 10 minutes or until the spritskransar are golden. Rest them for a minute or two before transferring them to a wire rack to cool. When completely cold, store in an airtight container.

*Syltkakor*, butter leaves, are another Swedish shortbread biscuit popular at Christmas time.

## Butter Leaves with Jelly – Syltkakor – Sweden

*Oven temperature Moderate 180° C, 350° F, Gas Mark 4*

*Makes about 40*

| | |
|---|---|
| 225 g/8 oz butter | 1 egg white |
| 75 g/3 oz castor sugar | 50 g/2 oz blanched almonds, |
| 1 egg yolk | chopped |
| ½ teaspoon almond essence | 50 g/2 oz granulated sugar |
| 275 g/10 oz plain flour | 175 g/6 oz redcurrant jelly |

In a large bowl cream together the butter and sugar until light and fluffy. Stir in the egg yolk and almond essence. Gradually add the sifted flour and mix thoroughly. Chill the dough for 2 hours.

On a lightly floured surface roll out the dough to a thickness of about 3 mm/⅛ inch and using a 5-cm/2-inch round cutter, stamp out circles of dough. Using a smaller round cutter, cut the centre out of half the circles of dough. Roll the centres and scraps again to make more circles and rings. Brush the rings only with egg white and sprinkle them with chopped almonds and sugar. Arrange the biscuits on buttered baking tins and bake them in a preheated moderate oven for about 10 minutes or until they are golden. Cool on a wire rack.

When the biscuits are cold, sandwich together the plain bases (circles) and nutty tops (rings) with redcurrant jelly. Unfilled syltkakor keep well for several weeks in an airtight container.

Basle in Switzerland has an unusual nut biscuit made for every festive occasion which is not unlike the famous *panforte di Siena*, another special-occasion confection from Italy.

### Basle Cinnamon Biscuits – Basler Leckerli – Switzerland

*Oven temperature Moderate 180° C, 350° F, Gas Mark 4*

*Makes about 24*

250 g/9 oz honey
175 g/6 oz castor sugar
1½ tablespoons powdered cinnamon
225 g/8 oz plain flour
4 tablespoons kirsch

50 g/2 oz blanched almonds, chopped
50 g/2 oz hazelnuts, chopped
50 g/2 oz candied orange and lemon peel, finely chopped
50 g/2 oz icing sugar

Put the honey in a large, heavy saucepan with the sugar and cinnamon and cook them together over a low heat until the sugar has dissolved. Remove from the heat and stir in half the sifted flour, the kirsch, nuts and peel. Turn the mixture on to a well-floured surface and knead in the remaining flour. Spread the mixture about 6 mm/¼ inch thick on one or more greased and floured rectangular baking tins and sprinkle the top lightly with flour. Bake in a preheated moderate oven for about 20 minutes or until golden brown.

Turn out of the tin, and while still warm, cut the leckerli in halves horizontally using a sharp knife. Brush off any excess flour and cut into bars. Dust the pieces with icing sugar and cool on a wire rack. When cold, store in an airtight container.

Caramel-filled coconut biscuits are made for Christmas in Peru.

## Caramel and Coconut Biscuits – Alfajores de Maicena – Peru

*Oven temperature Moderate 180° C, 350° F, Gas Mark 4*

*Makes about 25*

| | |
|---|---|
| 100 g/4 oz butter | 125 g/4½ oz cornflour |
| 75 g/3 oz castor sugar | 1 teaspoon baking powder |
| 1 egg | 300 ml/½ pint *natillas piuranas* |
| 1 egg yolk | (see page 115) |
| ½ teaspoon vanilla essence | 100 g/4 oz freshly grated coconut |
| 225 g/8 oz plain flour | |

In a large bowl, cream together the butter and sugar until light and fluffy. In a separate bowl beat together the whole egg, egg yolk and vanilla essence. Add them to the creamed mixture and beat until smooth. Sift together twice the flour, cornflour and baking powder, then add them gradually to the creamed mixture. Turn the dough on to a lightly floured surface and knead it lightly until it is smooth and slightly elastic. Roll it out to about 3 mm/⅛ inch thick, and stamp out 5-cm/2-inch circles using a plain round biscuit cutter. Arrange the biscuits on baking tins lined with baking parchment and bake in a pre-heated moderate oven for about 12 minutes or until they are firm but barely coloured. Cool on a wire rack.

Sandwich the biscuits together with a generous filling of natillas piuranas and roll them in the grated coconut so that it sticks to the exposed filling.

Scots shortbread is sent all over the world at Christmas and New Year and the commercial product has become such a popular export that its festive origins are often forgotten. In less affluent times when fresh butter and white flour were not everyday fare for most people, short-bread was a high days and holidays treat, traditionally made and baked in the manner of oatcakes. Like pastry, shortbread should be handled as little and lightly as possible as too much messing about with the dough toughens it. Carved wooden moulds are sometimes used to pat-tern shortbread, but plain circles with hand-crimped edges are more usual.

## Shortbread – Scotland

*Oven temperature Moderate 180° C, 350° F, Gas Mark 4*

*Makes 8 pieces*

| | |
|---|---|
| 100 g/4 oz plain flour | 100 g/4 oz butter |
| 50 g/2 oz rice flour | 50 g/2 oz castor sugar |
| ¼ teaspoon salt | 1 egg yolk |

Sift together into a large bowl the flour, rice flour and salt. Dice the butter, which should be chilled, into the flour, then using your finger-tips or a pastry blender, lightly work in the butter until the mixture resembles fine breadcrumbs. Blend in the sugar and bind the mixture with the egg yolk to form a stiff dough.

Press the dough lightly into a shallow 18-cm/7-inch round cake tin lined with baking parchment. Pinch the edges all round using your finger and thumb, mark into 8 wedges, and prick the shortbread neatly with a fork. Bake it in a moderate oven for 40 to 60 minutes or until it is a light, golden brown. Allow the shortbread, which will still be soft, to cool a little in its tin before turning it on to a wire rack. When it is quite cold and crisp dredge it with castor sugar and store in an airtight container.

A light, fragrant Christmas shortbread is made in Greece for which there are countless subtly varied family recipes. It is certainly of ancient origin, and a cake of *kourabiédes* is said to have been mentioned by St John Chrysostom in one of his sermons. Today it is usually made in the form of individual biscuits each spiked with a clove to represent the gift of spices which the wise men brought to the infant Christ.

The secret of kourabiédes is said to lie in beating the butter (which should ideally be goat butter) and sugar by hand for at least half an hour. I think this is a bit of Greek grannies' one-up-womanship and use an electric beater with perfect results. The following recipe uses ouzo which is not widely available outside Greece and Cyprus, but pastis and arrack in their many forms are very similar. There are also equally authentic recipes which leave out the alcohol altogether and use water and a few drops of rosewater.

## Butter Cookies – Kourabiédes – Greece

*Oven temperature Moderately hot 190° C, 375° F, Gas Mark 5*

*Makes about 40*

225 g/8 oz butter
75 g/3 oz castor sugar
2 tablespoons ouzo
¼ teaspoon vanilla essence
1 egg yolk

275 g/10 oz plain flour
½ teaspoon baking powder
40 whole cloves
icing sugar
rosewater

In a large bowl cream together the butter and sugar until light and fluffy. Beat in the ouzo, vanilla essence and egg yolk. Sift together twice the flour and baking powder and add them to the creamed mixture. Mix well to make a firm dough.

Form rounded tablespoonfuls of the mixture into balls and arrange them on a baking tin lined with baking parchment. The mixture spreads very little so there is no need to leave big spaces between the cookies. Press each piece of dough lightly with the ball of your thumb to flatten them in the middle, and spike the centre of each cookie with a clove. Bake them in a preheated moderately hot oven for about 20 minutes, or until they are a light, golden colour.

Transfer the kourabiédes immediately to a wire rack, and while they are still piping hot, sprinkle them twice with icing sugar and rosewater. When they are completely cold, store them in an airtight container.

There is also a nutty version of these cookies. Add 50 g/2 oz blanched, toasted and chopped almonds to the dough.


Another buttery recipe is for *S-Gebäck*, S-shaped ribbons of lemon-flavoured shortcake.

## S-Shaped Biscuits – S-Gebäck – Germany

*Oven temperature Moderately hot 200° C, 400° F, Gas Mark 6*

*Makes about 40*

100 g/4 oz unsalted butter
100 g/4 oz castor sugar
4 egg yolks
1 teaspoon finely grated lemon rind

225 g/8 oz plain flour
1 egg white
100 g/4 oz sugar cubes

In a large bowl cream together the butter and sugar until light and fluffy. Gradually beat in the egg yolks and lemon rind. Beat in the flour, a little at a time, to make a firm dough. Form the dough into a long roll about 5 cm/2 inches in diameter, wrap in greaseproof paper and chill it for about an hour. Shape slices of the dough into ribbons about 10 cm/4 inches long by 2 cm/¾ inch wide and 6 mm/¼ inch thick, and arrange them in S-shapes on a well buttered baking tin.

Beat the egg white until foamy and paint the biscuits with it. Coarsely crush the lump sugar and sprinkle a little on the top of each biscuit. Bake them in a preheated moderately hot oven for about 10 minutes or until they are firm but barely coloured. Cool on a wire rack and store in an airtight container.


Ring-shaped twists of dough make Sweden's *konjakskransar*, brandy rings.

### Brandy Rings – Konjakskransar – Sweden

*Oven temperature Moderate 180° C, 350° F, Gas Mark 4*

*Makes about 75*

275 g/10 oz butter
125 g/4½ oz castor sugar

3 tablespoons brandy
400 g/14 oz plain flour

In a large bowl cream together the butter and sugar until light and fluffy. Beat in the brandy and gradually add the sifted flour. Mix thoroughly to make a smooth, firm dough.

On a lightly floured surface roll the dough into thin ropes. Twist two ropes together, cut into 12-cm/5-inch lengths and form each piece into a ring. Arrange the rings on buttered baking tins and bake in a preheated moderate oven for about 15 minutes or until golden. Rest the brandy rings on their baking tins for about 5 minutes, then transfer them to a wire rack to cool completely. Store in an airtight container.

*Ruiskakkuja*, sweet rye biscuits baked to resemble miniature loaves of sour rye bread are a traditional offering on the Finnish Christmas coffee table.

## Rye Biscuits – Ruiskakkuja – Finland

*Oven temperature Moderately hot 200° C, 400° F, Gas Mark 6*

*Makes about 35*

| | |
|---|---|
| 100 g/4 oz butter | 100 g/4 oz rye flour |
| 5 tablespoons castor sugar | 50 g/2 oz plain flour |

In a large bowl cream together the butter and sugar until light and fluffy. Sift in the flours and mix well until the mixture looks like breadcrumbs. Knead into a firm dough. The warmth of your hands will make a dough without adding liquid.

On a lightly floured surface roll out the dough to a thickness of about 3 mm/⅛ inch. Using a plain-edged 7·5-cm/3-inch biscuit cutter stamp out rounds of dough. Cut a hole in each round, slightly off-centre, using a very small round cutter or the top of an essence bottle.

Arrange the ruiskakkuja on generously buttered baking tins and prick each biscuit several times with a fork. Bake them in a preheated moderately hot oven for about 7 minutes or until lightly browned. Cool on a wire rack and store in an airtight container.

Honey biscuits with a crunchy sugar topping are a traditional Christmas biscuit in Bulgaria.

## Honey Biscuits – Medeni Kurabii – Bulgaria

*Oven temperature Moderate 180° C, 350° F, Gas Mark 4*

*Makes about 25*

| | |
|---|---|
| 100 g/4 oz unsalted butter | 1 egg yolk |
| 6 tablespoons honey | 100 g/4 oz plain flour |
| 50 g/2 oz castor sugar | 100 g/4 oz cube sugar |
| 1 teaspoon bicarbonate of soda | |

Melt the butter, and when it is cool, but not solidified, mix it in a large bowl with the honey, sugar, bicarbonate of soda and egg yolk. Gradually add the sifted flour and mix well to make a firm dough.

On a well-floured surface, roll out rounded teaspoonfuls of the mixture into balls. Coarsely crush the lump sugar and dip the top of each ball of dough into it. Arrange the balls on a baking tin lined with baking parchment and bake in a preheated moderate oven for about 12 minutes or until golden brown. Cool on a wire rack and when completely cold, store in an airtight container.

# SAUCES AND SWEETMEATS

Plum pudding sauce and brandy butter are the only sauces made almost exclusively for Christmas. The remainder are used in, or to accompany, dishes made at other times of year as well. Béchamel sauce is included because it is needed for cannelloni (see page 15). Mayonnaise and many other classic sauces are omitted because no particular recipe calls for them and they can be found in any basic cookery book.

### Béchamel Sauce – Sauce Béchamel – France

*Makes about 600 ml / 1 pint*

| | |
|---|---|
| 50 g/2 oz butter | 1 sprig thyme |
| 1 medium onion | 1 small bay leaf |
| 3 tablespoons plain flour | white pepper |
| 900 ml/1½ pints milk | nutmeg |
| 50 g/2 oz lean veal or ham | salt |
| 1 stalk celery | |

In a heavy-based saucepan or in the top of a double-boiler melt 40 g/ 1½ oz butter over direct heat. Peel and finely chop the onion and sauté it gently in the butter until it is soft but not coloured. Add the flour and cook the roux, stirring constantly, for 2 or 3 minutes, taking care that it does not colour. Scald the milk and add it to the roux a little at a time, stirring constantly to make a smooth sauce. Keep warm.

In another saucepan melt the remaining butter. Add the veal or ham, and celery, finely chopped. Cook them together over a low heat for 2 or 3 minutes. Add the thyme and a generous seasoning of freshly ground white pepper and grated nutmeg.

Add the meat mixture to the sauce and bring the sauce to the boil over a direct heat. Cook the sauce over boiling water for about 1 hour or until it has reduced to about 600 ml/1 pint. Season to taste with salt and strain the sauce through a fine sieve, pressing the meat and onion residue to extract its juices. Use as directed.

Creole sauce is served with roast suckling pig in Jamaica.

## Creole Sauce – Jamaica

*Makes about 450 ml / ¾ pint*

| | |
|---|---|
| 3 tablespoons vegetable oil | 300 ml / ½ pint chicken stock or |
| 1 medium onion | dry white wine |
| 1 medium green pepper | salt |
| 3 tablespoons plain flour | black pepper |
| 2 medium tomatoes, peeled, | 1 teaspoon lime juice |
| seeded and chopped | 1 teaspoon vinegar |
| | hot pepper or Tabasco sauce |

Heat the oil in a heavy-based saucepan and cook the onion, peeled and finely chopped, and the pepper, de-seeded and finely chopped, until soft but not browned. Add the flour and cook, stirring constantly, until the flour has coloured a little. Add the tomatoes, peeled, de-seeded and roughly chopped, and mix well in. Gradually add the stock or wine, stirring constantly until the sauce thickens. Season to taste with salt, freshly ground black pepper, lime juice, vinegar and hot pepper sauce.

*Chimolé*, a basic Mexican chilli sauce can be made with fresh chillies, using several kinds ground to a paste. It is also made more simply with powdered chilli.

## Chilli Sauce – Chimolé – Mexico

*Makes about 250 ml / 8 fl oz*

| | |
|---|---|
| 1 tablespoon vegetable oil | 250 ml / 8 fl oz stock, meat or |
| 1 medium onion | chicken |
| 1 clove garlic | salt |
| 1 teaspoon chilli powder | black pepper |
| 1 large tomato | |

Heat the oil in a small, heavy-based saucepan and sauté the onion and garlic, peeled and very finely chopped, over a low heat until golden. Add the chilli powder and mix well. Peel, de-seed and roughly chop the tomato, add it to the pan and cook, stirring from time to time, until the mixture is thick and almost dry. Stir in the stock, bring to the boil, reduce the heat and cook the sauce gently for about 10 minutes. Season to taste with salt and freshly ground black pepper. Use as directed.

A cooked mustard is sometimes used to glaze the Christmas ham in Finland. It is also delicious served with hams glazed in other ways.

### Mustard – Sinappi – Finland

*Makes about 75 ml / 3 fl oz*

| | |
|---|---|
| 4 tablespoons powdered dry mustard | $\frac{1}{4}$ teaspoon salt |
| 3 tablespoons castor sugar | 4 tablespoons boiling water |
| | 1 tablespoon wine vinegar |

In a small bowl or cup combine the powdered dry mustard, sugar and salt. Add the boiling water and vinegar and, stirring constantly, cook over hot water until the mixture is smooth and slightly thickened. Store in an airtight glass or plastic container. This mustard keeps for a week or more in the refrigerator.

Bread sauce, subtly flavoured with onion, cloves and bay is one of the traditional accompaniments to roast turkey in England. It is also served with roast grouse, pheasant and quail.

### Bread Sauce – England

*Makes about 350 ml / 12 fl oz*

| | |
|---|---|
| 1 medium onion | 75 g / 3 oz fresh white |
| 6 cloves | breadcrumbs |
| 1 bay leaf | salt |
| 350 ml / 12 fl oz milk | black pepper |
| | single cream (optional) |

Peel the onion and stick the cloves into it near the base. Put it in a small saucepan with the milk and bay leaf and bring slowly to the boil. Remove from the heat immediately and set aside for at least 15 minutes.

Strain the milk and return it to the pan. Discard the onion and bay leaf. Add the breadcrumbs and bring the sauce slowly to the boil, stirring continuously to make a thick, smooth sauce. Season to taste with salt and freshly ground black pepper and cook very gently for a minute or two. Cream may be added to taste. Serve hot with roast turkey. The exact consistency of bread sauce is a matter of preference. It may be as soft as mayonnaise or a good deal thicker, and thickened or thinned with more breadcrumbs, milk or cream.

Cranberry sauce to accompany turkey is sold in jars and tins, but it is not difficult to make. Fresh cranberries are widely available during the Christmas season. Spiced cranberries are a delicious alternative to the plainer sauce.

### Cranberry Sauce – United States

*Makes about 350 ml / 12 fl oz*

450 g / 1 lb cranberries, fresh or        175 g / 6 oz castor sugar
   frozen                            150 ml / ¼ pint water

Put the cranberries in a pot with the sugar and water. Bring to the boil, lower the heat and simmer, covered, for about 20 minutes or until the cranberries are tender. Serve warm or cold.

### Spiced Cranberries – United States

*Makes about 350 ml / 12 fl oz*

450 g / 1 lb cranberries                          6 whole allspice
200 g / 7 oz dark brown sugar            6 cloves
2·5 cm / 1 inch root ginger, bruised     175 ml / 6 fl oz wine vinegar
5 cm / 2 inches cinnamon stick

Put the cranberries in a pot with the sugar, spices, bruised and tied loosely in muslin, and vinegar. Bring to the boil, lower the heat, cover and simmer for about 20 minutes or until the cranberries are tender. Remove the spice bag and leave to cool. Serve cold.

Spiced peaches and pears pickled in a syrup of sugar and vinegar may be made when the fruits are plentiful for Christmas eating. They are especially good with cold ham and poultry.

## Spiced Pears – England

*Makes 900 g/2 lb*

| | |
|---|---|
| 900 g/2 lb fresh hard pears | 10 cm/4 inches cinnamon stick |
| 450 g/1 lb granulated sugar | 8 cloves |
| 300 ml/½ pint malt or wine vinegar | 2 teaspoons whole allspice |

Peel, core and quarter the pears and set them aside in cold water acidulated with a teaspoon of vinegar.

Put the sugar and vinegar in a stainless steel or enamelled saucepan. Bruise the spices and tie them loosely in muslin. Put them in the pan. Dissolve the sugar over a low heat then add the strained pears and bring to the boil. Lower the heat, cover and simmer gently until the pears are tender but not mushy.

Using a draining spoon, lift out the pears and pack them into a large heated jar. Remove the spice bag from the syrup, and return the pan to a high heat. Boil the syrup until it thickens a little, then pour it over the pears. The liquid should cover the fruit. Make an airtight seal for the jar and store the spiced pears in a cool place for at least a month, or until needed.

## Spiced Peaches – England

*Makes 900 g/2 lb*

| | |
|---|---|
| 900 g/2 lb fresh peaches | 2·5 cm/1 inch root ginger |
| 450 g/1 lb granulated sugar | 10 cm/4 inches cinnamon stick |
| 300 ml/½ pint malt or wine vinegar | 8 cloves |
| | 1 teaspoon whole allspice |

To prepare the peaches, peel them after dipping for about 30 seconds in boiling water. Cut the fruit in halves and remove the stones.

Put the sugar and vinegar in a large stainless steel or enamelled saucepan. Bruise the spices and tie them loosely in muslin. Add them to the pan. Dissolve the sugar over a low heat, then bring the syrup to the boil and add the peaches. Simmer together very gently until the peaches are tender but not mushy.

Using a draining spoon, lift the peaches out of the syrup and pack them into a large, heated jar. Remove the spice bag from the pan and return the syrup to the heat. Boil rapidly until it thickens slightly, then pour the syrup over the peaches. The liquid should cover the fruit. Make an airtight seal for the jar, and store it in a cool place for at least a month, or until needed.

Apple sauce is the classic accompaniment to roast pork. In the Caribbean a mock apple sauce made with unripe papaya (pawpaw in Jamaica) or chayote, is served throughout the islands with roast suckling pig.

### Pawpaw Apple Sauce – Jamaica

*Makes about 350 ml / 12 fl oz*

450 g / 1 lb unripe papaya
350 ml / 12 fl oz water
4 cloves

2 tablespoons sugar
4 tablespoons lime juice

Peel the papaya, remove the seeds and roughly chop the flesh. Put the fruit in a heavy-based pot with the water, cloves, sugar and lime juice. Bring to the boil, cover and simmer for about 1 hour or until the fruit is soft and most of the liquid absorbed. Discard the cloves and rub the sauce through a sieve. Serve warm or cold.

Cumberland sauce, a hot mixture of wine and redcurrant jelly, is delicious with roast lamb or a hot Christmas ham. Its festive colour is an attractive bonus.

### Cumberland Sauce – England

*Makes about 475 ml / 16 fl oz*

1 orange
4 tablespoons port or red wine
500 g / 18 oz redcurrant jelly
2 teaspoons lemon juice

2 teaspoons powdered dry
  mustard
salt

Cut the orange rind into neat julienne strips, being careful to discard any white pith. Squeeze the juice from the flesh and reserve. In a small

186

saucepan heat the port or red wine and strips of orange peel to boiling point, then reduce the heat and stir in the redcurrant jelly. Stir over a low heat until the jelly has melted completely. Mix together the orange juice, lemon juice and dry mustard and stir them into the redcurrant mixture. Season to taste with salt and serve the sauce hot or cold.

Mincemeat was originally a means of preserving meat without smoking or salting it. It is seldom made with meat now, except in a few strong-holds of tradition, and only the suet remains to remind us of older recipes. The following recipe is particularly good and keeps for over a year. If mincemeat stored for long periods dries a little, revive it by adding a little more brandy or rum.

### Mincemeat – England

*Makes 2 kg/4 lb*

| | |
|---|---|
| 350 g/12 oz eating apples | 200 g/7 oz dark brown sugar |
| 225 g/8 oz stoned raisins | 225 g/8 oz shredded beef suet |
| 225 g/8 oz sultanas | 1 teaspoon mixed spice |
| 225 g/8 oz currants | ½ teaspoon grated nutmeg |
| 225 g/8 oz candied lemon peel | ½ teaspoon salt |
| 225 g/8 oz candied orange peel | 1 lemon |
| 25 g/1 oz blanched almonds | 6 tablespoons brandy or rum |

Peel and core the apples. Pass them through the coarse blade of a mincer together with the raisins, sultanas, currants, candied peel and almonds. Put the ground ingredients in a large bowl with the sugar, suet, spices and salt. Finely grate the lemon rind over the bowl, then squeeze the juice and add it with the brandy or rum. Mix all the ingredients very thoroughly together and pack the mincemeat into jars or plastic containers. Make airtight seals, and store the mincemeat in a cool place for at least a month before using.

Three different types of sauce are made to accompany Christmas pudding and each has its devotees. Dr William Kitchener writing in 1804 gives this recipe for a hot sauce in his famous and much plagiarised *Apicius Redivivus, The Cook's Oracle*. A similar Scots recipe is called caudle sauce.

### Plum Pudding Sauce – England

*Serves 4–6*

| | |
|---|---|
| 1 teaspoon grated lemon rind | 125 ml/4 fl oz brandy |
| 1 tablespoon castor sugar | 100 g/4 oz butter, melted |
| 125 ml/4 fl oz sherry | grated nutmeg |

Stir the lemon rind and sugar into the brandy mixed with the sherry and slowly stir the warm butter into the mixture. Keep warm over hot water and stir well just before serving in a sauceboat with a ladle. At the last minute sprinkle a little grated nutmeg over it.

Queen Victoria's chef, Francatelli, gave the following instructions for a German custard sauce for plum pudding. It is very like the frothy Italian pudding *zabaglione*, and is served hot.

Put four yolks of eggs into a bain-marie or stewpan, together with two ounces of pounded sugar, a glass of sherry, some orange or lemon peel (rubbed on loaf sugar), and a very little salt.

Whisk this sharply over a very slow fire until it assumes the appearance of a light, frothy custard.

Brandy butter is the best loved accompaniment to Christmas pudding. It should be served well chilled and can be made in advance.

### Brandy Butter – England

*Serves 4–6*

| | |
|---|---|
| 175 g/6 oz unsalted butter | 1 teaspoon grated orange rind |
| 175 g/6 oz castor sugar | 4 tablespoons brandy or rum |

Cream together the butter and sugar until pale and fluffy. Beat in the grated orange rind and gradually add the brandy or rum, beating well after each addition. Turn the mixture into a serving dish and chill well.

Marzipan or almond paste is a favourite Christmas sweetmeat originally mainly from Germany, but popular too in other parts of Europe, and an integral part of English Christmas cake. Sugar and ground almonds are the essential ingredients, with eggs and butter appearing in some recipes and not in others. The Danes have pink marzipan Christmas pigs, while Austrians save them for New Year. In Germany, where marzipan appears as almost anything but itself, it is fashioned into brightly coloured fruits, flowers and figures; and in Spain into huge, dragon-like monsters filled with dried fruit.

### Lubecker Marzipan – Germany

*Makes 450 g/1 lb*

225 g/8 oz ground almonds          orange flower water or rosewater
225 g/8 oz icing sugar

Work the ground almonds and sieved icing sugar into a firm paste with just enough orange flower water or rosewater to make it pliable.

Put the paste into a small saucepan and stir it over a low heat until it no longer sticks to the sides of the pan.

Turn the marzipan on to a sugar-dusted board. Shape it into figures or sweets. These may be left, lightly covered, in a warm place to dry a little, or dried in a very slow oven. The marzipan should remain both soft and white.

The next recipe is the one to use for Christmas cake. It can also be tinted with a few drops of food colouring to make sweets, stuffed dates and figures.

### Marzipan – England

*Makes 450 g/1 lb*

100 g/4 oz icing sugar          1 teaspoon lemon juice
100 g/4 oz castor sugar         almond essence
225 g/8 oz ground almonds       1 egg, beaten

Sift the icing sugar into a bowl and stir in the castor sugar and ground almonds. Add the lemon juice and a few drops of almond essence. Mix well, then gradually add enough beaten egg to make a firm paste. Knead the paste lightly on a sugar-dusted surface until it is smooth. Store the marzipan, well wrapped, in the refrigerator, for up to two months.

*Borstplaat* is an indispensable Christmas sweet in Holland. It is made in many colours, flavours, sizes and shapes, and special ring moulds are sold in the Netherlands for shaping it. However, round cake tins or the flat lids of biscuit tins work just as well. The liquid used may be water, milk or single cream. Flavourings can be varied by using essences or by adding cocoa or strong coffee.

### Christmas Fondant – Borstplaat – Holland

*Makes about 24 pieces*

225 g/8 oz granulated sugar
3 tablespoons single cream
1 tablespoon butter

orange essence
orange food colouring

In a small heavy saucepan stir the sugar and cream together. Heat slowly to boiling point and cook on a low heat, without stirring, until the syrup spins a thread or registers 115°C/240° F on a sugar thermometer. Remove from the heat immediately and add the butter and a few drops each of flavouring and colouring. Beat the mixture vigorously with a wooden spoon until it thickens and begins to make a scratchy sound. Pour it into a greased tin and leave it to set. Leave it until cold, then break it into bite-sized pieces.

*Turrón* is the Christmas sweet of the Spanish-speaking world. The famous turróns of Alicante and Jijona are so popular that they are now available all year round. But turrón used to be a special Christmas treat, and all the big houses and estates had family recipes for making it. Small bags or packets of turrón were distributed on Christmas Eve to the servants and tenants who had brought gifts to the mistress of the house.

The basic ingredients of turrón are almonds, sugar, and, or, honey, and egg yolks or whites. But there are numerous variations – powdered coriander, cinnamon, walnuts and pine kernels in Spain, hazelnuts and sesame seeds in Mexico. Sometimes the almonds are simply blanched and peeled, sometimes toasted, or ground to a paste. Often all three forms are included in a single recipe. A loaf tin will substitute for the wooden mould used in Spain.

# Almond Nougat – Turrón – Spain

*Makes 1 bar*

200 g/7 oz blanched almonds
300 g/10 oz castor sugar
275 ml/9 fl oz water

4 egg yolks
almond oil

Leave the almonds as they are or toast all or some of them. Grind at least two-thirds of the almonds to a paste. The remainder may be ground, chopped, slivered or left whole.

Heat the sugar and water slowly in a heavy-based saucepan and when the sugar has dissolved completely, boil the syrup rapidly for about 7 minutes or until small drops set hard instantly on a cold plate. Remove from the heat and add all the almonds, stirring until the mixture forms a thick paste which leaves the sides of the pan. Stir in the beaten egg yolks.

Line a loaf tin with paper brushed with almond oil and cut neatly to fit. Press the turrón into the tin and cover with another piece of oiled paper and a piece of heavy cardboard cut to fit. Weight the top and leave the nougat to set in a cool place.

Turn out the bar, remove the oiled papers, and dust the top with castor sugar. Use a very hot skewer to burn a traditional pattern of criss-cross lines on top of the turrón.

# DRINKS

If recipe books reflect the world's drinking practices then punches of varying potency are undoubtedly the most popular Christmas drinks. But books do not exactly mirror our drinking habits and for the most part people fill their glasses with what they drink on other days. So these recipes are for party drinks, special occasion brews to be made in quantity for festive gatherings of every kind. There are hot, spiced wines for travellers in cold northern winters, and long cool punches from places where the sun shines at Christmas.

### Christmas Punch – Jul Glögg – Denmark

*Serves 8–10*

1 litre/1¾ pints red wine
5 cm/2 inches cinnamon stick
4 cloves
8 cardamom seeds
75 g/3 oz castor sugar
rind of ½ lemon, cut in strips

50 g/2 oz blanched almonds, chopped
50 g/2 oz seedless raisins
250 ml/8 fl oz Cognac or Armagnac

Put the wine and all the other ingredients except the Cognac or Armagnac in a large saucepan and stir over a low heat until the sugar has dissolved. Bring almost to the boil and transfer to a serving bowl. Just before serving, add the spirit. Set alight with a match then ladle into handled punch glasses.

### New Year Punch – Neujahrspunsch – Germany

*Serves 12–14*

225 g/8 oz castor sugar
350 ml/12 fl oz rum

1·3 litres/2¼ pints white wine
350 ml/12 fl oz red wine

Soak the sugar in the rum and stand for several hours until the sugar dissolves. Put the wine in a saucepan and bring it almost to the boil. Add the sweetened rum and serve immediately.

Wassailing must have been going strong in England long before formal Christmas festivities took root. The word wassail comes from the Old Norse *ves heill*, good health, and a variety of wassailing traditions still survive in various parts of the country. A bubbling wassail bowl greeted the revellers who dragged the Yule log home from the woods on Christmas Eve. Gloucestershire wassailers downed it at New Year, and in the West Country and other fruit growing areas wassailing the apple tree survives in a number of noisy ceremonies sometimes known as apple howling and usually occurring on Twelfth Night.

There are many versions of the drink, some of which are made with cider. This recipe for a wassail bowl comes from *The Curiosities of Ale and Beer* by John Bickerdyke. The book was published in about 1860, but the recipe is almost certainly much older.

Into a bowl is first placed ½ lb sugar in which is placed one pint of warm beer; a little nutmeg and ginger are then grated over the mixture, and four glasses of sherry and five pints of beer added to it. It is then stirred, sweetened to taste and allowed to stand covered for two or three hours. Roasted apples are then floated on the creaming mixture and the wassail bowl is ready.

Het pint, the New Year's morning drink of urban Scots, used to be sold from bright copper kettles in the streets of Edinburgh and Glasgow. It is seldom made now, but this recipe is given in *The Scots Kitchen*.

Grate a nutmeg into two quarts of mild ale, and bring to the point of boiling. Mix a little cold ale with sugar necessary to sweeten this, and three eggs well-beaten. Gradually mix the hot ale with the eggs, taking care that they do not curdle. Put in a half-pint of whisky, and bring it once more nearly to the boil and then briskly pour it from one vessel into another till it becomes smooth and bright.

Atholl brose is one of those drinks that most of us have heard of but few have tried. Its strong associations with New Year's Eve – Hogmanay in Scotland where is is offered as a popular gesture of hospitality to first-footers in the Highlands – are excuse enough to give it a whirl. In *The Scots Kitchen* F. Marian McNeill says that the following recipe was 'made known' by the eighth Duke of Atholl.

To make a quart, take four dessertspoonsful of run honey and four sherry glassfuls of prepared oatmeal; stir these well together and put into a quart bottle; fill up with whisky; shake well before serving.

To prepare the oatmeal, put it into a basin and mix with cold water to the consistency of a thick paste. Leave for about half an hour, pass through a fine strainer, pressing with the back of a wooden spoon so as to leave the oatmeal as dry as possible. Discard the meal, and use the creamy liquor for the brose.

The proportions suggest that the eighth Duke didn't care to have his whisky too much messed about with.

From the same book comes another recipe served by Williamina Macrae at her angling inn at Lochailort. The quantities called for may seem more suitable for domestic experiment, but the result is more like a pudding than a drink.

Beat one and a half teacupfuls of double cream to a froth; stir in one teacupful of very lightly toasted oatmeal; add half a cup of dripped heather honey and, just before serving, two wine-glasses of whisky. Mix thoroughly and serve in shallow glasses.

Advocaat, a heavy, milkless eggnog, is the New Year's Day drink in Holland where it is served from a punchbowl.

### Eggnog – Advocaat – Holland

*Serves 16–20*

| | |
|---|---|
| 20 egg yolks | *Topping* |
| 225 g/8 oz castor sugar | 6 egg whites |
| 950 ml/32 fl oz brandy | 75 g/3 oz castor sugar |

In a large bowl whisk together the egg yolks and sugar until thick and fluffy. Gradually whisk in the brandy.

In another bowl whisk the egg whites until they hold a stiff peak. Fold in the sugar.

To serve the advocaat fill glasses with the brandy mixture and flip a blob of fluffy egg white on top of each portion.

For Puerto Rico's coconut rum punch, use the liquid from two or three fresh coconuts plus coconut milk made by straining the grated flesh soaked in water.

### Coconut Rum Punch – Ron con Coco – Puerto Rico

*Serves 20–25*

6 egg yolks
225 g/8 oz castor sugar
1 (475-ml/16-fl oz) tin evaporated
    milk

1·3 litres/2½ pints coconut milk
900 ml/1½ pints rum
vanilla essence (optional)

In a large bowl whisk the egg yolks and sugar until pale and thick. Gradually whisk in the evaporated milk, then the coconut milk and finally the rum. Chill well.

Whisk again immediately before serving in long glasses with or without ice, as an aperitif or at any other time.

### Coffee Punch – Cola de Mono – Chile

*Serves 18–20*

1·5 litres/2¾ pints milk
600 ml/1 pint water
8 cloves
rind of 1 orange, cut in strips
100 g/4 oz instant coffee

225 g/8 oz granulated sugar
1 teaspoon grated nutmeg
600 ml/1 pint aguardiente or
    vodka

Scald the milk and set it aside to cool. Put the water, cloves, strips of orange peel, instant coffee, sugar and nutmeg in a saucepan and bring to the boil. Lower the heat, cover, and simmer gently for about 20 minutes. Set aside to cool.

Strain the cold milk and spiced coffee into a large bowl or jug. Add the aguardiente or vodka. Mix thoroughly and chill well before serving as an aperitif.

Brazil's party punch is a cool, wine-based cup lavishly embellished with fresh fruit.

### Party Punch – Ponche Para Festas – Brazil

*Serves 6–8*

| | |
|---|---|
| 1 lemon | 3 tablespoons castor sugar |
| 1 orange | 90 ml/3 fl oz maraschino |
| ½ pineapple | 90 ml/3 fl oz curaçao |
| 2 peaches | 725 ml/1¼ pints red wine |
| 24 grapes | 350 ml/12 fl oz soda water |

Slice the lemon and orange very thinly and put them in a serving bowl or jug. Add the pineapple, peeled and thinly sliced, peaches and grapes, peeled, stoned and thinly sliced. Sprinkle the fruit with sugar and set it aside for an hour. Add the maraschino and curaçao, wine and soda water. Mix well and chill the punch for about 2 hours.

Serve with a large lump of ice in the bowl or jug. Freeze flowers or fruit into the ice for decoration.

Home-made ginger beer – a revelation to those who have only tasted the commercial product – is a popular drink throughout the English-speaking islands of the Caribbean. Start production two weeks before it is needed.

### Ginger Beer – Trinidad

*Serves 10*

| | |
|---|---|
| 50 g/2 oz fresh ginger root | 450 g/1 lb granulated sugar |
| 125 ml/4 fl oz lime juice | 1·8 litres/3 pints boiling water |
| rind of 1 lime | 2 teaspoons dried yeast |

Peel and crush the ginger root (or substitute 2 tablespoons of powdered ginger). Put the ginger, lime juice, lime peel cut in strips, and sugar in a large bowl or jug and pour the boiling water over them.

Dissolve the yeast in a small amount of lukewarm water, about 43° C/ 110° F. When the ginger mixture has cooled to the same temperature, add the yeast and stir well. Cover the container loosely and leave it to stand in a warm place for a week. Stir it daily.

Strain the liquid through a fine sieve lined with muslin and pour it into clean bottles. Cork them lightly and leave to stand at room temperature for another 4 or 5 days. Chill well before serving in tall glasses, with or without ice.

Another Christmas drink in Trinidad and Jamaica is a festive red infusion of sorrel – an annual plant also called rosella, which matures at this time of year. Dried sorrel sepals or fresh sorrel can be used for the following recipe. Sorrel syrup is also exported and should be diluted according to the instructions on the bottle.

### Sorrel Drink – Jamaica

*Serves 12–14*

25 g/1 oz fresh ginger root
25 g/1 oz dried sorrel sepals or
   225 g/8 oz fresh sorrel

450 g/1 lb granulated sugar
1·8 litres/3 pints boiling water
175-350 ml/6-12 fl oz dark rum

Peel and coarsely grate the ginger and put it in a large bowl or jug with the sorrel sepals and sugar. Add the boiling water, stir and cover loosely. Leave to stand at room temperature for at least 48 hours.

Strain the liquid through a fine sieve lined with muslin into a serving bowl or jug. Chill well before adding rum to taste.

In Trinidad cloves, cinnamon and orange peel replace the ginger.

# SELECTED BIBLIOGRAPHY

Eliza ACTON (editor Elizabeth Ray), *The Best of Eliza Acton*, Longmans, London, 1968.

Margarette de ANDRADE, *Brazilian Cookery*, Charles E. Tuttle, Rutland, Vermont, 1965.

Amanda ATHA (editor), *Good Housekeeping Home Baking*, Ebury Press, London, 1977.

Elisabeth AYRTON, *The Cookery of England*, André Deutsch, London, 1974.

Margaret BAKER, *Christmas Customs and Folklore, A Discovering Guide To Seasonal Rites*, Shire, England, 1972.

Isabella BEETON, *Beeton's Book of Household Management, A First Edition Facsimile*, Jonathan Cape, London, 1968.

Sula BENET, *Festival Menus Round the World*, Abelard Schuman, New York, 1957.

George C. BOOTH, *The Food and Drink of Mexico*, Dover Publications, New York, 1964.

Cora, Rose and Bob BROWN, *The South American Cook Book*, Dover Publications, New York, 1971.

Dale BROWN, *The Cooking of Scandinavia*, Time-Life Books, 1969.

Elizabeth CASS, *Spanish Cooking*, Mayflower Books, England, 1976.

Robert CARRIER, *Great Dishes of the World*, Thomas Nelson, England, 1963.

Robert CARRIER, *The Robert Carrier Cookery Course*, W. H. Allen, London, 1974.

Ann H. CURRAH, *Chef to Queen Victoria, The Recipes of Charles Elmé Francatelli*, William Kimber, London, 1973.

Elizabeth DAVID, *French Country Cooking*, Penguin, England, 1966.

Elizabeth DAVID, *Italian Food*, Penguin, England, 1975.

Elizabeth DAVID, *Spices, Salt and Aromatics in the English Kitchen*, Penguin, England, 1970.

Enriqueta DAVID-PEREZ, *Recipes of the Philippines*, D. M. Press, Philippines, 1967.

Peter S. FEIBLEMAIN, *The Cooking of Spain and Portugal*, Time-Life Books, 1970.

Michael and Frances FIELD, *A Quintet of Cuisines*, Time-Life Books, 1970.

Theodora FITZGIBBON, *The Food of the Western World*, Hutchinson, London, 1976.

Lilli GORE, *Game Cooking*, Weidenfeld & Nicolson, London, 1974.

Károly GUNDEL, *Hungarian Cookery Book*, Pannonia, Budapest, 1964.

Nika Standen HAZELTON, *The Cooking of Germany*, Time-Life Books, 1970.

Robin HOWE, *German Cooking*, André Deutsch, London, 1953.

Diana KENNEDY, *The Cuisines of Mexico*, Harper & Row, New York, 1972.

Jonathan Norton LEONARD, *Latin American Cooking*, Time-Life Books, 1968.

F. Marian McNEILL, *The Scot's Kitchen. Its Traditions and Lore with Old-Time Recipes*, Blackie, Glasgow, 1929.

Anna MIADHACHÁIN, *Spanish Regional Cookery*, Penguin, England, 1976.

Prosper MONTAGNÉ, *Larousse Gastronomique*, 15th impression, English edition, Hamlyn, London, 1974.

Countess MORPHY (Marcelle Azra Forbes), *Recipes of All Nations*, Michael Joseph for Selfridges, London, 1935.

Beatrice A. OJAKANGAS, *The Finnish Cookbook*, Crown, New York, 1964.

Elizabeth Lambert ORTIZ, *Caribbean Cooking*, André Deutsch, London, 1975.

Helen and George PAPASHVILY, *The Cooking of Russia*, Time-Life Books, 1969.

Edited by the READER'S DIGEST ASSOCIATION, *The Cookery Year*, Reader's Digest, London, 1973.

Waverley ROOT, *The Cooking of Italy*, Time-Life Books, 1969.

Sofka SKIPWITH, *Eat Russian*, David & Charles, England, 1973.

Katie STEWART, *The Times Calendar Cookbook*, Hamlyn, London, 1975.

Nicholas TSELEMENTES, *Greek Cookery*, D. C. Divry, New York, 1956.

Joseph WECHSBERG, *The Cooking of Vienna's Empire*, Time-Life Books, 1974.

Sam WIDENFELT (editor), *Swedish Food*, Wezäta Förlang, Gothenburg, 1946.

C. Anne WILSON, *Food and Drink in Britain*, Constable, London, 1973.

# INDEX

207